Da~~~~~~
GUIDE
to Vermont

Green Mountain Club

Day Hiker's

GUIDE

Vermont Hiking Trails Series

Volume 2

Fifth Edition

Green Mountain Club

4711 Waterbury-Stowe Road
Waterbury Center, Vermont 05677
www.greenmountainclub.org

Editions
First Edition 1978
Second Edition 1983
Third Edition 1987
Fourth Edition 2002
Fifth Edition 2006

The Green Mountain Club, Inc.
4711 Waterbury-Stowe Road
Waterbury Center, Vermont 05677
(802) 244-7037
gmc@greenmountainclub.org
www.greenmountainclub.org

Ben Rose, *Executive Director*

Dave Hardy, *Director of Field Programs*

Arthur Goldsweig, *Director of Finance*

Jennifer Karson, *Director of Communications*

Susan Shea, *Managing Editor*

GMC Publications Committee, 2006: Richard Andrews, Dave Blumenthal, Ruth Hare, Steve Larose, Mary Lou Recor, Val Stori

Information in this guide is based on the best efforts of the publisher, using information available at the time of printing. Changes resulting from maintenance, relocations, natural disturbance, etc., occur over time, and use of the information in this book is at the sole risk of the user.

Printed in Canada on recycled paper.

Fifth Edition
2006
ISBN 1-888021-14-4

Contributors

Dick Andrews, Kathy Astrauckas, Dave Blumenthal, Charlene Bohl, Scott Christiansen, Bill Clark, Bob Crossett, Kit Davidson, Daniel Dietz, Marcia Dunning, Wally Elton, Equinox Preservation Trust, Doug Fish, Marge Fish, Hubey Folsom, Joe Frank, Green Mountain National Forest-Manchester District, Chris Hanna, Ruth Hare, Roger Haydock, David Hooke, Gregory Judson, Jenn Karson, Katy Klutznick, Steve Larose, Matt Larson, Alice Mattison, Pat Meulemans, Larry Michaels, Paul Moffat, Matt Moore, Mary Noll, Jeff Nugent, Reidun Nuquist, Luke O'Brien, Herb Ogden, Trina Perkins, George Plumb, Sylvia Plumb, Mary Lou Recor, Barbara Rhoad, George Roy, Gary Salmon, Eric Scharnberg, Lexi Shear, Martha Steitelman, Val Stori, Harry Temple, Sue Thomas, Vermont Institute of Natural Science (VINS) Community Mapping Program, Paul Vidovich, Laura Wallingford, Greg Western, Arthur Westing, Kevin Williamson and Claire Wilson.

Cover and book design by The Laughing Bear Associates, Montpelier, Vermont.

Cover photograph by A. Blake Gardner, from *Untamed Vermont*, published by Thistle Hill Publications, North Pomfret, Vermont.

Title page watercolor painting by Helmut Siber, ca. 1955. Collection of Fairbanks Museum and Planetarium, St. Johnsbury, Vermont.

Text illustrations by Ed Epstein.

Format, indexing, and proofreading by Kate Mueller, Electric Dragon Productions, Montpelier, Vermont.

Copyediting by Mary Lou Recor.

Maps edited and revised by Dave Blumenthal. Maps for the Fifth Edition created by Daniel Currier and William Toussaint. Original maps compiled and digitized by Middlebury College Geography Department.

Dedication

This fifth edition of the *Day Hiker's Guide to Vermont* is dedicated to the clubs, associations, camps and other volunteer groups that build and maintain many of the footpaths enjoyed by Vermonters and visitors.

Few regions in the country are as richly endowed with opportunities for hikers and walkers as Vermont. But clear, maintained, and marked trails don't just happen. They require physical work and sweat, money, and nowadays detailed planning, paperwork, and continuous complex relationships with landowners as well. None of this would take place in the many places offering inviting footpaths without sustained effort by members of the organizations that generously create the trails.

The Green Mountain Club salutes these organizations and hopes that their members will find this guide as useful as we find their trails enjoyable.

Contents

Region 4

East Central

Region 5

Northwest

Region 6

Northeast

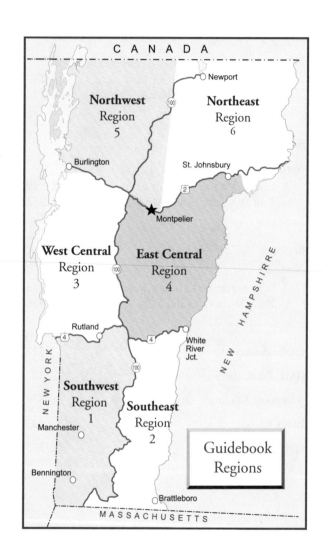

CANADA

Newport

Northwest
Region
5

Northeast
Region
6

Burlington

St. Johnsbury

★ Montpelier

West Central
Region
3

East Central
Region
4

NEW HAMPSHIRE

Rutland

White
River
Jct.

NEW YORK

Southwest
Region
1

Southeast
Region
2

Manchester

Guidebook
Regions

Bennington

Brattleboro

MASSACHUSETTS

Using This Guide

The Six Regions

The state of Vermont has been divided into six regions, roughly from west to east by Vt. 100 and from north to south by U.S. 4 and U.S. 2. In a few instances, trails are included in neighboring regions for geographic reasons; however, this happens rarely. Region boundaries are indicated on the map on the opposite page. The six regions are:

- Region 1: Southwest

- Region 2: Southeast

- Region 3: West Central

- Region 4: East Central

- Region 5: Northwest

- Region 6: Northeast

Region Components

Each region has three components: (1) a region map, (2) a map locator key, and (3) trail descriptions and maps.

1. Region Map

The region map depicts the location of the trails that are described in the region. It is meant as a quick reference, not as an exact locator of trails.

2. Map Locator Key

The map locator key lists the trails indicated on the region maps and the page numbers where they are found in the guide.

3. Trail Descriptions and Maps

Within each region, trails are grouped by (1) trails in general and (2) rambles. Some trails are only described and not depicted on a map.

Trails are described from trailhead to destination or terminus. Hiking distance, elevation change, and estimated hiking time are given. If an exact elevation gain is not provided, the elevation gain is described as minor, moderate, or difficult. Departures from this norm are noted.

The scales of the maps vary as shown on each map. The contour interval is 200 feet. Trails are shown as dotted lines. Dashed lines distinguish roads that are not driveable. In Vermont, the compass points about 15 degrees west of true north.

Abbreviations

AMC . . . Appalachian Mountain Club

AT . . . . Appalachian Trail

ATC . . . Appalachian Trail Conference

CCC . . . Civilian Conservation Corps

CVT . . . Cross Vermont Trail

DOC . . . Dartmouth Outing Club

ft. . . . . feet

GMC . . . Green Mountain Club

GMNF . . Green Mountain National Forest

hr. . . . . hour(s)

km . . . . kilometer(s)

LT . . . . Long Trail

mi. . . . . mile(s)

min. . . . minutes

Mt. . . . Mount

Mtn. . . . Mountain

NEPCO . New England Power Company

USFS . . . U.S. Forest Service

WHPA . . Windmill Hill Pinnacle Association

WMA . . Wildlife Management Area

yds. . . . yards

Welcome to the Mountains of Vermont

The *Day Hiker's Guide to Vermont* describes the many trails scattered about the state that are suitable for day hikes and is a companion to the *Long Trail Guide*, which concentrates on Vermont's largest hiking network.

More than 200 trails are presented here; they include high peaks, natural areas, state parks, nature centers, and multiuse recreation paths. Many of the spots in this book are old favorites, while others are less well known. There are hikes that are perfect for half-day outings; others will take a day to complete.

Many of the trails lead to ecosystems rare to Vermont, with oak or mountain laurel, pitch pines, and bogs with rare plants. There are trails to suit most anyone—from the outdoor athlete to the casual walker. While concentrating on footpaths, this guide also describes many of the recreation paths in the state.

Together, the *Day Hiker's Guide* and the *Long Trail Guide*, the official guide to the Long Trail, describe the majority of the publicly accessible hiking trails in Vermont.

Long Trail

Known as the "Footpath in the Wilderness," the Long Trail follows the main ridge of the Green Mountains for more than 270 miles from the Massachusetts line to the Canadian border. Along the way, it passes more than forty of Vermont's highest peaks, follows streams, skirts ponds, and traverses areas of aesthetic or historical interest. More than 175 miles of side trails complete the 445-mile Long Trail System.

Built by the Green Mountain Club (GMC) between 1910 and 1930, the Long Trail is the oldest long-distance hiking trail in the country. It was the inspiration for the Appalachian Trail, which coincides with the Long Trail for 100 miles. As the protector, manager, and maintainer of the Long Trail, the Green Mountain Club works to ensure that the trail—one of Vermont's most significant natural and recreational features—is protected and maintained for the enjoyment of future generations.

Appalachian National Scenic Trail

Vermont and the Long Trail hold a prominent place in the history of the Appalachian Trail; it was on the summit of Stratton Mountain that the idea of an extended footpath linking the scenic ridges of the East crystallized in the mind of Appalachian Trail visionary Benton MacKaye.

The Appalachian Trail extends 2,172 miles from Mt. Katahdin in Maine to northern Georgia's Springer Mountain. The Appalachian Trail Conference, founded in 1925, works with its member clubs and federal and state agencies to preserve and maintain the Appalachian Trail, the world's longest linear national park.

More than 145 miles of the Appalachian Trail pass through Vermont. The Appalachian Trail coincides with the Long Trail from the Massachusetts border to Maine Junction, north of Sherburne Pass at Vt. 4, then swings easterly to cross the Connecticut River near Hanover, New Hampshire. The Appalachian Trail in Vermont is described in the GMC's *Long Trail Guide*. For more information about the Appalachian Trail, contact the Appalachian Trail Conference, P.O. Box 807, Harpers Ferry, West Virginia 25425; (304) 535-6331; atconf.org.

Trails Beyond the Long Trail

Although the Long Trail System is the largest trail network in Vermont, there are other wonderful hiking opportunities throughout the state. These trails are the subject of this guide. Please contact the GMC with any changes, corrections or additions to this guide.

Support Vermont's Trail Organizations

Many of the trails in this guide are cared for by small, local trail organizations. Like the GMC, these organizations need monetary and volunteer support to ensure the continued existence of these trails. To learn more, contact the organizations mentioned throughout the text and listed on pages 327 to 330.

Trail Markings

Because the trails are maintained by many different agencies, trail markings vary. The Long Trail and Appalachian Trail are marked with white rectangular blazes and their side trails are marked with blue blazes. Other trail markers run the gamut from yellow paint to blue metal disks and from scarce to abundant.

Staying Found

Some of the trails in this guide are minimally maintained and used and have marginal trail markings. A well-defined trail bed and indications of past clearing and blowdown removal are usually apparent. Occasionally, trails are neglected for so long that they become difficult to follow. The guidebook maps serve only for reference and should not be considered suitable for map and compass work.

Hiking Gear Checklist

The following checklist is recommended for a safe and enjoyable day hike:

- ❏ guidebook and/or map
- ❏ lunch and snacks
- ❏ water—and plenty of it!
- ❏ sturdy boots or hiking shoes
- ❏ wind jacket or rain gear with breathable shell (it is considerably colder at higher elevations)
- ❏ warm layer (wool or synthetic fleece)
- ❏ hats and mittens (even in summer)
- ❏ flashlight or headlamp (extra bulb and batteries)
- ❏ compass
- ❏ first-aid kit
- ❏ waterproof matches
- ❏ insect repellent and sunscreen
- ❏ toilet paper and trowel
- ❏ whistle

Mileages and Hiking Times

Mileages used in the summaries and trail descriptions are actual hiking distances, including twists and turns. Hiking times given in the book are based on the age-old formula: a half-hour for each mile plus a half-hour for each 1,000 feet of ascent. These figures are for actual walking time; allowances should be made for lunch breaks, viewing and resting, ruggedness of terrain, hiking experience and for trips to summits and other viewpoints reached via side trails. Actual times are likely to differ from "book times."

Climate and Weather

Never underestimate the variability of Vermont weather. Conditions on mountain summits are rarely the same as in the lowlands; temperatures often vary dramatically, sometimes as much as 5 degrees Fahrenheit per 1,000 feet. There is also a marked increase in the amount of precipitation at higher elevations. Rain, fog, and sudden drops in temperature can occur at any time, even in the summer.

Hypothermia

The threat of hypothermia, a dangerous and potentially deadly condition, exists year-round. Hypothermia is the cooling of the body's core temperature caused by heat loss and the body's inability to keep its internal temperature constant. This condition is not limited to winter. In fact, what is often referred to as hypothermia weather is not minus 20 degrees Fahrenheit, but those rainy, windy 40- to 50-degree or even 60-degree Fahrenheit days that occur in Vermont's mountains at any time of the year.

Symptoms of hypothermia include poor judgment, forgetfulness, and confusion. Motor control may suffer, leading to problems with coordination (such as being unable to fasten one's clothing), an unsteady gait, or slurred speech. Other warning signs include being unable to keep one's fingers and toes warm, uncontrollable shivering, or extreme unexpected fatigue. If untreated, hypothermia can result in coma and even death.

Prevention is the key to avoiding hypothermia. Always eat and drink plenty. Dress in layers, including, as needed, wicking underwear, an insulating layer, and a wind- and waterproof shell. Wear wool or synthetics like polypropylene or pile or, if it's warm, keep some of these in your pack, just in case. Regulate body temperature by adding and removing layers as needed.

Immediately get the chilled person out of the wind and into dry and warm clothing, including a hat. Give him or her food and water and keep the person moving. For more information about hypothermia or other backcountry emergencies, consult *Medicine for the Backcountry*, by Buck Tilton and Frank Hubbell, or take a course in backcountry first aid.

Lightning

Injury from lightning, although fortunately rare, is a serious risk to hikers. Whenever there is a threat:

• avoid open summits, ridges, and fields,
• if in the forest, seek an area amid shorter trees,

- avoid wet gullies and crevices, and stay out of small depressions where ground currents may travel,
- stay out of small caves (large, dry ones are usually good, however),
- sit or crouch on insulating objects, such as a dry sleeping bag or mattress, making yourself as small as possible, and
- set aside exposed metal objects (things inside a pack are usually all right).

About 70 percent of people hit by lightning survive. If a person is still conscious and breathing after being struck, the chance of survival is excellent. Even if a lightning victim is not breathing or has no pulse, prompt and effective CPR may save him or her. Continue CPR as long as possible—there is a much greater chance of survival in this situation than in most other cases of cardiac arrest.

Hunting

Most trails in this guide cross land that is open to hunting, a time-honored Vermont tradition. Hunting seasons extend from September 1 through mid-December. Deer rifle season runs from mid- to late November. Wear bright, visible colors, preferably fluorescent orange. Avoid wearing brown, tan, black, or patches of white that might be mistaken for the white tail of a deer. For information on hunting in Vermont, contact the Department of Fish and Wildlife, 103 South Main Street, Waterbury, Vermont, 05671-0501; (802) 241-3700; anr.state.vt.us/fw/fwhome/index.htm.

Leave No Trace

You can help preserve Vermont's backcountry and wilderness by practicing the seven Leave No Trace principles:

- **Plan Ahead and Prepare.** Prepare for extreme weather, hazards, and emergencies; bring appropriate clothing; carry and know how to use a map and compass; purify drinking water; know local regulations.

- **Travel on Durable Surfaces.** Travel only on foot and stay on the trail—shortcuts erode soil and damage vegetation; walk single file in the middle of the trail, even when it is wet or muddy; stay on rocks above tree line to avoid fragile vegetation.

- **Dispose of Waste Properly.** If you packed it in, pack it out; pick up trash others have left behind; when provided, use toilets; otherwise, bury human and pet waste in six- to eight-inch cat holes at least seventy steps from water sources and trails. Pack out toilet paper and sanitary products.

- **Leave What You Find.** Take only pictures, leave only footprints; do not disturb plants, flowers, rocks, and wildlife; leave natural objects and cultural artifacts.

- **Minimize Campfire Impacts.** Build fires only where permitted and only in established fire rings; use a portable stove instead of fire.

- **Respect Wildlife.** Don't feed or disturb wildlife; if you bring a pet, keep it leashed.

- **Be Considerate of Others.** Travel quietly, allowing nature's sounds to prevail; take breaks on durable surfaces away from the trail and other visitors.

Leave No Trace, Inc. is a national program dedicated to promoting responsible recreation by teaching minimum-impact practices and wildland ethics. For more information, contact the GMC.

Water

The quality and quantity of drinking water cannot be guaranteed. During dry weather, water sources may fail. Water may look and taste clean but still be unsafe to drink. Giardiasis, caused by the intestinal parasite *Giardia lamblia*, is just one of many illnesses caused by drinking contaminated water. Other bacteria and viruses may also be present in water sources. To kill all viruses and bacteria, all water must be chemically treated or boiled for five minutes.

Spring and Fall Mud Seasons

The Green Mountain Club and the state of Vermont encourage hikers to avoid higher elevation trails during the spring and late fall mud seasons (usually late March through the end of May and late October until snowpack). Snow melt creates extremely muddy trails and makes them vulnerable to damage from foot traffic, which is often compounded when hikers walk beside the trail to avoid the mud.

Camping

While this guide focuses on day hikes, camping is usually allowed on state and national forestlands. Guidelines for each type of land ownership are described below. Unless you know you are on federal or state land and in an area where primitive camping is permitted, camp only at designated sites. For more information, contact the appropriate state or federal agency listed on pages 327 to 330.

STATE LANDS. With the exception of state lands north of Mount Mansfield State Forest and some areas on Camel's Hump and Mount Mansfield, primitive camping is permitted below 2,500 feet if Leave No Trace practices are followed. Groups larger than ten require a state primitive camping permit. For more information, contact the state regional offices of the Department of Forests, Parks and Recreation listed on page 329.

FEDERAL LANDS. Camping is permitted in the Green Mountain National Forest if Leave No Trace practices are followed.

PRIVATE LANDS. Always seek permission if planning to camp on private land.

Group Hiking Guidelines

To help your group minimize negative impacts on the land and the experiences of other hikers, follow these guidelines:

- **Keep Groups Small.** The maximum group size for day use is twenty people (including leaders); for areas above tree line, fragile areas, and popular destinations, groups should be no larger than ten. Overnight camping should always be limited to no more than ten.

- **Experienced Leaders Are Essential.** Groups should include one leader for every four hikers.

- **Avoid Overcrowding.** If possible, plan your trip for weekdays instead of weekends and holidays.

- **Obtain Necessary Permits.** Organized groups hiking in the Green Mountain National Forest may need an Outfitter Guide Special Use permit. Groups of eleven or more planning to camp on state land should contact the Department of Forests, Parks and Recreation to obtain a primitive camping permit. (See page 329 for contact information.)

Wildlife

PEREGRINE FALCONS. After almost a thirty-year absence, peregrine falcons have returned to nest in Vermont. But they are still rare, with only twenty-three nesting sites reported in 2001. Peregrines prefer high cliffs and outcrops, and they are easily disturbed, especially by hikers above their cliff-side nests. During the nesting season, from mid-March to mid-August, hikers may encounter trails that have been closed or relocated. Please give these areas a wide berth until the young have fledged.

For information, contact the Department of Fish and Wildlife, 103 South Main Street, Waterbury, Vermont 05671-0501; (802) 241-3700; anr.state.vt.us/fw/fwhome /index.htm or vtfishandwildlife.com.

BLACK BEARS. Although black bears exist in Vermont, they are generally not a problem, being shy and seldom seen. Don't feed them, and please follow Leave No Trace practices so bears do not become a problem.

INSECTS. Black flies, mosquitoes, and ticks can make hiking in the Green Mountains very uncomfortable. Black flies are most abundant in early summer, usually disappearing by mid-July. Mosquitoes and ticks are around most of the summer. The best defense is to wear long-sleeved shirts and pants.

RABIES. Like other areas in the Northeast, rabies is present in Vermont. Although human cases are rare, and the danger of contracting the disease remains greater at home than on the trail, it is best to take precautions. Hang your food, keep your campsite clean to avoid attracting animals, carry out food wastes and trash, refrain from feeding animals, and stay away from any wild animal that is acting strangely, such as too tame or unafraid or too aggressive. Leave dead animals alone.

Winter Use

Winter conditions occur from October to May in the mountains, with snow lasting until early June at higher elevations just below tree line. At 3,800 feet, feet snow lingers for eight to twelve weeks longer than at 1,800 feet. Maximum snow depth usually occurs in March. Use skis or snowshoes to avoid post-holing through the snow. These knee-deep holes can make it unpleasant and even dangerous for the person who comes next.

To gain winter hiking experience, go on outings with friends who have experience, take a class, or join a guided hike. GMC sections offer winter trips with experienced leaders. Several good books on the subject are available (see pages 331 to 334), including the GMC publication, *Snowshoeing in Vermont: A Guide to the Best Winter Hikes.*

WINTER CATAMOUNT TRAIL. The Catamount Trail traverses the length of Vermont from Massachusetts to Canada, linking cross-country areas with long stretches of back-country trail. For more information about the Catamount Trail, contact Catamount Trail Association, P.O. Box 1235, Burlington, Vermont 05402; (802) 864-5794.

Trail Access

Although directions to all the trails are given in this guide, hikers should refer to road maps to find their way to trailheads. The official highway map of Vermont is available from the Department of Travel and Tourism, P.O. Box 1471, 134 State Street, Montpelier, Vermont, 05601-1471; (802) 828-3236 or (800) VERMONT.

Parking and Fees

Trailhead parking varies from large lots to roadside pull-offs. Wherever you park, avoid obstructing traffic or blocking access to homes, farms or woodlots.

To prevent trailhead vandalism, try not to leave your car at trailheads overnight. Leave valuables at home, or, at the very least, keep them locked in the trunk or otherwise hidden. Remove or hide your stereo, if possible. Don't leave a note on the car advising of your plans. Leave the glove compartment open and empty and park in the open and parallel to the highway if possible. If you have a problem at a trailhead, call the local or state police.

Although most hiking trails in Vermont are free to the public, some state parks and nature centers do charge a nominal fee for hiking on their trails.

Public Campgrounds Near the Trail

For a listing of Vermont campgrounds, contact the Department of Travel and Tourism.

Green Mountain Club

Membership and Volunteers

Membership in the GMC is an important way to support hiking opportunities in Vermont and is open to anyone with an interest in hiking and the preservation of Vermont's backcountry. Annual membership dues support trail maintenance, trail protection, education, and publications.

Those wishing to participate in outings and organized trail maintenance activities may choose to join a GMC section. Sections provide four-season schedules of outings, including hiking, biking, cross-country skiing, and canoeing. They also maintain portions of the Long Trail and its shelters. The club offers an at-large membership for those who wish to support the work of the GMC but are not interested in affiliating with a local section. Both section and at-large members enjoy the same benefits including a subscription to the club's quarterly newsletter, the *Long Trail News*, which provides information on trail and shelter conditions, hiking, statewide trails, club history, and club activities. Members receive discounts on club publications and items carried in the GMC bookstore, reduced fees at some overnight sites served by GMC caretakers, opportunities to participate in a wide range of club activities, and discounts on admission to most GMC events. Section members also receive their section's newsletter and activity schedule.

There are fourteen GMC sections. Twelve are based in Vermont: Bennington, Brattleboro, Bread Loaf (Middlebury), Burlington, Killington (Rutland), Laraway (Northwestern Vermont), Manchester, Montpelier, Northeast

Kingdom, Northern Frontier (Montgomery), Ottauquechee (Woodstock), and Sterling (Stowe-Morrisville). Two sections are based out of state: Connecticut and Worcester (eastern Massachusetts).

To join the GMC, send payment for dues ($35 individual, $45 family, $20 student/volunteer/limited income) to the Green Mountain Club, 4711 Waterbury-Stowe Road, Waterbury Center, Vermont 05677 or call the GMC with your VISA or MasterCard number at (802) 244-7037. Memberships can also be purchased online at greenmountainclub.org.

Headquarters

Information and Education Services

The Green Mountain Club headquarters are on Route 100 in Waterbury Center, Vermont, midway between Waterbury and Stowe. To reach the GMC from I-89 in Waterbury (exit 10), take Vt. 100 north four miles. The headquarters is in the Herrick Office Building on the west (left) side of Vt. 100. From the intersection of Vt. 108 and 100 in Stowe, the GMC is six miles south on Vt. 100.

The hiker center in the Herrick Office Building is open seven days a week (9:00 A.M. to 5:00 P.M.) from Memorial Day to Columbus Day. Business hours are Monday through

Friday from 9:00 A.M. to 5:00 P.M. year-round. Hikers are encouraged to stop by the center for trail information.

Protecting Vermont's Mountain Lands

Long Trail Protection Campaign

In 1986, the GMC launched the Long Trail Protection Campaign in an ambitious effort to acquire land or easements where the trail crossed private land. More than 21,000 acres of backcountry land with wildlife habitat and recreational value have been safeguarded. This effort has been made possible in large part through state legislative appropriations for Long Trail acquisitions. Much of the acquired land has gone into state ownership. Help preserve the trail for future generations with a donation to the Long Trail Protection Campaign.

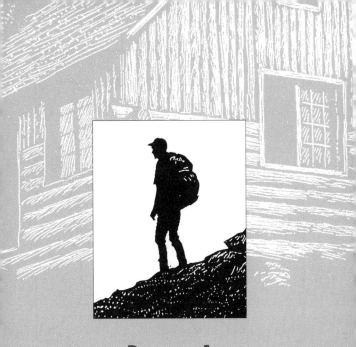

REGION 1

Southwest
Vermont

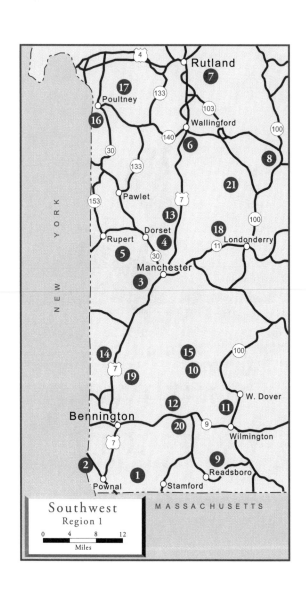

4

Rutland
7

17
Poultney

133

16

103

Wallingford

140

30

6

100

133

8

153

Pawlet

7

21

100

13

153

Rupert

Dorset

4

18

Londonderry

5

11

30

Manchester

3

14

15

100

7

19

10

12

11   W. Dover

Bennington

20

9

Wilmington

7

2

9

1

Readsboro

Pownal   Stamford

Southwest
Region 1

MASSACHUSETTS

0   4   8   12
Miles

N E W   Y O R K

REGION 1
Southwest Vermont

REGION 1
Southwest Vermont

The geography of southwestern Vermont is largely defined by the Taconic Mountains on the west and the Green Mountains on the east. In between, the Valley of Vermont, which originates in northwest Massachusetts, extends north 85 miles to Brandon. This lowland distinctly separates the two mountain ranges and is several miles wide in the Bennington area, narrowing dramatically to a few hundred yards near Emerald Lake in Dorset. Within this valley lie Otter Creek, the longest river entirely within Vermont, and the Batten Kill, a world-famous trout stream.

Of uncertain geologic origin, the Taconic Mountains rise steeply from the Valley of Vermont. Beginning as low hills in northwest Connecticut, the Taconics reach their greatest height at Mt. Equinox in Manchester before dwindling to insignificant hills north of Brandon.

A part of the Appalachian Mountains that extend from the southeastern United States to Canada, the Green Mountains run the length of Vermont. East of the Valley of Vermont, they continue southward into Massachusetts where, together with the Taconics, they are known as

1

the Berkshire Hills. Unlike northern Vermont, where the Green Mountains form two or three parallel ranges, in southern Vermont the mountains spread out in an irregular manner to form a highland plateau. Much of the area has been relatively inaccessible and unsuitable for permanent settlement. As a result, more wild country is found in southern Vermont than anywhere else in the state except the Northeast Kingdom (see Region 6).

POWNAL AREA

Lying in the southwest corner of Vermont and the northwest corner of Massachusetts, this large trail network offers many loop hikes. These trails are maintained by the Williams Outing Club and the Green Mountain Club. They lead to several peaks with wonderful views across Vermont's southern Green Mountains, New York's Taconics, and Massachusetts's Mt. Greylock and the Berkshires.

Most of these trails lie within a watershed area owned by the city of North Adams, Massachusetts. Camping is allowed only at Seth Warner Shelter on the Long Trail and at Sherman Brook Primitive Campsite on the Appalachian Trail in Massachusetts.

THE DOME

Distance: 2.6 mi. (4.2 km)
Elevation Change: 1,650 ft. ascent
Hiking Time: 2½ hr. (reverse 1¼ hr.)

Although most of the broad ridge of this mountain has a dense cover of spruce and balsam, an exposed rock area on the summit (2,748 ft.) offers limited views of the southern Green Mountains, the Hoosic Range to the east,

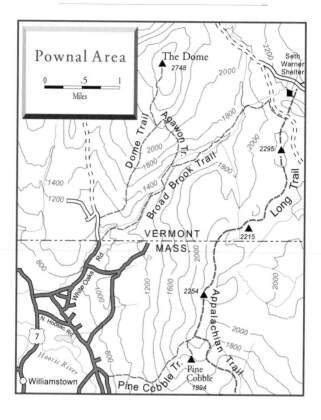

Mt. Greylock and the Berkshires to the south, and the
Taconic Range to the west. The trail is maintained by the
Williams Outing Club.
TO THE TRAIL: From U.S. 7 in Williamstown, Massachu-
setts, 1.6 mi. north of its junction with U.S. 2, or 0.8 mi.

1

south of the Vermont state line, turn east on Sand Springs Road (0.0 mi.). Bear right at a fork on Bridges Road, then turn left (0.6 mi.) on White Oaks Road at a four-way intersection. Continue north to the end of the pavement at the Vermont state line (1.7 mi.). Continue 0.3 mi. beyond the parking lot for the Broad Brook Trail (described in the *Long Trail Guide*) to a logging road, which enters from the right where White Oaks Road veers left. Parking is available along the apron of the logging road. A trail sign is posted on a tree set back from the road.

DESCRIPTION: From White Oaks Road (0.0 mi.), the trail follows the logging road past a chain barring motor vehicles, through a large log landing and into the hardwood forest. After following the logging road for a distance along a moderate ascent, the trail veers left into the woods (0.5 mi.) following yellow blazes. (The logging road continues straight ahead onto posted land.) The trail eventually reaches a junction on the right with the Agawon Trail, a few feet below Meeting House Rock (1.2 mi.). The Agawon Trail leads 0.7 mi. southeast to the Broad Brook Trail.

Bearing left at the junction, the trail climbs easily for some distance, then descends gradually to a shallow sag (1.7 mi.) where it turns right and follows an occasionally muddy woods road. (No trespassing signs in this area are intended to keep out unauthorized hunters.) The trail follows the woods road past a spur road left, then within 50 ft., bears left itself, leaving the woods.

The trail climbs out of the hardwoods into a spruce-fir forest before beginning a steep and circuitous climb over a series of quartzite outcrops to a false summit on a narrow ridge with a limited view through the trees (2.4 mi.). The trail then passes through a heavily wooded wet area before swinging to the east side of the ridge and climbing easily through scrub growth to the open summit (2.6 mi.). The view from the summit is limited as the surrounding trees have grown up significantly.

AGAWON TRAIL

Distance: 0.7 mi. (1.1 km)
Elevation Change: 880 ft. descent
Hiking Time: 20 min. (reverse 45 min.)

This yellow-blazed trail connects the Dome Trail with the Broad Brook Trail.

TO THE TRAIL: This trail leaves the Dome Trail just below Meeting House Rock, 1.4 mi. below the Dome summit.

DESCRIPTION: From the Dome Trail junction (0.0 mi.), the Agawon Trail ascends gradually toward the northeast on an old woods road. Soon turning sharply right (0.1 mi.), the trail makes a steep and winding descent, crosses a small stream, which later disappears underground (0.2 mi.), and continues its steady winding descent to a wooded knoll overlooking Broad Brook (0.6 mi.). Here, the trail turns right and continues on easier grades to a junction with the Broad Brook Trail (0.7 mi.). Via the Broad Brook Trail, it is 1.4 mi. to White Oaks Road, 0.3 mi. south of the Dome trailhead. In periods of heavy rain and wet weather, the stream crossings of Broad Brook can be challenging, if not impossible and it may not be possible to complete the loop hike.

• • • • • • • • • • • • • • • •

TACONIC CREST TRAIL

Distance: 7.8 mi. 12.5 (km)
Elevation Change: 2,520 ft. ascent
Hiking Time: 5¼ hr. (reverse 4½ hr.)

The Taconic Mountains extend from northwestern Connecticut until they dwindle to small hills near Brandon, Vermont. The Taconic Crest Trail, maintained by the Taconic Hiking Club of Troy, New York, follows the west

1

and central ridges of the Taconic Range southward for about 30 mi. from N.Y. 346 in Petersburg, New York, to Berry Pond in the Pittsfield Massachusetts State Forest. While there are few trail signs, the route is well marked with metal diamonds and white-paint blazes. A trail guide with maps is available from the Taconic Hiking Club (see page 329 for contact information).

The only Vermont portions of the trail are two short sections leading south to N.Y. 2 at Petersburg Pass, which is just west of the New York–Massachusetts line (USGS North Pownal, Berlin). A blue-blazed approach trail once led to the ridge from North Pownal, but until landowner issues are resolved, the trail is closed.

Never far from the ridgeline, this section of the Taconic Crest Trail generally remains in mature hardwoods, but several large clearings and other vantage points offer wide views of the Adirondacks, Catskills, Taconics, and Berkshires. Water sources are scarce along the ridge. Camping is permitted off trail on lands belonging to, and marked by, the New York Department of Environmental Conservation.

To the Trail: From North Pownal, travel west on N.Y. 346 to the New York–Vermont border. A large Department of Conservation sign on the south side of N.Y. 346 marks the northern end of the Taconic Crest Trail, approximately 200 yds. west of the bridge over the Hoosic River where there is a parking lot for ten cars and a kiosk.

Description: The trail begins at the southwest corner of the lot (0.0 mi.), west of the kiosk. (avoiding the jeep trail on the east side.) The trail ascends steeply for approximately 0.25 mi. on an old woods road, then breaks sharply left (south), still climbing, to emerge into a brushy open area marked by small evergreens.

The trail then reenters the trees, curves west, and crosses the earlier mentioned jeep trail at right angles. Steadily climbing through the woods, it crosses wet sections to emerge on a ridge where it turns left, crosses over a small knoll and descends, on the far side, to a woods road that continues to the true Taconic Ridge crest (1.5 mi.).

From here, the trail travels along the broad and meandering ridge. After passing over two minor knobs (2.3 mi. and 3.3 mi.), the trail briefly returns to the Vermont side of the state line in the vicinity of a wooded knob (3.9 mi.) and descends into the saddle north of Bald Mtn. (4.1 mi.). The trail then begins a steady climb to the wooded summit (4.4 mi.) and continues around its east shoulder to a spur, which leads 250 ft. to a lookout where there are views of the Pownal Valley, the Dome, and Mt. Greylock. The main trail descends past two other lookouts to a sag (4.7 mi.) and follows an old road uphill to a junction (4.9 mi.). To the left (east), a spur descends about 250 ft. to the Snow Hole, a deep fissure in the rocks where tradition holds that snow and ice may be found year-round.

From the Snow Hole spur, the trail continues uphill along the old road, eventually crossing to the west side of the ridge, bypassing the wooded summit of White Rock, and passing through two large clearings (5.4 mi. and 5.5 mi.), both offering good views west and south. Returning to the woods after passing through two smaller clearings, the trail continues with minor elevation changes to a nameless peak (2,485 ft.) on the Vermont side of the state line (5.8 mi.). The trail then descends across the boundary into a wet sag (6.1 mi.) and climbs easily east of a wooded peak (6.4 mi.). Descending to a junction on the left with the red-blazed Birch Brook Trail (6.5 mi.), the trail continues through an overgrown clearing (6.6 mi.) before reaching the north end of the extensive White Rocks clearing (6.8 mi.). The open summit of Jim Smith Hill (2,330 ft.), a few yards east of the trail, offers extensive views south and west. Soon returning to the woods (7.2 mi.), the trail descends steadily on a woods road to two small

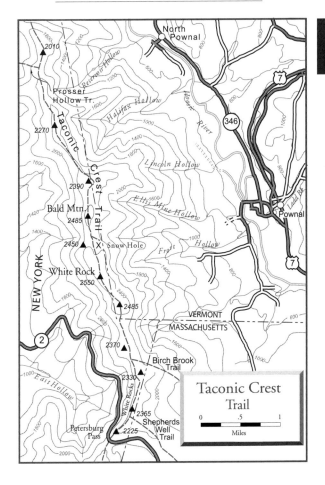

Taconic Crest
Trail

0   .5   1

Miles

springs on the left (7.4 mi.). A short distance beyond, the trail turns right off the road and rises to a large open area (7.7 mi.). Descending in the open, the trail soon reaches N.Y. 2 at the summit of Petersburg Pass, opposite the Taconic Trails Ski Area (7.8 mi.) and continues through the ski area.

From Petersburg Pass, the highway descends about 4.0 mi. east to U.S. 7, south of Williamstown, Massachusetts. To the west, it is about 5.0 mi. to N.Y. 22 at Petersburg.

• • • • • • • • • • • • • • • •

MOUNT EQUINOX

With an elevation of 3,825 ft., Mt. Equinox (USGS Manchester, West Rupert) is the highest peak in the Taconic Mountains and also the highest peak in Vermont not in the Green Mountain Range. Common theory holds that the origin of the mountain's name is a corruption of Native American words meaning either "place of fog" or "place where the very top is."

Access to the summit is by foot along the Blue Summit Trail, formerly known as the Burr and Burton Trail, as well as by car along the paved Equinox Sky Line Drive (toll charged). From the parking area at the summit, trails from the Sky Line Inn (which is now closed) lead to several points of interest. Additionally, the Equinox Preservation Trust (EPT), established in 1993 to protect and maintain the lands of Mt. Equinox, maintains several multiuse trails in the vicinity of Equinox Pond. For a brochure and trail map, contact the EPT at P.O. Box 46, Manchester Village, Vermont 05254; (802) 362-4700; ept@sover.net, or stop by the Equinox Resort.

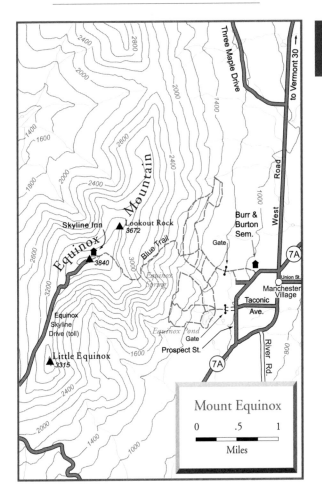

Mount Equinox

0   .5   1

Miles

BLUE SUMMIT TRAIL
(PREVIOUSLY THE BURR AND BURTON TRAIL)

Distance: 2.7 mi. (4.3 km)
Elevation Change: 2,730 ft. ascent
Hiking Time: 3 hr. (reverse 1½ hr.)

This trail was first established and later maintained for many years by students from the Burr and Burton Seminary, now a semipublic high school renamed the Burr and Burton Academy, in the village of Manchester. The trail is maintained by the Friends of Equinox Preservation Trust, a dedicated group of volunteers who maintain all the trails on the Mt. Equinox Preserve. The trail is rated difficult by the EPT because it is steep for most of the way.

TO THE TRAIL: Parking for the Blue Summit Trail is available at the Equinox Hotel on Vt. 7A in Manchester Village. Hikers should leave their cars at the upper (west) end of the large parking lot at the hotel. Park behind the Hotel and follow the West Union Trail (blazed in green) to the top of West Union Street. Turn right onto a dirt road and follow the Red Gate Trail to the Blue Summit Trail. There are three other small parking lots for the preserve; please consult the EPT map for directions.

DESCRIPTION: From the red gate (0.0 mi.), the signed Blue Summit Trail follows a woods road westerly and reaches successive junctions on the left with the Snicket Trail, which trends southerly on parallel routing for about 0.5 mi. to the Pond Loop Trail and the Black Gate access from Pond Road and Prospect Street. The Blue Summit Trail continues uphill past a grassy woods road on the left to reach a fork (0.2 mi.). Here, the Red Gate Trail takes the left fork and descends southerly for about 0.75 mi. to the Pond Loop and the main gate.

The Blue Summit Trail takes the right fork and ascends on the woods road to a clearing and an unmarked trail crossing (0.4 mi.).

Junction: Here, the Trillium Trail departs left and descends southerly for about 0.6 mi. to Equinox Pond. To the right, the Trillium Trail leads to the Southern Vermont Art Center Loop, which accesses the lower slopes of the Southern Vermont Art Center and connections with its local trails.

The Blue Summit Trail continues straight through the junction, and after some steady climbing, it crosses the Maidenhair Trail (0.5 mi.).

Still following the woods road, the trail begins a steep and winding climb northwest. Eventually swinging southwest (1.0 mi.), the trail continues its steady ascent to the end of the road and a junction (1.4 mi.) where a marked but somewhat brushy spur trail descends 250 ft. to the gushing torrent of Equinox (Upper) Spring, which can be easily heard from the junction.

The Blue Summit Trail, now a rough and narrow footpath, takes the right fork and continues its steady southwesterly climb past several limited but increasingly revealing views of the Manchester area and the Green Mountains. Eventually reaching the south shoulder of the mountain, the trail swings right (2.0 mi.) and ascends westerly on easier grades through spruce woods.

After passing limited views to the east, it makes an easy ascent to the ridge.

From the junction, the Blue Summit Trail continues in the woods and soon crosses the terminus of a narrow gravel road at a television repeater station. The trail skirts the left side of the fenced-in facility and continues 100 ft. to its end.

To the left, the Lookout Rock Trail leads uphill to the Sky Line Inn, the upper end of the Toll Road and the summit of Mt. Equinox (0.1 mi.), with some of the finest views in southern Vermont.

• • • • • • • • • • • • • • • • •

DORSET AREA

West of the Valley of Vermont, at the headwaters of the Battenkill and Otter Creeks, rises an impressive series of summits and ridges, long a site of quarrying activity. A variety of old roads, revived hiking trails, and snowmobile trails provide access to abandoned quarries and rocky outcrops, as well as to the summits of Dorset's higher peaks. Portions of a ridge trail connecting Owl's Head, Mt. Aeolus, Dorset Peak, and other significant summits surrounding Dorset Hollow have been reopened. Note: the trails to the peaks in the Dorset region can be difficult to follow due to a large number of ATV trails, logging roads and poor blazing.

DORSET PEAK

Although this mountain (USGS Dorset) is one of New England's 100 highest peaks, the south (3,730 ft.) and north (3,770 ft.) summits are wooded and provide only limited views. A local flood and resultant landslides ravaged the Dorset Hollow area in late 1976, but the forest has reclaimed most of the damaged areas, leaving only traces of the event. Two trails provide good access to the peak. It is also possible to ascend by a series of woods roads from North Dorset, but much of this route is very steep, eroded, or wet, and some of the turns are confusing.

DORSET HOLLOW APPROACH

Distance: 3.4 mi. (5.5 km)
Elevation Change: 2,320 ft. ascent
Hiking Time: 3 hr. (reverse 1¾ hr.)

TO THE TRAIL: In the village of Dorset, just west of the Barrows House on Vt. 30 (0.0 mi.), turn right (north) on the paved Dorset Hollow Road. Turn right at the first junction

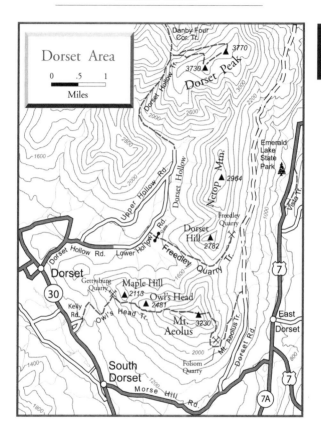

Dorset Area

0   .5   1
Miles

(0.8 mi.) and continue past a fork on the left (1.0 mi.) on Lower Hollow Road. Continue beyond the end of the pavement (1.7 mi.), past a fork on the left (3.6 mi.) where the road's name changes to Tower Road. Limited roadside parking is available at the end of this public road in Dorset

Hollow (4.2 mi.). The trail proceeds up the woods road, which quickly becomes quite rough, on the left. Special care should be taken not to block any driveways.

DESCRIPTION: From the end of the public road (0.0 mi.), the unsigned, unblazed trail ascends easily on an obvious woods road through areas of logging activity and passes right of a hunting cabin (1.1 mi.). The trail continues following the logging road, ascending steeply uphill. It crosses Jane Brook (1.5 mi.) before reaching the saddle (2.0 mi.) between Jackson Peak on the left and Dorset Peak on the right. To the left, the woods road continues to a public road at Danby Four Corners, providing access from the north. Ascent via this trail begins on page 35.

In the saddle, the trail bears right along an obvious snowmobile trail marked by an orange caution sign. The trail soon comes to a fork in the snowmobile route marked by a small cairn (2.4 mi.) where it turns right and ascends steeply along this route, which is sporadically marked with silver squares. At a second cairn (2.7 mi.), the trail turns right, leaving the snowmobile trail, and ascends through the ferns on an unblazed foot trail to a clearing on the south summit of Dorset Peak (2.8 mi.). An alternative access to the summit is reached by continuing straight past the cairn a short distance where another snowmobile trail departs right and makes a short ascent to the summit. The clearing contains the remains of a steel tower erected in the 1930s. To the north there are good views of the Taconics.

Ignoring a smaller trail leaving the clearing to the east, the trail exits the summit clearing to the north and descends to rejoin the snowmobile trail, now marked with orange diamonds. Continuing north past a trail to the right, it reaches a sign at another snowmobile trail crossing (3.2 mi.), which descends steeply to North Dorset. Continuing straight through this junction, the trail becomes smaller and climbs to the wooded north summit of Dorset Peak at the remains of an old cabin (3.4 mi.). A short spur south provides limited views.

Danby Four Corners Approach

Distance: 3.7 mi. (6.0 km)
Elevation Change: 2,354 ft. ascent
Hiking Time: 2½ hr. (reverse 1½ hr.)

This trail uses an unmarked but obvious woods road to ascend to the saddle between Dorset and Jackson Peaks and offers an alternate final ascent to the north summit of Dorset Peak

To the Trail: From Danby village, 0.2 mi. west of U.S. 7, follow the paved Brook Road west toward Danby Four Corners. At 2.8 mi. from the village, take a sharp left on the gravel Keeler Road. Continue south 0.6 mi. before turning sharply left on Edmunds Road. The trailhead is 0.6 mi. south where Edmunds Road curves left. Limited roadside parking is available. Avoid blocking the driveway of the nearby house or parking on the lawn.

Description: The trail begins on the south side of the road (0.0 mi.), passes through a gate in 150 ft., follows a logging road, and, after passing through another gate, continues through an overgrown field where there is a log landing. After veering left, the trail leaves the field and enters the woods (0.8 mi.). It remains on the obvious woods road and climbs steeply in places before reaching the saddle between Dorset and Jackson Peaks (2.2 mi.). The woods road continues straight ahead, descending into Dorset Hollow. In the saddle, a well-defined snowmobile trail leads east (left). An ascent to the south and north summits of Dorset Peak may be made following the path previously described in the ascent from Dorset Hollow.

An alternate ascent to the north summit may also be made using this trail. Turning left in the saddle and ascending gently, the trail crosses a small stream (2.4 mi.), then continues past a snowmobile trail on the right, leading to the south summit. Continuing east and passing a poorly defined trail on the right (2.7 mi.), the trail offers limited views of the Tinmouth Valley and Danby Four

Corners through the trees. The trail arrives at a junction indicated by a red marker on a tree (3.5 mi.) where a short spur left leads to a lookout with views east to the Green Mountains. Turning sharply right at the marker, a rocky trail ascends to the north summit of Dorset Peak at the remains of an old cabin (3.7 mi.).

MOUNT AEOLUS

Distance: 2.8 mi. (4.5 km)
Elevation Change: 1,850 ft. ascent
Hiking Time: 2½ hr. (reverse 1¾ hr.)

This approach from the east, over a limited section of the Dorset Ridge Trail, ascends Mt. Aeolus and connects to the Owl's Head Trail (described on page 38) at Gilbert Lookout. For guidebook purposes, the quarry roads leading to the trail are considered part of the trail, which can be difficult to follow to the summit.

TO THE TRAIL: From South Dorset on Vt. 30, follow the paved Morse Hill Road east 2.5 mi. to Dorset Hill Road/Quarry Road on the left. To reach this same point from the east, follow U.S. 7 south from the East Dorset General Store 0.7 mi. to an intersection on the right with the same Morse Hill Road and proceed 1.2 mi. west to this junction. From Morse Hill Road, follow the unpaved Quarry Road (also Dorset Hill Road) 1.9 mi. north to a woods road on the left, across from a white house. Two large road signs at this junction indicate that the side road is open to the public. Roadside parking is available.

DESCRIPTION: From the trailhead (0.0 mi.), the Mount Aeolus Trail follows the quarry road, soon reaching a fork (0.1 mi.) at a gate across a gravel road on the left. While the woods road continues to the right (leading about 1.0 mi. to the abandoned Freedley Quarry), the Mount Aeolus Trail turns sharply left, passes through the gate, and follows an old quarry road in a southerly direction. At a second fork (1.0 mi.), the trail bears left onto a narrow

1

woods road, leaving the gravel road, which turns sharply right to a microwave transmitter. To the right of the trail, a short spur leads to the abandoned Folsom Quarry (2,060 ft.) (1.3 mi.). Opened in 1854, the quarry is now a great roofless man-made vault with vertical work faces extending about 100 ft. high. A short distance beyond is a level area atop quarry dumps with good views of the Manchester area and Bromley Mtn.

The trail turns right and ascends steadily, circling above the quarry before meeting another road junction (1.8 mi.) where metal arrows point to the right. Bearing right, the trail continues along a series of switchbacks to a point east of the entrance to the Dorset Bat Cave (2.0 mi.), which is easily overlooked. Because of the importance of this cave as a hibernaculum for many bat species, including the endangered Indiana bat, there is an iron gate at the cave entrance to minimize disturbance of these timid creatures. This area is owned by The Nature Conservancy, which asks that the cave entrance remain undisturbed during the September-to-May hibernation period.

A short distance above the cave, the trail passes left of a lookout providing views east and south from leveled quarry rubble. The trail then turns left off the road (2.1 mi.) and ascends along a narrower footbed to a short rocky path, which climbs to the summit of Mt. Aeolus, formerly Green Peak (3,230 ft.) (2.8 mi.). A short distance south of the summit is a rocky lookout with views south of the Dorset-Manchester area, Stratton Mtn., Haystack Mtn., Mt. Equinox, and Mt. Greylock.

DORSET RIDGE TRAIL

Distance: 2.0 mi. (3.2 km)
Elevation Change: 980 ft. ascent
Hiking Time: 1½ hr. (reverse 1¾ hr.)

Early last century, George Holly Gilbert scouted and blazed the Dorset Ridge Trail, which formed a lengthy loop over Owl's Head, Mt. Aeolus, Dorset Peak, and other significant summits surrounding Dorset Hollow (USGS Manchester, Dorset). Portions of this trail remain obvious or have been reopened and are described here. This section of the Dorset Ridge Trail connects Mt. Aeolus with Owl's Head and Gilbert Lookout (page 39).

TO THE TRAIL: See description for Mt. Aeolus Trail (page 36).

DESCRIPTION: Beyond the summit of Mt. Aeolus (0.0 mi.), the trail is variously marked with tape, metal trail markers, and faded paint blazes. Leaving the summit, the trail continues in a westerly direction along the narrow rocky summit ridge through stunted evergreens. Passing several views north and south, the trail leaves the ridge on a rocky path (0.6 mi.) and descends south along a fern-filled route, eventually veering west and descending to an old woods road (1.6 mi.) heading in a north–south direction in the notch between Owl's Head and Mt. Aeolus.

Turning sharply left (south) onto the woods road, the trail ascends over the height of land at the top of the notch, then leaves the woods road right (west) at a marked junction soon after starting a descent. The trail then ascends, climbing through dense spruce forest and following the south side of Owl's Head, but remaining well below the summit. The trail makes a short rocky descent to Gilbert Lookout (2,300 ft.) (2.0 mi.) where a stone plaque bearing that name is cemented to the cliff face. From this point, there are good views of Dorset Hollow, the Mettawee Valley, and the Adirondacks.

OWL'S HEAD TRAIL

Distance: 2.2 mi. (3.5 km)
Elevation Change: 1,260 ft. ascent
Hiking Time: 1¾ hr. (reverse 1 hr.)

This approach to Gilbert Lookout from the west follows a portion of the aforementioned former Dorset Ridge Trail.

1

Combined with the approach to Gilbert Lookout from the east over the summit of Mt. Aeolus via the Dorset Bat Cave and Folsom Quarry (described previously), these trails offer a lengthy day hike.

To the Trail: The trail begins on Kelly Road on the north side of Vt. 30, 1.3 mi. south of the Dorset Inn in Dorset and 1.4 mi. north from South Dorset village, or 4.7 mi. north of Manchester Center. A pull-off along Kelly Road provides roadside parking for several cars.

Description: From the parking area (0.0 mi.), the un-signed and unblazed trail follows a private dirt road east, toward a sign for Black Rock Farm. Past a white pine plantation, the road forks (0.3 mi.), and the trail bears right following a gravel road and continuing past two new houses until turning sharply right onto an old logging road across from the second house (0.6 mi.). The trail then follows this logging road on easy grades to an old hunting cabin (1.0 mi.) where it turns sharply left immediately before the camp. Here, the trail may be overgrown but begins to be marked by yellow and orange flagging. After crossing a pair of old woods roads (1.3 mi.), the trail ascends steadily to the open face of the abandoned Gettysburg marble quarry (1,720 ft.) (1.4 mi.), opened in 1866. The quarry dump, reached by a rough path on the left, offers views of the Dorset Valley.

From the quarry, the trail bears right and within 150 ft. turns left, then ascends steeply for another 150 ft. before turning abruptly right on a gently ascending woods road along a ledge. The trail may be poorly maintained but is marked with yellow and orange flagging and tin disks. There are limited views from along the ridge, south to the upper Batten Kill Valley and west to Mother Myrick Mtn.

Eventually, the trail reaches a flat-topped ridge (1.9 mi.), which provides a good view of Owl's Head, then crosses into the saddle between Maple Hill and Owl's Head (2.1 mi.), before turning sharply left at a 12-ft.-high boulder on the right. A steep zigzag climb up the cliff, marked with reddish orange blazes, tin disks, and yellow and orange flagging, ends at Gilbert Lookout (2,300 ft.) (2.2 mi.), named for the father of the Dorset area trails, George Holly Gilbert. From the lookout, there are good views of Dorset Hollow, the Mettawee Valley, and the Adirondacks.

FREEDLEY QUARRY

Distance: 2.1 mi. (3.4 km)
Elevation Change: 900 ft. ascent
Hiking Time: 1½ hr. (reverse 1 hr.)

This unmarked trail ascends moderately along a series of old roads to reach the long-abandoned Freedley Quarry (2,020 ft.), originally opened in 1808.

TO THE TRAIL: From the village of Dorset on Vt. 30 (0.0 mi.), follow the paved Dorset Hollow Road north, turn right at the first junction onto Elm Street (0.7 mi.) and bear right at a second junction where the Upper Hollow Road leaves left (0.9 mi.). Continue on the right fork (Lower Hollow Road) to a large barn on the left (2.3 mi.). The trailhead is immediately across the road at the start of a farm lane.

DESCRIPTION: From the trailhead (0.0 mi.), the unsigned and unblazed trail passes through a gate and proceeds along a farm road for 600 ft. before bearing left and passing through a tree line into a meadow. Turning left, the trail follows the meadow around its margin to an obvious road (0.4 mi.), which it then follows, turning right and continuing into the woods. Ascending gradually, the trail reaches a height of land in the notch between Mt. Aeolus and Dorset Hill.

In the notch, the trail bears left on a woods road (1.4 mi.), then right at a second intersection (1.5 mi.), and descends to intersect the quarry road itself (1.9 mi.). Bearing left into the Freedley Quarry, the trail continues to a large water-filled opening in the side of the mountain, which can remain frozen after cold winters until July. A marble dump just east of the quarry offers good views of the Valley of Vermont with the Green Mountains beyond. On a clear day, the view from this point extends all the way to Mt. Monadnock in southern New Hampshire.

MOTHER MYRICK MOUNTAIN

Distance: 3.8 mi. (6.1 km)
Elevation Change: 2,020 ft. ascent
Hiking Time: 3 hr. (reverse 2 hr.)

This unmarked trail follows logging roads and snowmobile trails to a wooded summit where there are limited views from a nearby lookout.

TO THE TRAIL: From Vt. 30 in South Dorset, follow the Dorset West Road west for 2.1 mi. to a junction on the left with the Nichols Hill Road then proceed 1.3 mi. to the end. Parking for several vehicles is available in a small lot provided by a landowner.

DESCRIPTION: From the parking area (0.0 mi.), the unblazed and unsigned trail proceeds through a gate along a woods road, soon reaching junctions with roads on the right and left. Ignoring these roads, the trail continues straight, passes a log landing, and skirts the front of a hunting camp (0.3 mi.), before beginning a steep ascent. Ignoring logging trails off the main woods road, the trail crests a ridge in an area of active logging (1.0 mi.) and bears left along a road. In a short distance, the road curves right, but the trail bears left onto an older logging road. Ascending on gentle grades southwest and south, the trail then turns abruptly right (1.8 mi.), climbs more steeply, and reaches the Taconic ridge and a second hunting cabin. At a snowmobile trail beyond the cabin, the trail turns left and descends a short distance before coming to a major three-way intersection where it bears left and begins a moderately steep climb to an intermediate summit (2.7 mi.) and ridge.

Continuing along the crest of the ridge and ignoring a series of trails to the right, the trail reaches an intersection at a sign incorrectly identifying the summit as located to the northwest. Bearing left and ascending moderately, the trail reaches the summit of Mother Myrick Mtn. (3,010 ft.) (3.8 mi.). A small, rocky lookout is 50 ft. northeast of the trail, and it provides views across the Mettawee Valley to Dorset Mtn. and Mt. Aeolus. A short distance beyond the lookout are the remnants of a wing from a small plane that crashed near the summit in the 1970s.

•••••••••••••••••

MERCK FOREST AND FARMLAND CENTER

Located in the town of Rupert (USGS Pawlet, West Rupert), the Merck Forest and Farmland Center (Merck Forest) encompasses more than 3,100 acres of fields and forests in the Taconic Mountains. George Merck founded Merck Forest in 1950 as a nonprofit conservation organization devoted to environmental education and recreation and funded by memberships and contributions. The center's lands are open for public use during daylight hours throughout the year, and several backcountry cabins and shelters are available for rent. Although there are no fees for day use of the area, donations, left in the contribution boxes at each entrance, are appreciated.

The trails described are a small part of an intricate network of more than 28 mi. of forest roads and trails providing access to all parts of the forest. Closed at all times to motorized vehicles, most are ideally suited for walking and cross-country skiing. For more information, contact Merck Forest and Farmland Center, P.O. Box 86, Rupert, Vermont 05768; (802) 394-7836; merck@vermontel.net; merckforest.org.

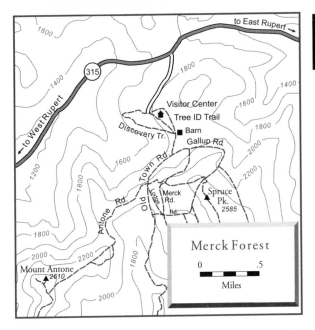

To the Trail: From the junction of Vt. 30 and Vt. 315 in East Rupert, follow Vt. 315 west 3.0 mi. to a height of land. Turn left (south) on an unnamed gravel road with a sign for Merck Forest. A map of the trail system is available at the Joy Green Visitor Center or at the entrance sign nearby.

MOUNT ANTONE

Distance: 2.5 mi. (4.0 km)
Elevation Change: 820 ft. ascent
Hiking Time: 1¾ hr. (reverse 1¼ hr.)

Description: The ascent to the summit of Mt. Antone follows a series of roads. From the visitor center (0.0 mi.), the route follows Old Town Road, past sweeping views south, to the barn and the upper end of the Discovery Trail (0.3 mi.). After descending for some distance, the road ascends through the woods to a junction with Lodge and Antone Roads (0.8 mi.).

From the junction, Antone Road takes the right fork and follows easy grades along the ridge, passes through Clark's Clearing (1.3 mi.), and continues to a shelter at a junction (1.4 mi.) where the Clark's Clearing Trail departs left and a ski trail (which offers alternate routing) leaves right. The Antone Road continues straight ahead and soon begins a steady, winding climb left of the ridge. After gaining the ridge, the trail continues on easier grades, is rejoined on the right by the ski trail (1.9 mi.), then begins a steady ascent past the Wade Lot Road and Lookout Road (2.1 mi.) to a junction with the Masters Mountain Trail and the Beebe Pond Trail (2.3 mi.). Here, the Mount Antone Trail turns sharply right and ascends steeply to a junction with a spur trail, which leads left 0.1 mi. to a lookout. A short distance beyond, the main trail reaches the summit (2,610 ft.) (2.5 mi.) with views of Dorset Peak, the southern Adirondacks, the northern Catskills, and the White Creek Valley.

SPRUCE PEAK

Distance: 1.7 mi. (2.7 km)
Elevation Change: 750 ft. ascent
Hiking Time: 50 min. (reverse 1¼ hr.)

DESCRIPTION: From the visitor center (0.0 mi.), the route follows Old Town Road, past sweeping views south, to the barn and the upper end of the Discovery Trail (0.3 mi.). After descending for some distance, the road ascends, enters the woods, passes the Gallup Road on the left and the McCormick Trail on the right, and reaches a junction with

1

Lodge and Antone Roads (0.8 mi.). Following Lodge Road left, the trail soon begins a winding ascent to a four-way junction (1.2 mi.).

Junction: To the right, a spur leads 300 ft. to a clearing where there is a good view of Mt. Antone. To the left, the Merck Road descends 0.3 mi. to Gallup Road, from which it is 0.4 mi. to the barn.

Straight ahead through the junction, the trail slabs through the woods following Lodge Road left past the Kouwenhoven, Meyer, and Hammond Roads (which lead south) before turning sharply right (1.7 mi.) on the Barton Trail and a steep and winding climb to the summit (2,585 ft.). From the open rock, there is a fine view including Mt. Antone and the Merck Forest. A longer but less steep approach is to turn right (south) from the Lodge Road onto the Hammond Road, which ends at the Gallup Road. Follow the Gallup Road about 0.1 mi. left (northeast) to the Barton Trail, which leads north to Spruce Peak.

NATURE TRAILS

At the Merck Forest and Farm Center, there are also two self-guided nature trails, the Discovery Trail and the Tree Identification Trail, which begin at the upper parking lot and make good walks for young families. Each trail is about 1.0 mi. long, and both trails lead to the center's working 60-acre farm. Open to the public, this area includes an organic garden and barnyard animals. Discovery Trail guides can be found at the visitor center.

• • • • • • • • • • • • • • •

WHITE ROCKS NATIONAL RECREATION AREA

The Ice Beds Trail accesses the beautiful and interesting White Rocks National Recreation Area (USGS Wallingford). Several hiking trails leave the common trailhead at the U.S. Forest Service's White Rocks Picnic Area. The Ice Beds Trail is described here. The *Long Trail Guide* has information on the other trails in this area.

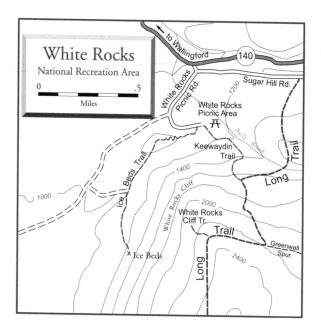

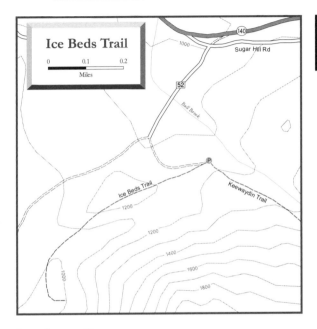

ICE BEDS TRAIL

Distance: 0.8 mi. (1.3 km)
Elevation Change: 160 ft. ascent
Hiking Time: ½ hr. (reverse ¾ hr.)

This trail leads to spectacular views of White Rocks Cliff as well as a spot at the base of a rockslide where ice persists throughout the year. The cliff is made of Cheshire quartzite exposed by glacial action in the last Ice Age, about 12,000 years ago.

TO THE TRAIL: From U.S. 7 in Wallingford, follow Vt. 140 east. Turn south on Sugar Hill Road (2.3 mi.), then turn right on White Rocks Picnic Road (USFS Road 52) (2.4 mi.) and continue to the picnic area and parking (3.0 mi.). Overnight parking at the picnic area is not permitted. White Rocks Picnic Road is not plowed in winter.

DESCRIPTION: From the southwest side of the parking area (0.0 mi.), the blue-blazed trail quickly crosses a small stream and reaches the base of a rocky hogback. The trail then follows a series of switchbacks to a saddle (0.2 mi.). To the left, a spur leads a few feet to the Parapet where there is an impressive view of White Rocks Cliff.

From the saddle, the trail ascends past several views of the cliffs to the summit at the top of the knoll (0.3 mi.) where there is a good view west of the Otter Creek Valley and the Taconics. Continuing over the knoll, the trail descends to an old woods road (0.6 mi.). Turning left and following the road, the trail descends to cross a brook (0.7 mi.), then quickly crosses a second, smaller brook and follows it upstream to its source in the Ice Beds at the base of an old rockslide (0.8 mi.). The ice beds lie within this pile of rocks. Winter ice lasts late into summer and melts slowly, keeping the air cool.

•••••••••••••••••

BALD MOUNTAIN, MENDON

EAST LOOP

Distance: 3.3 mi. (5.4 km)
Elevation Change: 750 ft. ascent
Hiking Time: 2 hr. (reverse 1 hr. 40 min.)

Occupying most of Aiken State Forest in the town of Mendon (USGS Rutland), Bald Mtn. has twin summits that are linked by a blue-blazed trail loop maintained by the Department of Forests, Parks and Recreation. While no

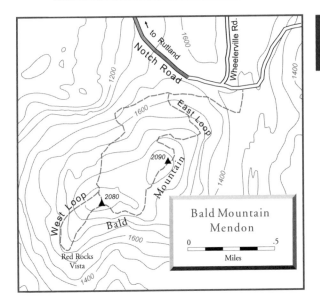

longer bald, the summit does have several lookouts with excellent views of the surrounding mountains and valleys. The West Loop is poorly maintained and may be hard to follow.

TO THE TRAIL: From the convergence of Woodstock Avenue (U.S. 4) and Main Street (U.S. 7) in Rutland, follow Main Street south a short distance to a traffic light at an intersection where Killington Avenue leaves east. Follow Killington Avenue 1.8 mi. to its end at the junction of Town Line Road and Notch Road. Turn right on the paved Notch Road (0.0 mi.), continue past the end of the pavement (1.5 mi.) through Tamarack Notch, and bear right at a fork (1.9 mi.) where the Wheelerville Road departs left. The trailhead is soon reached on the right (2.1 mi.) where Notch Road levels out just before crossing a brook. Roadside parking is available for a half-dozen vehicles.

DESCRIPTION: From Notch Road (0.0 mi.), the trail descends gradually south on a woods road beside a small brook. After crossing a tributary stream, it turns right off the road (0.1 mi.) and climbs to a junction (0.4 mi.) at the head of the East Loop.

Turning left at the junction and soon reversing direction, the trail climbs to another junction (0.7 mi.) where a spur trail left leads 100 ft. to Pico Vista (1,800 ft.). From this point, there are views, from north to south, of Pico, Mendon, and Little Killington Peaks, as well as Shrewbury Peak, Salt Ash Mtn., and the more distant Ludlow Mtn., also known as Mt. Okemo.

Continuing on the main trail by bearing right at the junction, the trail slabs around the shoulder of the ridge and reaches another spur trail left, leading 150 ft. to Cold River Vista (2,060 ft.). The views from this vantage point are similar, but now include Killington Peak. The East Loop then continues with little change in elevation to the wooded north summit (2,090 ft.) (1.2 mi.). The trail soon turns sharply left, descends a short distance, then bears left of a scenic bog on easy grades. Reaching a lookout (1.5 mi.) where there are views over the Cold River Valley to Mt. Equinox and Dorset Peak, the trail passes through a rocky ravine before reaching a junction in an open area on the south summit (2,080 ft.) (1.8 mi.).

Junction: To the left the West Loop (description follows) follows an occasionally obscure footpath 0.9 mi. around the western side of the mountain, rejoining the East Loop about 0.1 mi. north of the south summit.

To the right at the junction atop the south summit, the East Loop descends gently over ledges to reach the junction with the West Loop. A short distance left lies Rutland Lookout (1.9 mi.) where there is a good view of Rutland

and the Otter Creek Valley to the north, as well as the Adirondacks and northern Taconics. Bearing right at the junction, the East Loop then leaves the ledges and descends, steeply at first, before reaching an old woods road (2.1 mi.). The trail descends along the road, soon reaching another woods road (2.4 mi.), which it follows to the right. After only 200 ft., it leaves this road right at an easily missed junction and ascends to a more recent logging road. Following this road through tall spruces, the trail reaches the junction at the head of the East Loop (2.9 mi.). Continuing straight, it comes to Notch Road (3.3 mi.).

WEST LOOP

Distance: 0.9 mi. (1.4 km)
Elevation Change: 380 ft. ascent
Hiking Time: ½ hr. (reverse 40 min.)

This trail extends the East Loop hike and includes a vista with impressive views east and west.

DESCRIPTION: Leaving the south summit at the southern junction of the East and West Loop, (0.0 mi.), the West Loop continues over brushy ledges, soon reaching a vista to the south (0.1 mi.). The trail descends past two more limited views before reaching Red Rocks Lookout (0.3 mi.) where there are extensive vistas of Mendon and Little Killington to the east and of the Taconics, Mt. Equinox, Dorset Peak, and the Adirondacks to the west.

From the lookout, the trail descends steeply, passing under a cliff on the left, before reaching the low point of the West Loop (0.4 mi.). The trail passes atop a small cliff before ascending a switchback and reaching Rutland Lookout and the East Loop (0.9 mi.).

• • • • • • • • • • • • • • • •

OKEMO STATE FOREST

HEALDVILLE TRAIL

Distance: 2.9 mi. (4.7 km)
Elevation Change: 1,900 ft. ascent
Hiking Time: 2½ hr. (reverse 1½ hr.)

The Healdville Trail was built in the summers of
1991–1993 by the Vermont Youth Conservation Corps.
The view from the summit fire tower encompasses the
major peaks in southern Vermont.

TO THE TRAIL: From its junction with Vt. 104 in East
Wallingford (0.0 mi.), follow Vt. 103 east to Station Road
(6.4 mi.) and turn right. Follow Station Road 0.8 mi. to a
graded crossing of the Green Mountain Railroad (7.2 mi.).
A parking lot for ten cars is just past the tracks on the left.
Alternately, follow Vt. 103 west from its junction with Vt.
100 (0.0 mi.) north of Ludlow to a right turn on Station
Road (2.7 mi.).

DESCRIPTION: The blue-blazed trail follows the railroad
tracks a short distance, then turns right, away from the
tracks. It crosses a bridge (0.2 mi.), passes a cascade (0.6
mi.), and climbs gently on switchbacks to a plateau (1.5
mi.). At 1.9 mi., an unmarked spur leads 0.2 mi. to the
paved summit road. The trail descends gradually, then begins a steeper climb to an overlook (2.3 mi.) with views
west of Salt Ash Mtn., Shrewsbury Peak, Killington Peak,
Little Killington, Mendon Peak, and the Taconics in the
distance. Beyond the overlook, the trail continues upward
to a small marsh (2.7 mi.) on the left. At 2.9 mi., it turns
sharply left to a northern view of Killington Peak. The trail
levels, coming to the remains of a forest ranger's cabin
and, just beyond, a sign on a tree that points right to the
summit fire tower (3.0 mi.). The view from the tower includes Okemo Ski Area below, Mt. Ascutney to the east,

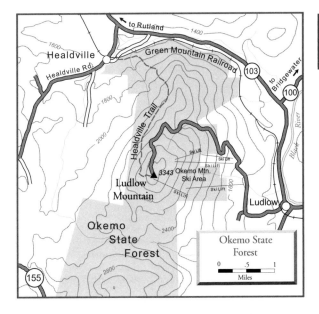

Killington Peak to the north, Stratton and Bromley Mtns. to the south, and Dorset Peak and the Taconics to the southwest.

• • • • • • • • • • • • • • • •

DEERFIELD RIVER WATERSHED

Deerfield River watershed encompasses a large area of southwestern Vermont and northwestern Massachusetts. The river has been dammed in many places for power generation, creating several reservoirs along the way. Near East Greenfield, Massachusetts, the Deerfield

River empties into the Connecticut River. Well upstream lies Sherman Reservoir, straddling the Vermont-Massachusetts border (USGS Rowe, Readsboro), Harriman Reservoir, and the much smaller Searsburg Reservoir. Just north of Searsburg Reservoir, the river branches; upstream along the East Branch is Somerset Reservoir, a large man-made impoundment. Beyond Somerset, along an unnamed stream, is Grout Pond. The National Grid USA and the U.S. Forest Service maintain a variety of footpaths and multiuse trails along the reservoirs.

HARRIMAN TRAIL

Distance: 7.2 mi. (11.6 km)
Elevation Change: 200 ft. ascent
Hiking Time: 3¾ hr. either direction

Also known as the Westside Trail, this route is maintained by National Grid USA, the parent company for the New England Power Company who built the trails. The trail follows a mostly unblazed but obvious path along the west side of Harriman Reservoir, between a power company picnic area near the north end of the reservoir west of Wilmington and a small parking area at the base of Harriman Dam in Whitingham (USGS Readsboro). Blue plastic markers of the Catamount Trail are found along parts of the route where the two trails coincide. Walking and cycling are allowed on the trail. While the trail is described from north to south, directions to both trailheads are given.

The trail provides frequent views across the reservoir to the surrounding mountains and passes stonewalls, foundations, and other reminders of past settlement. Like all other recreational facilities on NEPCO lands, this trail is open only during daylight hours; overnight parking, camping, and open fires are not permitted.

Except for short bypasses of the original stream crossings, the trail follows the roadbed of the former Hoosic

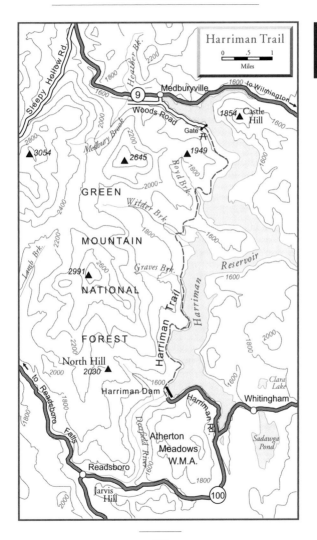

Harriman Trail

0   .5   1
Miles

1

Tunnel and Wilmington Railroad. This section of track, with its roller coaster grades and a switchback crossing of Harriman Dam, was constructed in 1923 to replace original routing flooded by the newly created reservoir. It remained in service until the line was abandoned in 1937. The story of the railroad is told in Bernard R. Carman's *Hoot, Toot and Whistle* (Brattleboro, Vt.: Stephen Green Press, 1963).

TO THE TRAIL (NORTHERN ACCESS): The northern end of the trail is at the power company's Mountain Mills West picnic area. From Vt. 9, about 0.3 mi. east of the Searsburg-Wilmington town line, or 2.9 mi. west of the traffic lights in Wilmington, turn south on Woods Road and cross the Deerfield River on a steel bridge. Turn left at a junction just beyond the bridge and follow the narrow gravel road for 1.0 mi. to the picnic area where there is an impressive view of Haystack Mtn. The trail begins at a gate barring the road to vehicular traffic.

TO THE TRAIL (SOUTHERN ACCESS): The southern trailhead is located at the Harriman Dam. From Vt. 100, about a mile west of the Whitingham post office, or about 4.0 mi. east of the center of Readsboro, turn north on the paved Harriman Road (also Dam Road) and continue 1.9 mi. to its end at a parking area at the bottom of a hairpin turn. The trail begins at an inconspicuous opening in the chain-link fence. This access is about 60 ft. left of the main gate, opposite a birch tree. The trail follows a paved road, which crosses the lower face of the dam and then ascends to its top. Here, the trail bears left on a dirt road, which follows the path of the railroad bed and continues along the shore toward a prominent rock cut.

DESCRIPTION (SOUTHBOUND): From the gate at the picnic area (0.0 mi.), the trail and a coinciding truck road ascend steadily south. After passing camps on the right and left (0.8 mi.), the trail continues with minor elevation changes, crosses a gate (1.1 mi.), and begins a brief swing west (1.6 mi.). It then resumes a southerly course before crossing high above Boyd Brook (1.9 mi.). Passing through two prominent rock cuts, then several less obvious ones, the trail enters a much longer, deeper, and occasionally wet cut where the railroad ties are still in place (2.7 mi.). Beyond this cut, it reaches a junction (2.8 mi.). The truck road forks right, and the trail bears left along the undisturbed railroad bed.

Continuing through another cut in the rocks (2.9 mi.), the trail leaves the railroad bed to the right and follows yellow blazes into the woods (3.0 mi.). Here, it arrives at a junction with the Catamount Trail, which it follows left. Descending to cross Wilder Brook on a footbridge (3.1 mi.), the trail then ascends left to cross a stonewall (3.2 mi.) before continuing through an old farm clearing and into a reforested area.

Returning to the railroad bed (3.4 mi.), the trail crosses the former stage road to Heartwellville (3.5 mi.) and gradually approaches the reservoir. It then leaves the railroad bed again (4.0 mi.), descending left to cross Graves Brook a few feet from the reservoir (4.1 mi.). It then briefly follows the shore before returning to the railroad bed (4.3 mi.).

After rounding a pleasant point (5.2 mi.) and paralleling a long stonewall on the left, the trail swings right off the railroad bed (5.3 mi.), briefly ascends in open woods, then passes through an overgrown clearing near the massive foundations of former farm buildings. The trail joins and follows a dirt road (5.4 mi.) used by power company vehicles to its end at Harriman Dam, generally along the now-obscure route of the old roadbed.

Passing through a prominent rock cut (6.4 mi.), the trail descends gradually along the shore of the reservoir to the north end of Harriman Dam (6.9 mi.). Here, the trail jogs to the right a few feet, then descends on a paved roadway, which soon swings left and crosses the lower face of the dam to a closed gate in a chain-link fence. The trail follows the fence to the right for about 60 ft. to a white birch tree where an inconspicuous narrow opening provides access to the parking lot (7.2 mi.).

WILMINGTON-SOMERSET TRAILS

Traveling alongside large reservoirs and rivers, these trails often follow old railroad beds. The trails were established and are maintained by the New England Power Company (NEPCO). In addition to the reservoir trails, the trails up Haystack Mtn. and Mt. Snow are described.

EAST BRANCH TRAIL

Distance: 5.0 mi. (8.1 km)
Elevation Change: 550 ft. ascent
Hiking Time: 2¾ hr. (reverse 2½ hr.)

This trail is marked for its entire length with faded diagonal double yellow blazes. Since nearly all the trail is on power company property, overnight camping and open fires are prohibited. The trail generally parallels the Catamount Trail, which is blazed with blue diamonds.

TO THE TRAIL: The East Branch Trail and Flood Dam Trail (page 61) (USGS Mt. Snow) share a common trailhead on Somerset Road (USFS Road 71), which leads to Somerset Reservoir. This road leaves Vt. 9 (0.0 mi.) about 1.5 mi. east of its junction with Vt. 8 and 5.6 mi. west of the traffic lights in Wilmington. After reaching the end of the pavement (0.3 mi.), the road passes the dam at Searsburg Reservoir (1.0 mi.) before reaching a small lot where limited parking is available at the trailhead (2.1 mi.).

DESCRIPTION: Descending from Somerset Road (0.0 mi.), the trail crosses the West Branch of the Deerfield River on a suspension bridge and proceeds gradually uphill. It soon turns sharply uphill to the right at a junction with the Flood Dam Trail (0.1 mi.), which departs left.

The East Branch Trail continues across a low ridge and crosses the East Branch of the Deerfield River on a suspension bridge (0.4 mi.). The trail reaches an old railroad bed and joins the Catamount Trail as it comes in from the right.

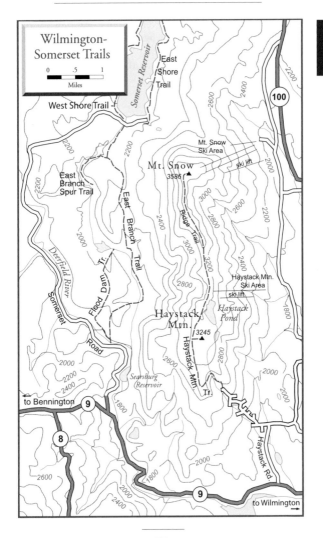

Wilmington-
Somerset Trails

0   .5   1
Miles

Somerset Reservoir

East
Shore
Trail

West Shore Trail

100

East
Branch
Spur Trail

Mt. Snow
Ski Area

ski lift

Mt. Snow
3586

Ridge Trail

Deerfield River

East Branch Trail

Flood Dam Tr.

Somerset Road

Haystack Mtn.
Ski Area

ski lift

Haystack
Pond

Haystack
Mtn.

3245

Haystack Mtn. Tr.

Searsburg
Reservoir

to Bennington

9

8

9

Haystack Rd.

to Wilmington

Along this railroad bed are several scenic overlooks of the river as well as views northeast of Mt. Snow. The trail crosses several streams (1.2 to 1.6 mi.), some at fords and others on hewn timbers that span the stream channel.

After crossing the last brook, the trail bears right, leaves the railroad bed (1.6 mi.), and crosses another brook on a hewn timber. The trail returns to the railroad bed (2.0 mi.), crosses two more streams, and bears right off the main roadbed (2.3 mi.). Following a spur railroad bed running up a stream, the trail quickly bears right, away from the river.

After crossing the brook (2.7 mi.), it crosses a red-blazed boundary and enters the Green Mountain National Forest (2.9 mi.) where the route was formerly marked with blue blazes. The trail follows the brook channel and crosses it (3.0 mi.), then bears right at the first fork in the brook (3.1 mi.) and left at the second fork (3.2 mi.). (The trail is difficult to follow in this area, so care should be taken to look for blazes.) The trail begins to level and crosses the brook for the last time (3.3 mi.). Descending across a red-blazed boundary line, it crosses back onto NEPCO land (4.1 mi.) where there are views of Mt. Snow and several beaver ponds. The trail continues to descend gradually along a small stream into a large clearing (4.5 mi.) where the East Branch Spur Trail leads left to the East Branch of the Deerfield River.

The main East Branch Trail turns sharply right at this junction and follows the upper edge of a small meadow. After returning to the woods (4.6 mi.), the trail once again reaches the East Branch (4.7 mi.), following its east bank for several hundred feet, then again turning away to the right. Climbing a moderate grade, the trail levels and passes to the right of an old mill foundation (4.9 mi.), then ascends to the right and reaches the Somerset Reservoir access road (5.0 mi.), just below the east end of the dam.

To the left, the access road descends a short distance to the dam's outlet and continues south, past the parking lot to the southern end of the West Shore Trail (page 63). The access road leads 9.7 mi. back to Vt. 9.

To the right on the access road, it is a few hundred feet uphill to the top of the dam. It is about 0.3 mi. to parking and boat launching areas and 0.5 mi. to a picnic grove and the southern end of the East Shore Trail (page 62).

FLOOD DAM TRAIL

Distance: 2.3 mi. (3.7 km)
Elevation Change: 280 ft. ascent
Hiking Time: 1¼ hr. (reverse 1¼ hr.)

Marked with single yellow blazes, the trail is sporadically maintained and may be overgrown in places.

TO THE TRAIL: This trail diverges from the East Branch Trail 0.1 mi. from the trailhead on Somerset Road (page 58).

DESCRIPTION: A short distance north of the Deerfield River suspension bridge, the Flood Dam Trail branches left where the East Branch Trail makes an abrupt right turn (0.0 mi.). The Flood Dam Trail passes through overgrown clearings and woods along an old roadbed (0.1 mi.) and continues parallel to the Deerfield River on level ground before arriving at a fork (0.4 mi.). To the left, a dead-end spur continues along the river a short distance. The Flood Dam Trail follows the right branch of the fork away from the river. The trail continues to the base of a hill (0.5 mi.), turning more northerly as it begins a gradual climb up a rocky section. Climbing through mature hardwood forests, the trail reaches its highest point at the unmarked Windham-Bennington county line (1.2 mi.).

It continues generally to the northeast across this flat-topped mountain, begins a very gradual descent, then levels out (1.7 mi.). Turning sharply right, the trail descends again to the bottom of a hill, crosses a small stream (1.8 mi.), and continues northeasterly around a spruce and hardwood forest to another stream (1.9 mi.). The trail meets an old railroad bed (2.0 mi.) and turns sharply left where there are views of a large area of beaver activity. The trail follows the railroad bed and ends at a clearing on the shore of the pond (2.2 mi.). The foundations of the old flood dam, which dates back to at least the turn of the past century, can be seen from this point. The dam and railroad beds found in this area are remnants of logging activity in the nineteenth century.

EAST SHORE TRAIL

Distance: 5.7 mi. (9.2 km)
Elevation Change: minor
Hiking Time: 3 hr. (reverse 3 hr.)

This trail follows high ground near the east shore of scenic Somerset Reservoir (USGS Mt. Snow, Stratton Mtn.), dropping down to skirt many coves. The trail offers views across the water to Mt. Snow, Stratton Mtn., and other area landmarks. The double-yellow-blazed route follows, in part, the Catamount Trail (a cross-country ski trail) and a former woods road. At the northeast arm of Somerset Reservoir, the Catamount Trail leaves the East Shore Trail to continue 0.5 mi. to Grout Pond where several trails lead 1.2 mi. to the Grout Pond parking area. From the point where the Catamount Trail departs, the East Shore Trail continues 4.0 to 5.0 mi. to its end on the north shore of the reservoir and the West Trail Loop, part of the Grout Pond network. However, this portion of the East Shore Trail is overgrown and difficult to follow.

TO THE TRAIL: The East Shore Trail begins at the end of the Somerset Reservoir access road, 10.0 mi. from the junction of Somerset Road and Vt. 9, and about 0.3 mi. north of the dam. From Vt. 9, turn north on Somerset Road (USFS Road 71) and continue past the trailhead for the East Branch Trail (2.1 mi.) (page 58). Bear right at a fork (6.3 mi.) onto the Somerset Reservoir access road and continue to a small trailhead parking area just beyond a larger parking lot on the right, near the end of the road (10.0 mi.).

DESCRIPTION: From the end of the road (0.0 mi.), the trail crosses a small stream on a bridge and follows an old road to a cove. After swinging around the east end of the cove (0.2 mi.), the trail enters the woods, passes between several large rocks (0.7 mi.), and crosses a small stream. It then skirts a small cove on puncheon (1.1 mi.) before ascending a small knoll (1.6 mi.), descending to another cove and climbing another knoll (1.8 mi.). Dropping to yet another cove, the trail follows the shore to the right, partly on puncheon, before leaving the cove (2.0 mi.) to cross a brook on a wooden bridge (2.2 mi.). Turning northerly, the trail ascends and crosses an old woods road (2.5 mi.), then slabs a slope to reach the high ground atop a ridge. From the high point in winter, there is a view of the Mt. Snow–Haystack Mtn. ridge. The trail descends to the shoreline and joins with the Catamount Trail (3.2 mi.) before crossing a large brook.

The trail continues on higher ground, enters a clearing on the shore (3.5 mi.), and continues north to a point on the shore closest to Streeter Island (4.2 mi.). The trail swings right around a cove before crossing a small brook (5.0 mi.), then a rocky stream (5.3 mi.) where a bridge has washed out. It crosses the stream and reaches a sign (5.7 mi.) indicating 6.0 mi. back to the dam at the outlet of Somerset Reservoir.

WEST SHORE TRAIL

Distance: 5.6 mi. (9.0 km)
Elevation Change: 130 ft. ascent
Hiking Time: 3 hr. (reverse 2¾ hr.)

This trail follows the high ground on the west side of Somerset Reservoir to an indefinite terminus on the reservoir's shoreline. The trail is overgrown and unblazed along much of the route and peters out after 5.5 mi. Care must be taken to stay on the trail. Map and compass and the knowledge of how to use them are recommended. For an alternate route that is easier to follow, walk along the grassy service road, which continues north on gentle grades for a couple of miles—out of sight of Somerset Reservoir—and makes a pleasant path through the woods.

TO THE TRAIL: Follow directions to the East Shore Trail (page 62). The trail begins at the junction of the access road and a chained service road at the base of the west end of the dam. Parking is available at the trailhead and other nearby locations. (A NEPCO sign for the West Side Trail may be seen nearby.) The route is marked with double yellow blazes.

DESCRIPTION: From the access road (0.0 mi.), the trail follows the service road up the face of the dam for about 150 yds. before turning left onto a woods road. Soon after leaving the service road (0.2 mi.), the trail descends toward the reservoir, reaching the water's edge at a rock ledge (0.4 mi.). The trail continues around two small coves (0.7 mi. and 0.8 mi.) and crosses a large brook, entering another cove (1.3 mi.) before rising to higher ground.

After returning to the shore and crossing another stream (1.7 mi.), the trail again leaves the reservoir at a rocky cove (1.9 mi.) and slabs the slope for some distance on occasionally rough ground before continuing with minor elevation changes to a former town road (2.5 mi.). It follows the old road and its paralleling stonewalls uphill to the left through an overgrown farm site (2.8 mi.), then descends gradually, bearing right at an old woods road junction (3.2 mi.) and soon reaching a trail junction (3.3 mi.). To the left, a red-blazed snowmobile trail follows old roads.

The West Shore Trail descends on the right fork and returns to the reservoir (3.4 mi.). Continuing along or near the shore, the trail crosses a large brook at the entrance to a cove (4.2 mi.) and swings right, away from a woods road, which also uses the brook crossing. Once again turning into the woods (4.4 mi.), the occasionally obscure trail goes a short distance inland, crosses a low spur ridge (4.9 mi.), and gradually descends to the shore (5.2 mi.). The trail follows the rocky beach a short distance, returns to the shore-line and continues on higher ground to become ill-defined in the woods (5.6 mi.). Note: From here, the trail is un-maintained and very difficult to follow to its ending on the west bank of the East Branch of the Deerfield River. On the east bank of the East Branch is the East Shore Trail; do not cross the river; it is deep and the currents are strong.

HAYSTACK MOUNTAIN

Distance: 1.8 mi. (2.9 km)
Elevation Change: 1,025 ft. ascent
Hiking Time: 1½ hr. (reverse 1 hr.)

From the partially wooded, conical summit (3,445 ft., USGS Mt. Snow), there are views of Haystack Pond and Mt. Snow (formerly Mt. Pisgah) to the north and Harriman Reservoir and Lake Sadawga to the south (USGS Reads-boro). More distant views include Mt. Ascutney to the northeast, Mt. Monadnock in New Hampshire to the southeast, Mt. Greylock to the south, and Glastenbury Mtn. to the north. For most of its length, this is a combi-nation hiking and cross-country ski trail, marked with oc-casional blue diamonds.

TO THE TRAIL: From Vt. 9, 1.0 mi. west of the traffic light in Wilmington, or 5.8 mi. east of Vt. 8, turn north into the Chimney Hill Development on Haystack Road (0.0 mi.). Bear right at a turn where Town Farm Road leaves left (0.3 mi.), continue north on Haystack Road, past junctions on the right and left, until reaching a four-way intersection (1.2 mi.).

Turn left on Chimney Hill Road, then right at the next junction (1.4 mi.) on Binney Brook Road. Bear left at a fork and begin a steep and winding climb past several roads to the right and left. At the junction where Binney Brook Road ends on Upper Dam Road (2.3 mi.), turn right and proceed uphill to another intersection (2.4 mi.).

Bear left, still on Upper Dam Road, to reach the trailhead, which is on the right (2.5 mi.) and marked with a U.S. Forest Service sign. Limited roadside parking is available in the vicinity.

DESCRIPTION: From Upper Dam Road (0.0 mi.), the trail ascends northwesterly on a gated jeep road. The trail turns left off the road at a crossing of Binney Brook (0.6 mi.), and then trends southwesterly for some distance before climbing steadily in a northwestward direction to the west slope of the mountain (1.5 mi.). This section of trail is mostly a snowmobile route, following the orange snowmobile signs. At the summit trail junction, the trail turns right and follows the blue-blazed route to the summit (1.8 mi.), which is partially wooded but offers views of Harriman Reservoir and the windmills to the south. Note: As indicated by postings in the area, this is a watershed protection zone for the town of Wilmington. Camping is not allowed along the trail or on the summit.

RIDGE TRAIL

Distance: 3.5 mi. (5.6 km)
Elevation Change: 385 ft. ascent
Hiking Time: 1¾ hr. (reverse 2 hr.)

This combination cross-country ski and hiking trail connects Haystack Mtn. with Mt. Snow. Although it is minimally marked, it is an obvious path and is as wide as a road.

DESCRIPTION: From a junction below the summit of Haystack Mtn. (0.0 mi.), the Ridge Trail continues straight ahead to the north. The trail follows easy up and down routing just west of the height of land to reach the Haystack Mountain Ski Area near the upper lift station (1.0 mi.). The trail then continues in a northerly direction, on or near the ridgeline, to the summit facilities of the Mount Snow Ski Area (3.5 mi.). Although the trail does not cross the summit of Mt. Snow, it does connect here with a network of trails maintained in season by the Mount Snow Adventure Center at Crisports, a shop in the Grand Summit Resort Hotel. Hikers may obtain trail maps for self-guided interpretive hikes, take a guided hike, or rent hiking boots. There is a trail access fee of $5.25 (in 2001) to hike from this center. The center is open May 29 through October 11, from 8:00 A.M. to 5:00 P.M. For more information, call the center at (802) 464-4040.

LITTLE POND

Distance: 2.6 mi. (4.2 km)
Elevation Change: 330 ft. ascent
Hiking Time: 1¾ hr. (reverse 1¼ hr.)

TO THE TRAIL: This secluded pond (USGS Woodford) is reached by an unblazed and unsigned woods road that leaves a U.S. Forest Service parking lot on the north side of Vt. 9 at a height of land about 1.6 mi. east of the Prospect Mountain Ski Area and about 1.6 mi. west of Woodford State Park.

DESCRIPTION: From the highway (0.0 mi.), the trail follows Forest Road 275 in a gradual ascent through the woods to a power line crossing (0.5 mi.) where there are views east and west. After dipping into a hollow, the road continues through overgrown fields to a fire ring at the site of an old camp (0.8 mi.). Nearby, there are limited views east to Haystack Mtn. and the Hoosic Range. The road then ascends gradually through the woods around a shoulder of Hager Hill and ignores a snowmobile trail departing right. The road then reaches a fork (2.4 mi.) where a more recent logging road veers left. To the right an older road descends to the west shore of the pond (2,602 ft.) (2.6 mi.).

• • • • • • • • • • • • • • • •

RAMBLES

EMERALD LAKE STATE PARK

Elevation Change: 200 ft. ascent
Hiking Time: ½ hr. either direction

The 430-acre Emerald State Park encircles Emerald Lake, the headwaters of Otter Creek, which flows north through the Valley of Vermont on a 100-mi. journey to Ferrisburg and Lake Champlain. The park offers swimming, fishing, motorless boating, and camping. In addition to the Vista Trail, several shorter trails are shown on a trail map of the park, available without charge at the contact station.

TO THE TRAIL: Emerald Lake State Park is on the west side of U.S. 7 in North Dorset, on the flank of Dorset Mtn.

DESCRIPTION: The blue-blazed Vista Trail begins at a sign on the park access road, 200 ft. east of the contact station. From the trailhead, the trail travels easterly to cross the railroad tracks under the U.S. 7 highway bridge, then turns south and climbs through the woods to ledges above the highway (0.6 mi.). Here, there is a good view of Emerald Lake and Netop Mtn. The trail continues along the ledge, descending gradually to recross U.S. 7 and reenter the park at the south end of Emerald Lake. Continuing near the shore through a marshy area, the Vista Trail continues around the west side of the lake and ends at the park beach (1.0 mi.), a short distance from the contact station.

LAKE SHAFTSBURY STATE PARK

This 84-acre park surrounds small and picturesque Lake Shaftsbury. The park has group camping facilities and a day-use area, with a fee charged in season.

TO THE TRAIL: State Park Road leaves Vt. 7A just north of the village of Shaftsbury about 10.5 mi. north of Bennington and leads 0.5 mi. to the park contact station.

DESCRIPTION: A brochure is available at the contact station describing the 0.75-mi. Healing Springs Nature Trail, which nearly circles the lake. The trail begins at the western end of the dam, which forms the lake's outlet, and follows the north shore for a distance before crossing a boardwalk onto Hemlock Island. The trail follows the ridge of this glacial esker to another bridge where it crosses to a peninsula on the south shore of the lake. The trail continues through an oak forest to a boardwalk over Warm Brook before ending at the group picnic shelter near a parking lot southeast of the lake.

GROUT POND RECREATION AREA

A major logging site until it was purchased by the Boy Scouts of America in 1950, Grout Pond was acquired by the U.S. Forest Service in 1979. The 1,600-acre area is managed for a variety of recreational uses. Nine campsites and three lean-tos are available on a first-come, first-served basis. Some of the sites are accessible by car, others only by foot or boat. The area also offers swimming and boating (electric motors only, with a portage required for access). A U.S. Forest Service caretaker may be in residence during the summer and fall. Additional information and a trail map are available from the U.S. Forest Service's Manchester office and at the trailhead.

More than 10.0 mi. of multipurpose trails encircle the 70-acre pond along mostly flat terrain. The trails connect with the extensive trail system at nearby Somerset Reservoir. The trails are marked with blue diamond-shaped blazes and are open year-round. In the winter, snowmobiles are restricted to USFS Road 262 and a portion of the trail system designated by orange diamond blazes.

TO THE TRAIL: To reach the Grout Pond Recreation Area from the east, follow the Stratton Road (also known as the West Wardsboro–Arlington Road) west from Vt. 100 in West Wardsboro for 6.3 mi. to Grout Pond Road (USFS Road 262). From the west, follow Kelley Stand Road (also known as the West Wardsboro–Arlington Road) east from U.S. 7 in Arlington for about 12.0 mi. to reach the same spot. Turn south on Grout Pond Road and continue 1.3 mi. to a parking lot near the pond.

DESCRIPTION: From the parking lot, the Pond Trail Loop heads southeast to make a 2.5 mi. counterclockwise circuit around the pond. From a junction near the south end of the pond, about 0.75 mi. from the parking lot, it is 0.5 mi. along the Catamount Trail to a junction with the East Shore Trail. This trail, described on page 62, originates from the dam at the outlet of Somerset Reservoir about 6.0 mi. south.

LAKE ST. CATHERINE STATE PARK

Lake St. Catherine State Park occupies 117 acres on the east shore of Lake St. Catherine. Formerly the site of a slate quarry, the remains of old slate mills and their rubble piles are still visible. Camping facilities and a day-use area, including a beach, are available. A fee is charged in season.

TO THE TRAIL: The park entrance is 3.0 mi. south of Poultney on the west side of Vt. 30.

DESCRIPTION: A brochure is available at the park contact station describing the 1.0-mi. Big Trees Nature Trail loop, which ascends gently to a low ridge in old pastureland. The trail passes a series of labeled trees, many rare for their exceptional size, before ending at the site of an old farmstead. From this point, a hiking trail continues west to the lake where a spur leads to the swimming area. The hiking loop then turns east and passes the park campground before returning to the contact station.

DELAWARE AND HUDSON RAIL TRAIL

1

Comprised of two discontinuous but nearly equal lengths of converted roadbed, the Delaware and Hudson Rail Trail follows the Vermont portion of a rail route that once connected the slate-producing regions near Rutland with Albany, New York. As it passes through the pastoral Vermont landscape of western Rutland and Bennington Counties, it encounters seventeen bridges and overpasses, including two railroad bridges nearly 100 ft. long in Poultney and West Pawlet. This 19.8-mi. multiuse trail is owned by the Vermont Transportation Agency and maintained by the Department of Forests, Parks and Recreation. An excellent flyer describing the access, history and permitted uses of the trail is available from the Pittsford office of the Vermont Department of Forests, Parks and Recreation (see page 329).

To the Trail: The northern segment of the trail runs from Castleton to Poultney. Parking is available at Castleton State College on Vt. 4A, and the trail can be accessed immediately west on South Street. The trail follows a southerly course and eventually reaches a southern access for the northern segment in Poultney, just east of the junction of Vt. 30, Vt. 31 and Vt. 140.

The northern end of the southern segment of the trail is several miles south in the village of West Pawlet on Vt. 153. The trail continues south, at first following the Indian River, before arriving at the village of Rupert. Here, the trail bears west and reaches a terminus in West Rupert on Vt. 153 where very limited parking is available.

The trail leaves Vermont to enter New York in three places. Since the New York sections of the trail have not been developed for recreational use, and in some cases ownership of the rail bed has reverted to adjacent private landowners, passage over these portions of the old roadbed is not assured.

HAPGOOD POND RECREATION AREA

The U.S. Forest Service's Hapgood Pond Recreation Area with a picnic area, campground and swimming area is reached from the village of Peru, located a short distance north of Vt. 11, east of the Bromley Mountain Ski Area. From Vt. 11, turn into Peru village and bear left on Hapgood Pond Road in front of the village church. Continue 1.7 mi. to the entrance of the recreation area. The Forest Service maintains a booth in summer. Currently, no fees are charged, but there is a donation box. Parking is beyond the booth and additional parking is available about 100 yds. beyond the entrance on Hapgood Pond Road. The Land and Man Forest Trail, 0.8 mi. long, circles the pond through mature woods and across the inlet to the pond. The trail begins straight beyond the entrance booth on the eastern side of the pond. Recent beaver activity has inundated the area around the inlet, but the trail through the campground is open and returns to the parking area.

BIG BRANCH TRAIL

This U.S. Forest Service trail descends to the Big Branch River from the Big Branch Picnic Area in the Green Mountain National Forest. Many dramatic views of the river are afforded from an adjoining trail.

TO THE TRAIL: From U.S. 7 in the village of Danby, turn on Brooklyn Street. Cross the railroad tracks and continue on the paved Mount Tabor Road/USFS Road 10 (seasonal) through the village of Mt. Tabor to the signed Big Branch parking area (2.6 mi.) on the south side of the road.

DESCRIPTION: The picnic area provides a good vantage point high above the Big Branch River with a broad southwestern view of the Otter Creek Valley and Dorset's peaks. At a break near the center of a split-rail fence, the Big Branch Trail begins a steep descent via switchbacks to the boulder-filled river (0.2 mi.). At the river's edge, narrow trails proceed in both directions, giving impressive views of the rushing water and gargantuan boulders in the riverbed.

WOODFORD STATE PARK

Woodford State Park occupies 398 acres on a mountain plateau surrounding Adams Reservoir. At an elevation of 2,400 ft., it is the highest Vermont state park and is covered by a high-altitude spruce-fir-birch forest. A number of campsites are available, and a day-use fee is charged in season.

TO THE TRAIL: The park entrance is on the south side of Vt. 9, about 11.0 mi. east of Bennington and 3.2 mi. west of Vt. 8. Out-of-season, parking is available at a U.S. Forest Service parking lot on Vt. 9, north and east of the park entrance.

DESCRIPTION: A blue-blazed hiking trail located mostly within the park encircles the 23-acre reservoir, closely following its western shore. Following a clockwise loop, the trail may be found at two points along an access road that leaves the contact station to the left and continues to the park campgrounds. The first access is a left into the woods at the top of the hill and adjacent to a playground. The second access is on the left 100 yds. farther, just before the access road descends a hill.

The hiking trail heads south, closely following the eastern park boundary, then bears west through a small section of the George Aiken Wilderness where there are limited views to beaver ponds. The trail recrosses state park land to enter the Green Mountain National Forest, reaching a junction at the south end of Adams Reservoir. The distance from the access road to the reservoir is about 1.0 mi. (1.6 km).

Junction: To the right, a trail returns to the state park, reaching the campground at site 64 where the access road leads back to the contact station.

To the left, the trail follows the west side of the reservoir, reentering state park land and eventually reaching a junction where the Atwood Trail leaves right, and provides a short alternate route along the shoreline. The trails converge several hundred feet ahead and reach a parking lot at the park day-use area (1.7 mi.). The contact station lies a short distance beyond.

GREENDALE TRAIL

This 4.0-mi. loop travels through a mixed forest along gravel roads and trails.

TO THE TRAIL: From Vt. 100 in Weston, take Vt. 100 north for 2.0 mi. Turn left on Forest Road 18, also known as Greendale Road. Follow it 3.0 mi. to the campground. The road ends a half mile beyond the campground. Limited parking is available at the end of the road. The trail is straight ahead over an unused concrete bridge.

DESCRIPTION: The trail, also a cross-country ski trail, crosses Greendale Brook and follows blue blazes along the brook. It climbs a moderately steep grade for the next mile. At a junction with an old road, now the Jenny Coolidge Trail, the trail turns left to follow Forest Road 17 for 2.0 mi. back to Greendale Road/Forest Road 18. This stretch follows Jenny Coolidge Brook. The route turns left on Greendale Road and follows it back to the campground.

REGION 2
Southeast
Vermont

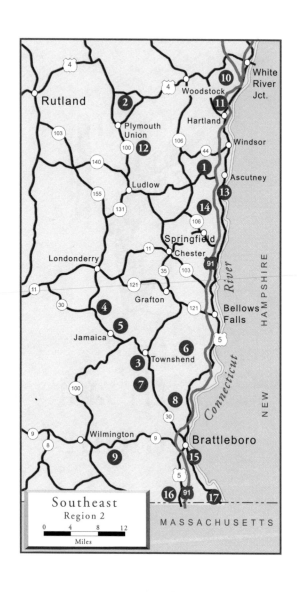

White
River
Jct.

Rutland

Woodstock

Hartland

Windsor

Plymouth
Union

Ascutney

Ludlow

Springfield

Chester

Londonderry

Grafton

Bellows
Falls

Jamaica

Townshend

NEW HAMPSHIRE

Connecticut River

Wilmington

Brattleboro

Southeast
Region 2

0   4   8   12
Miles

MASSACHUSETTS

Southeast Vermont

REGION 2
Southeast Vermont

Although this part of Vermont lacks the larger north–south mountain ridges of much of the rest of the state, there are plenty of places to explore by foot. Trails wend their way along rivers, climb to the few peaks, and wander through natural areas with rare plant species. Many trails are multiuse and good for walking, cross-country skiing, hiking, and often cycling.

To the west, the main range of the Green Mountains has petered to foothills; to the east, the broad Connecticut River separates the state from neighboring New Hampshire. Mixed in between is a jumble of hills and rivers draining to the great Connecticut. Throughout the region, rivers flow southeast in a tree-branch pattern, creating an unorganized-looking topography. Mt. Ascutney is the largest and most prominent mountain in the region.

MOUNT ASCUTNEY

A monadnock, Mt. Ascutney (3,150 ft.) is the dominant physical feature of southeastern Vermont and is rich in history. The mountain's quartz syenite rock has withstood the erosion and glaciation that has worn away

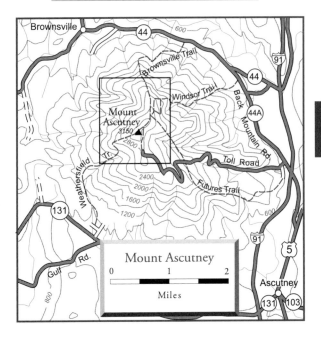

Mount Ascutney

0   1   2

Miles

2

the softer rocks of the surrounding Piedmont peneplane. Located in the towns of Windsor and West Windsor (USGS Mt. Ascutney), the mountain derives its name from the Algonquin words *Cas-Cad-Nac* or *Mahps-Cad-Na*, meaning "mountain of the rocky summit," or *Ascutegnik*, meaning "meeting of the waters."

The mountain's first hiking trail was built in the 1850s. Today, four trails approach from the base and connect near the summit. The Brownsville, Windsor, and Weathersfield Trails derive their names from the towns or villages that roughly mark their town of origin. The Futures Trail ascends through Ascutney State Park, which occupies about 2,000 acres on the eastern slope of the mountain. All trail descriptions include mileages to the summit. The Civilian Conservation Corps (CCC) developed the park between 1935 and 1939, constructing the original stone buildings as well as a 3.8-mi. paved auto road, which ascends some 2,250 ft. to within 0.75 mi. of the summit. There are camping facilities near the base of the mountain and picnic facilities along the mountain road and near the summit. Day-use and camping fees are charged in season. The park entrance is on the west side of Vt. 44A, which runs between U.S. 5, north of Ascutney, and Vt. 44, east of Brownsville.

The trail system is maintained largely by the Ascutney Trails Association, established in 1967. They have restored and improved these historic trails, and they publish a guidebook, the *Mount Ascutney Guide*, which describes the trails in detail and gives historical information and natural history of the area. It is available from the association (see page 327) or from the Green Mountain Club.

WINDSOR TRAIL

Distance: 2.7 mi. (4.3 km)
Elevation Change: 2,520 ft. ascent
Hiking Time: 2½ hr. (reverse 1¼ hr.)

TO THE TRAIL: Marked with white blazes, this trail begins at a small parking lot on the southwest side of Vt. 44A, also known as Back Mountain Road. From U.S. 5 in Windsor, head west on Vt. 44 for roughly 2.5 mi. to the intersection with Vt. 44A. Turn sharply left onto Vt. 44A, and continue south 0.2 mi. to reach the trailhead and parking lot on the right, marked by a small, white Ascutney Trails Association (ATA) sign on the opposite side of the road. The lot is 1.5 mi. north of the entrance to Ascutney State Park, also located on Vt. 44A.

DESCRIPTION: From Vt. 44A (0.0 mi.), the white-blazed trail follows the southern boundary of an open field. Beyond the upper end of the field, the trail passes through birches and pines and enters the woods. It then begins an increasingly steep climb on a wide woods road to a spur on the left (0.8 mi.), which leads a short distance to Gerry's Falls on Mountain Brook.

Continuing past the side trail, the Windsor Trail crosses the right branch of the brook (0.9 mi.), then follows the left branch upstream a short distance before swinging right and slabbing westerly to recross the right branch (1.1 mi.). The trail then continues over and around a low shoulder of the mountain to reach a trail junction at Halfway Spring (1.6 mi.), the former site of a logger's cabin.

2

> **Junction:** From the junction, two ascent routes diverge, rejoining in 0.2 mi. To the right, the 1857 Route climbs to a spring and log shelter, built in 1968 by the ATA, then rejoins the Windsor Trail a short distance beyond.

From Halfway Spring, the Windsor Trail follows the 1903 Route left at the fork, then turns sharply left and ascends steeply south to a junction with the Blood Rock Trail (1.7 mi.).

> **Junction:** To the left, this blue-blazed trail climbs steeply for about 0.25 mi. to Blood Rock where there is a good view north. Caution should be exercised around the face of the ledge, which has been blocked by a railing. The trail then swings west to rejoin the Windsor Trail about 0.5 mi. above the junction.

Bearing right at the junction, the Windsor Trail is rejoined by the 1857 Route (1.8 mi.). It then begins a steady climb past the upper end of the Blood Rock Trail (2.0 mi.) and reaches a junction with the Futures Trail a short distance beyond (2.2 mi.). The Windsor Trail then reaches another junction (2.4 mi.) where a spur on the left leads to Castle Rock and a view of the Connecticut River Valley.

The Windsor Trail reaches yet another junction where it is joined on the right by the Brownsville Trail. From this

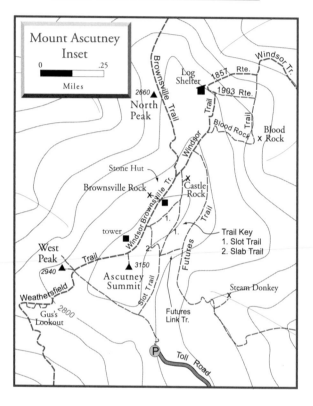

Mount Ascutney
Inset

0   .25

Miles

Brownsville Trail

Log
Shelter

1857 Rte.

1903 Rte.

Windsor Tr.

2660 ▲
North
Peak

Windsor Trail

Blood Rock Trail

Blood
X Rock

Stone Hut

Brownsville Rock

X
Castle
Rock

Windsor Brownsville Tr.

tower ■

1.

1.

Futures Trail

Trail Key
1. Slot Trail
2. Slab Trail

West
Peak
2940 ▲

Trail

2.

Ascutney
Summit ▲
3150

Slot Trail

Steam Donkey
X

Weathersfield

2800

Gus's
Lookout

Futures
Link Tr.

P

Toll Road

point, the trails coincide in a final ascent to the open area at
the Stone Hut site (3,110 ft.) (2.5 mi.). To the right, a short
spur leads to Brownsville Rock where there are extensive
views of much of the Green Mountain Range. As the trail
continues on the ridge toward the true summit, it passes a
junction with the Slot Trail on the left, which descends 0.7
mi. to the Mountain Road parking lot. The Windsor/
Brownsville Trail continues through the woods to a public

observation tower, then reaches a junction with the Weathersfield Trail at the bottom of a short spur, which ascends to Ascutney summit (3,150 ft.) (2.7 mi.).

Two communications towers dominate the mountain's highest summit, making views from this area mediocre. Hikers will be more satisfied with the vistas from Brownsville Rock, Castle Rock, and the nearby observation tower.

A cabin and tower were originally constructed on the summit of Mt. Ascutney in 1920 for forest fire surveillance. The CCC built a new steel tower in 1938 to 1940, and the site remained operational until 1952, when airplane patrols were established in the area. The concrete footings from this 1940 tower, which was removed in 1988, can be found about 300 ft. south of the present 24.5-ft. observation tower (without a cabin), constructed in 1989 by the state of Vermont using steel elements of the old tower. It affords panoramic views from treetop level to the White Mountains, Green Mountains, Berkshires, and Taconics.

BROWNSVILLE TRAIL

Distance: 3.2 mi. (5.2 km)
Elevation Change: 2,400 ft. ascent
Hiking Time: 2¾ hr. (reverse 1¾ hr.)

TO THE TRAIL: This trail begins on the south side of Vt. 44, 4.3 mi. west of its junction with U.S. 5 in Windsor and 1.1 mi. east of the Mt. Ascutney Ski Area. From the south, the trailhead is 2.8 mi. north of Ascutney State Park and 1.2 mi. north of the beginning of the Windsor Trail, making a loop hike over these two trails possible. Parking for the Brownsville Trail is available off the highway in a gravel lot with a trailhead bulletin board.

DESCRIPTION: From the parking lot (0.0 mi.), this white-blazed trail crosses a short grassy stretch in a former pasture before entering the woods in a southerly direction. It bears left to cross a wooden bridge over a seasonally dry wash before ascending briefly on wooden stair treads. At the top of the stairs, the trail bears right and zigzags steeply uphill to an old road. Turning right to follow the road, the trail continues on easier grades, soon reaching the former Norcross granite quarry (1.1 mi.), one of four that operated at various times in the area.

Beyond the grout (granite waste) pile, the old road ends and the trail turns sharply left, climbing steeply to a spur leading a short distance to Quarry Top Lookout, which offers views north (1.2 mi.). Climbing steadily through the woods, the trail eventually approaches a ski trail (1.6 mi.). Here, it swings sharply left and climbs on switchbacks to Knee Lookout (2.0 mi.) where there is a view east. The trail then continues on easier grades to the summit of North Peak (2.4 mi.) and a nearby vista where there are views west. Continuing on easy grades for some distance, the trail resumes a steep climb via switchbacks to a junction with the Windsor Trail (2.9 mi.).

Bearing right at the junction, the Brownsville and Windsor Trails coincide in their ascent to the Stone Hut site (3.0 mi.) atop the summit ridge. Here, a short spur trail right leads to Brownsville Rock where there are extensive views west to the Green Mountain Range and the hamlet of Brownsville. On the ridge, the trail continues south on easy grades, passes the observation tower, and reaches a junction with the Weathersfield Trail at the bottom of a short spur leading to Ascutney summit (3.2 mi.). Additional information on the summit area may be found in the description for the Windsor Trail.

FUTURES TRAIL

Distance: 4.8 mi. (7.7 km)
Elevation Change: 2,600 ft. ascent
Hiking Time: 3¾ hr. (reverse 2½ hr.)

Marked with blue blazes, this trail leads from Ascutney State Park to the Windsor Trail, about 0.5 mi. below the summit of Mt. Ascutney. Although it takes longer to ascend via this route, the trail offers several interesting views that compensate for the additional effort.

To the Trail: Follow the directions to Ascutney State Park on page 80. From the contact station near the park entrance, follow the signs for the Futures Trail, which point to the first road on the left, then follow the campground road to the trailhead at campsite 22.

Description: From the campsite (0.0 mi.), the trail winds south past the ruin of a stone fireplace dating to the 1930s. It continues climbing south and west through a series of switchbacks before reaching Bare Rock Vista (1.0 mi.), which offers views of the summit to the northwest and south to the Connecticut River Valley below.

Bearing right, the trail descends to traverse a mature hardwood forest before reaching a small stream (1.5 mi.) and then another small stream on the left (2.0 mi.). Ascending, it crosses under power lines to a parking lot along the Mountain Road (2.1 mi.) where a picnic shelter is located opposite. Without crossing the road, the trail bears west and returns to the woods, crossing two additional power lines (2.4 mi.) and the Mountain Road (2.8 mi.).

The trail ascends gently to a pair of streams (3.2 mi.). Just beyond the second stream, it reaches a junction (3.4 mi.) where a spur trail leads 0.1 mi. right to a "steam donkey." This steam engine was used in the early 1900s to pull logs up the mountain for use in building the road and fire tower. The Futures Trail bears left at the junction, soon reaching another junction (3.6 mi.) where the Futures Link Trail bears left.

Junction: The Futures Link Trail leads 0.1 mi. to a four-way intersection with the Slot and Slab Trails, which provide two shortcuts to the summit. The four-way intersection lies at about the midpoint of the Slot Trail (0.7 mi. long), which links the parking area atop the Mountain Road to a point on the Windsor/Brownsville Trail near the summit of the mountain. Continuing straight ahead at the intersection, the Slab Trail provides an additional shortcut to the summit, bypassing the upper half of the Slot Trail and reaching the Windsor/Brownsville Trail (0.2 mi.) in a saddle a short distance north of the observation tower and Ascutney summit.

The Futures Trail bears right at the junction and ascends steeply, finally reaching its terminus at a junction with the Windsor Trail (4.2 mi.). To the left, the Windsor Trail soon reaches a junction with the Brownsville Trail, and these two trails coincide to make a final ascent to the Stone Hut site and Brownsville Rock, a short distance below the observation tower and Ascutney summit (4.8 mi.). Additional information on the summit area may be found in the description of the Windsor Trail on page 80.

Slot Trail

Distance: 0.7 mi. (1.1 km)
Elevation Change: 350 ft. ascent
Hiking Time: ¾ hr. (reverse ½ hr.)

The Slot Trail begins at the top of the Mountain Road and climbs on moderate grades to the Windsor/Brownsville Trail in a saddle a short distance north of the Ascutney summit. It gets its name from a portion of the trail that passes through a high-walled slot.

Description: From the parking area (0.0 mi.), the trail ascends gradually to a four-way intersection (0.3 mi.).

Junction: To the right, the Futures Link Trail descends 0.1 mi. to reach the Futures Trail at a point 3.6 mi. above the trailhead in Ascutney State Park. To the left, the Slab Trail ascends 0.2 mi., rejoining the Slot Trail just below the ridge.

Continuing straight ahead, the Slot Trail soon reaches another junction (0.5 mi.) with the southern end of the Castle Rock Trail.

Junction: The Castle Rock Trail provides a short link (0.1 mi.) connecting the Slot Trail in the south with the Windsor Trail in the north. Castle Rock lies at the midpoint of the trail and provides an excellent view east to the Connecticut River Valley.

Turning left at the junction, the Slot Trail makes a winding ascent, is rejoined by the Slab Trail, and reaches the white-blazed Windsor/Brownsville Trail in a saddle 0.1 mi. north of the Ascutney summit (0.7 mi.).

2

WEATHERSFIELD TRAIL

Distance: 2.9 mi. (4.7 km)
Elevation Change: 2,062 ft. ascent
Hiking Time: 2½ hr. (reverse 1½ hr.)

This white-blazed trail ascends the southwestern side of the mountain and is on state and town (West Windsor) forestlands.

To the Trail: From Vt. 131, 3.3 mi. west of I-91 exit 8, and 3.8 mi. east of Vt. 106 at Downers Four Corners, turn north onto Cascade Falls Road. Bear left at High Meadow Road and continue 0.3 mi. to a right turn leading to a parking area and the trailhead.

Description: From the parking area (0.0 mi.), the trail begins a gradual ascent following an old woods road, soon crossing Little Cascade Falls (0.4 mi.). Ascending steeply over a rock outcrop, the trail enters a deep rock cleft, then ascends on easier grades, passing several overlooks (0.6 mi.). Descending, it reaches Crystal Cascade Falls (1.1 mi.) where Ascutney Brook tumbles 84 ft. over a sheer cliff. The trail then turns sharply right and continues up the east side of the brook. After crossing Cascade Brook, it meets and follows an old woods road strewn with boulders.

Following the road as far as Halfway Brooks (1.7 mi.), the Weathersfield Trail turns left and begins a winding and moderately steep climb through the woods. (Here, a bypass right leaves the trail to join it again at Gus's Lookout.) After passing several lookouts, the trail crosses an open rock area at the base of West Peak and continues a short distance to Gus's Lookout (2.3 mi.) where there is an excellent view of the Connecticut River Valley. The lookout is named for Augustus Aldrich, a charter director of the ATA and man of many talents who died at 86 while hiking Mt. Katahdin in 1974.

Beyond the lookout, the trail resumes its steady, winding climb past a spur to West Peak Spring (2.4 mi.), then reaches two more spurs. One leads a few hundred feet to West Peak (2,940 ft.) (2.6 mi.), while the other leads to a hang-glider launching site. Passing the spurs, the Weathersfield Trail makes a final winding climb to reach a junction with the Windsor/Brownsville Trail at the bottom of a short spur below the communications antennas on Ascutney summit (2.9 mi.). The summit area and nearby observation tower offer extensive views of the White Mountains, Green Mountains, Berkshires, and Taconics. Other features in the summit area are in the description of the Windsor Trail, page 80.

• • • • • • • • • • • • • • • •

COOLIDGE STATE PARK, SLACK HILL

Distance: 3.6 mi. (5.8 km)
Elevation Change: 500 ft. ascent
Hiking Time: 2¼ hr. (reverse 1¾ hr.)

Coolidge State Forest was first established in 1925 and now encompasses 16,166 acres scattered through seven towns. For management purposes, the forest is divided into eastern and western districts by Vt. 100. Camp Calvin Coolidge was established in Coolidge State Forest in Plymouth on June 9, 1933, as the third Civilian Conservation Corps (CCC) camp in Vermont, on the present site of

Coolidge State Park. Now occupying about 500 acres in the forest's eastern district, the park has camping and day-use facilities, with a fee charged in season. The several hiking trails include a 3.6-mi. loop that passes near the summit of Slack Hill (2,174 ft., USGS Plymouth).

TO THE TRAIL: The paved access road to Coolidge State Park leaves the east side of Vt. 100A, 4.3 mi. south of Bridgewater Corners and 2.7 mi. north of Plymouth Union. From Vt. 100A, travel 0.9 mi. uphill to the park contact station.

DESCRIPTION: Marked with blue blazes, the clockwise trail loop to the summit begins at the park contact station. To the right of a firewood shed (0.0 mi.), it follows the signed Slack Hill Trail, which climbs gently through open woods to a signed junction (0.5 mi.). Bearing left at the junction, the trail climbs moderately through a mixed hardwood forest before leveling off and passing east of the summit, which has been plagued with blowdowns. The trail then descends to a vista (1.5 mi.) where there is a narrow view southeast of Mt. Ascutney. It continues to descend gently, through hardwood forest, then a stand of white pine with little elevation change, eventually reaching the paved park access road (2.5 mi.).

Junction: The access road leads about 0.75 mi. right to the contact station.

Continuing the loop across the road, the CCC Trail leads from the park picnic area to a picnic pavilion with massive fireplaces at either end. Passing through the pavilion, the trail reaches a junction (3.0 mi.) where a spur right leads 0.1 mi. to the park tenting area. Continuing straight, the trail descends into a ravine to cross a stream, then climbs to another junction (3.5 mi.).

Junction: To the left, a 0.5-mi. spur trail descends fairly steeply to a picnic shelter (currently closed) and Vt. 100A, at the beginning of the park access road, 0.9 mi. below the contact station.

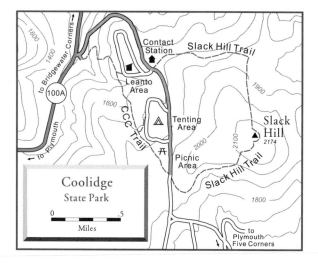

to Bridgewater Corners

to Plymouth

100A

Contact
Station

Slack Hill Trail

Leanto
Area

CCC Trail

Tenting
Area

Picnic
Area

Slack Hill Trail

Slack
Hill
2174

1600

1400

1200

1900

2000

2100

1800

to
Plymouth
Five Corners

Coolidge
State Park

0   .5

Miles

Bearing right at the junction, the trail quickly ends on a gravel roadway forming the western side of a road loop through the park's lean-to area. It bears right again along the road and continues straight through a junction forming the head of the loop where it is a short distance to the contact station on the park access road (3.8 mi.). Alternatively, by bearing left along the road to walk the longer leg of the road loop, there are occasional views west to Killington Peak and other summits in the Green Mountain Range. This route adds about 0.5 mi. to the distance.

● ● ● ● ● ● ● ● ● ● ● ● ● ● ● ● ●

WEST RIVER AREA

BALD MOUNTAIN, TOWNSHEND

Distance: 1.7 mi. (2.7 km)
Elevation Change: 1,100 ft. ascent
Hiking Time: 2 hr. (reverse 1 hr.)

2

This small mountain is in Townshend State Forest. Although the fire tower that once graced the summit (1,680 ft., USGS Townshend) is long gone, several small clearings offer views of Townshend Reservoir, the West River Valley, Stratton Mtn., Bromley Mtn., and New Hampshire's Mt. Monadnock.

Townshend State Park occupies about 41 acres in the 856-acre Townshend State Forest. The park was established as a CCC camp during the Great Depression and currently offers camping facilities. A fee is charged in-season. Access to swimming picnicking and the Ledges Overlook Trail (description follows, see maps on pages 92 and 97) is available at the Townshend Dam Recreation Area, managed by the Army Corps of Engineers.

TO THE TRAIL: To reach the trailhead in Townshend State Park, follow Vt. 30 north 2.1 mi. from the Townshend village common or south for 2.4 mi. from the post office in West Townshend to Townshend Dam. At the dam, turn west to cross the spillway on a narrow bridge and continue straight to an intersection. Turn left on the gravel West Hill Road, which leads to Scott Covered Bridge (the longest single-span covered bridge in Vermont). Bear right at the bridge on the state forest road and continue to parallel the West River to the park entrance on the left. Parking is available inside the park near the contact station.

DESCRIPTION: The blue-blazed trail starts at the contact station (0.0 mi.) and follows the paved campground road toward campsite 25 where it turns left to cross a brook on a

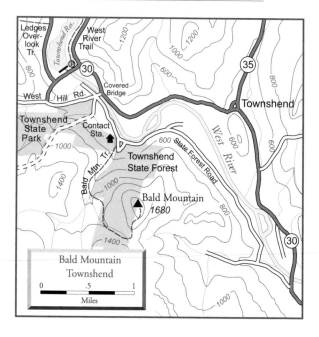

Bald Mountain
Townshend

0   .5   1
Miles

wooden bridge (0.1 mi.). It bears left to follow an old
woods road south, parallel to the brook, then ascends on
moderate grades. Eventually reaching a sign, the trail recrosses the brook on stones (0.5 mi.) and starts up a moderately steep grade. It leaves the woods road left, following
a smaller skid road. After a switchback left, the trail leaves
the skid road and continues, crossing two woods roads before passing through a hemlock forest. It reaches an old cellar hole (1.1 mi.), climbs moderately to a rocky section
before leveling off and bearing left (1.2 mi.). Turning
northeast, the trail passes an alder swamp on the right (1.5
mi.), then makes a steep climb north, mostly on bedrock, to
the summit of Bald Mtn. (1.8 mi.).

This spot was one of the earliest forest fire lookouts in Vermont. The station was established in 1912, and soon an observation tower was built. Between 1932 and 1934, the CCC constructed a steel tower at the site. In 1949 to 1950, this tower was relocated to Mt. Olga in Wilmington where it still stands as an observation tower for the general public.

In 1996, the eastern return leg of the old loop trail, which continued over the summit and down the north side of the mountain, was closed due to severe erosion. Until this section is reopened, hikers should use only the western half of the trail and not proceed beyond the summit.

LEDGES OVERLOOK TRAIL

Distance: 1.7 mi. (2.7 km)
Elevation Change: 450 ft. ascent
Hiking Time: 1½ hr. either direction

Maintained by the U.S. Army Corps of Engineers, this trail loop begins and ends at a wooded picnic grove on the west shore of Townshend Reservoir (USGS Townshend). Refer to the map on page 97.

TO THE TRAIL: From Townshend village, follow Vt. 30 north 2.1 mi. to Townshend Dam. At the dam, turn west and cross the spillway on a narrow bridge. Turn right onto an access road (0.0 mi.) and pass the beach (0.5 mi.) and picnic area (0.6 mi.) to the signed trailhead on the left. Ample parking is available on the east side of the road.

DESCRIPTION: The two ends of this yellow-blazed trail are separated by a short section of the paved access road. A register box at the southern trailhead contains brochures with a map outlining the clockwise loop.

From the register box (0.0 mi.), the trail enters the forest to follow a woods road, quickly crosses another woods road, then begins a steady ascent west, eventually reaching a stonewall, which it follows for a distance. The trail bears left off the road (0.2 mi.) on a southerly course through a mixed hardwood-softwood forest. It soon reaches and follows another road left on easier grades (0.3 mi.) before turning sharply west and crossing another stonewall. After resuming a steady climb, the trail turns north (0.5 mi.) to the end of the woods road (0.6 mi.). Following easier grades, it soon comes to a rock outcrop and picnic table (0.7 mi.), then continues to an old clearing at the top of a rock ledge (0.8 mi.). From this vantage point, there is a panorama of the West River Valley, including Townshend Reservoir and Dam and Scott Covered Bridge. Bald Mtn. lies to the southeast, and the long ridge of Rattlesnake Mtn. lies to the east.

Continuing north from the lookout, the trail climbs a short steep grade, then meanders along the top of the ridge parallel to the marked property line. In this woodland savannah, a grassy lawn lies beneath a grove of hophornbeam trees. Leaving the property line (1.0 mi.), the trail gradually descends, following a well-worn footpath marked with faded yellow blazes. It bears right onto a woods road, which it follows for a steady descent east, then southeast. Bearing slightly left off the woods road, the trail reaches another woods road, which it follows to the right. It passes some old foundations on the right (1.5 mi.) before again leaving the woods road. The trail crosses another woods road, then descends on easier grades to a dirt road. Bearing left on this road, it quickly turns right at a road junction before reaching the paved access road (1.7 mi.) across from the Burrington Picnic Pavilion, about 400 ft. north of the register box.

WEST RIVER TRAIL

When complete, the multiuse West River Trail will stretch 16.0 mi. from Townshend Dam, located between the villages of Townshend and West Townshend, west and north to South Londonderry. Walkers, cyclists, and cross-country skiers enjoy the route, which closely follows the West River and in many places uses the former bed of the West River Railroad. Marked with lavender and green West River Trail markers, four sections of the trail are open and maintained by the Friends of the West River Trail (page 327). Conditions may change as sections are rerouted or improved. The trail is divided into four sections described from south to north. Some portions of the trail are subject to flooding; camping and fires are not allowed; the trail closes at dusk; and dogs must be leashed.

Conceived as a connecting link between the Connecticut River and Lake Champlain, the West River Railroad operated from 1879 to 1935 between Brattleboro and South Londonderry, first as a narrow gauge line and later as a standard gauge railroad. Much of the route from Jamaica southward remains well defined; many sections of roadbed and several bridge abutments are readily visible from Vt. 30. The story of the West River Railroad is told in Victor Morse's *36 Miles of Trouble* (Brattleboro, Vt.: Stephen Greene Press, 1959).

TOWNSHEND DAM TO WEST TOWNSHEND

Distance: 3.0 mi. (4.8 km)
Elevation Change: minor
Hiking Time: 1½ hr. either direction

Using the old railroad bed and an abandoned section of Vt. 30, this section of the West River Trail (USGS Townshend) traverses the river bottomland along the east side of Townshend Reservoir and the West River. Located entirely on U.S. Army Corps of Engineers property, much of the first half of the trail may be underwater in the spring or when the Townshend Dam inundates the area for flood control purposes. Contact the corps office at the dam at (802) 365-7703 for trail information.

Townshend Dam was constructed between November 1958 and June 1961 and is 1,700 ft. wide and 133 ft. high.

With a drainage area of 278 square miles, the 1,010-acre lake has a maximum impoundment of 11 billion gallons.

TO THE TRAIL: At this time, this portion of the West River Trail is only accessible from the south. The trail starts at a large paved parking area on the southwest side of Vt. 30 at the Townshend Dam, 2.1 mi. west of the common in Townshend village or 2.4 mi. south of the post office in West Townshend.

DESCRIPTION: From a sign at the western end of the parking area (0.0 mi.), the trail descends steeply through a young forest to a cleared area behind the concrete spillway of the dam, then turns right on an old roadway. It then descends more gradually to the edge of the reservoir and into open, brushy land amid many broken tree limbs caused by ice damage from stored water.

With Rattlesnake Mtn. lying straight ahead and the West River Railroad bed visible in the trees to the right, the trail continues north to follow the blacktop roadway of a former section of Vt. 30 (0.2 mi.), abandoned when Townshend Dam was constructed.

The trail crosses a log boom and yellow gate (0.7 mi.) before arriving at a junction with a road on the right. Bearing left at the junction, the trail soon reaches the top of the reservoir where the waterway narrows and the West River veers to the far side of the valley. The trail follows a winding course past a series of small rock outcrops before eventually meeting the river again where both turn right (1.7 mi.). The West River Trail soon turns left off the old Vt. 30 roadbed (1.9 mi.), passes through a yellow gate, and crosses Ranney Brook on a wooden bridge. (Continuing along the roadbed for an additional 0.4 mi. leads to the present Vt. 30, 0.3 mi. south of the post office in West Townshend.)

The trail, now a footpath, wends its way through a brushy area before crossing a large open field where the route is marked by West River Trail markers mounted on posts. At the far side of the field (2.2 mi.), the trail enters

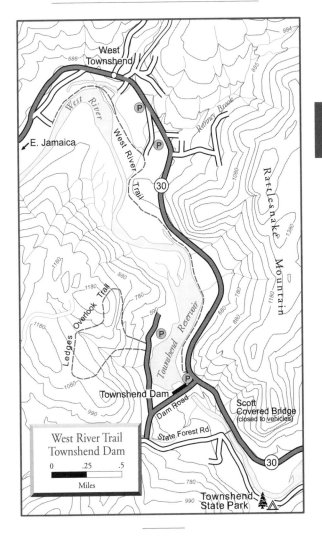

West
Townshend

688

984

635

Rainey Brook

E. Jamaica

West River Trail

West River

P

P

30

2

1080

Rattlesnake Mountain

1380

1180

890

1180

780

1080

590

Overlook Trail

Ledges

680

780

880

1180

Townshend Reservoir

1180

P

P

1080

Townshend Dam

Scott
Covered Bridge
(closed to vehicles)

990

Dam Road

State Forest Rd

30

**West River Trail
Townshend Dam**

0   .25   .5
Miles

780

990   Townshend
State Park

another brushy area and follows the barely discernible West River Railroad bed past a row of tall white pine trees on the right. Just beyond the trees lies the site of the former West Townshend railroad station. The trail leaves the roadbed briefly to cross a small stream then rejoins it before coming to a washout (2.6 mi.).

The trail enters a wooded area and leaves the almost imperceptible railroad bed to parallel a channel of the West River. It turns right to follow an old road a short distance to a gate where it turns left and soon reaches Vt. 30 at the Jamaica-Townshend town line. The trail follows the left side of Vt. 30 about 200 yds., passing a convenience store on the right, then bears left into the woods on a dirt road. This road ends in 500 yds. at the junction of Vt. 100 and Vt. 30 where parking is available.

JAMAICA STATE PARK TO COBB BROOK

Distance: 1.9 mi. (3.1 km)
Elevation Change: 350 ft. ascent
Hiking Time: 1½ hr. (reverse 1 hr.)

This segment of the West River Trail follows the roadbed of the former West River Railroad east and north for about 2.0 mi. along the West River (USGS Jamaica, Londonderry) and climbs over the U.S. Army Corps of Engineers' Ball Mountain Dam. The West River Trail also connects with the Overlook Trail and the Hamilton Falls Trail in Jamaica State Park, described on pages 103 to 106.

TO THE TRAIL: Jamaica State Park is located about 0.5 mi. from Vt. 30, 4.5 mi. west of West Townshend village, and about 9.0 mi. south and east of South Londonderry. From Jamaica village, turn north off Vt. 30 at a sign for the state park, pass the elementary school, and cross a bridge over the West River to reach the park entrance on the left. The park offers a variety of camping and day-use facilities with a fee charged in season.

DESCRIPTION: From a gate at the northern end of the state

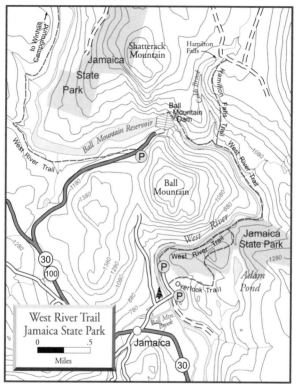

West River Trail
Jamaica State Park
0   .5
Miles

park day-use parking area (0.0 mi.), the West River Trail
follows the old railroad grade upstream and passes a series
of wire cables, which are used for setting slalom courses for
kayak races, stretched to the opposite bank of the West
River (0.5 mi. to 0.8 mi.). The trail then reaches a junction (1.0 mi.) where the north end of the Overlook Trail
(page 104) departs right to ascend Little Ball Mtn. before
returning to the state park campground.

The roadbed crosses several small streams, passes old foundations hidden in thick undergrowth on the left (1.6 mi.), then skirts the posted boundary of private property for some distance before reaching a junction with an old road on the right (1.9 mi.). Here, a sign marks the beginning of the Hamilton Falls Trail (described on page 105).

The trail continues on the old railroad bed straight ahead to cross Cobb Brook on rocks beside the ruins of old bridge abutments (2.0 mi.). It narrows to a foot trail as it reaches the base of the Ball Mountain Dam (2.2 mi.). The trail climbs the downstream face of the dam by a series of switchbacks, surmounts the top of the dam (2.3 mi.), then descends the upstream face on a traversing dirt road. At the dam tower (2.6 mi.), the trail follows a paved road under the bridge, which connects the tower to the dam, passes a gate, then continues on the paved road to the next section of trail (2.9 mi.).

BALL MOUNTAIN DAM TO WINHALL CAMPGROUND

Distance: 4.1 mi. (6.6 km)
Elevation Change: minor
Hiking Time: 2 hr. either direction

This section of the West River Trail (USGS Jamaica, Londonderry) starts on the access road to the Ball Mountain Dam and follows a woodland path along the slopes above Ball Mountain Reservoir before dropping to the river's edge. The trail then follows a road along the former bed of the West River Railroad on the south and west shores of the West River to reach the Army Corps of Engineers' Winhall Campground. This section is blazed with lavender paint as well as with West River Trail markers.

TO THE TRAIL: The Ball Mountain Dam access road leaves the north side of Vt. 30/100, 1.5 mi. west of the general store in the village of Jamaica or 3.4 mi. east of the junction of Vt. 100 and Vt. 30 in Rawsonville. The trailhead is located at a break in the guardrail on the west side of the access road, 1.5 mi. north of Vt. 30/100, beyond a yellow gate and adjacent to a sign describing the Ball Mountain Dam. Parking is available in a lot near a building on the right, 0.1 mi. south of the trailhead or just beyond the trailhead on the left. Note: The Ball Mountain Dam access road is closed from 3:00 P.M. to 7:00 A.M.

DESCRIPTION: From the yellow gate (0.0 mi.), the route follows a narrow paved road a short distance to a sign for the West River Trail. Departing the road left, the trail descends gradually through a young forest to a junction with an old road. It turns left and immediately meets a gravel road on the outside edge of a hairpin turn (0.1 mi.). Following the left leg of the road uphill for a very short distance, the West River Trail bears right onto the broad grassy roadbed. Remaining on level grades, the trail narrows to a footpath to traverse a steep hillside then crosses a rocky, washed-out area before entering an aspen-birch forest. It continues through rocky swales before descending to cross several small brooks on a bank overlooking Ball Mountain Reservoir.

The trail, now marked with occasional orange blazes, enters a hemlock forest (0.9 mi.) and makes a short but steady climb before dropping to cross a larger brook on a broad rock slab. Turning right onto an old woods road (1.2 mi.), it soon leads to open lands where the West River enters the head of the Ball Mountain Reservoir. The rocky slopes of Shatterack Mtn. can be seen to the east across the water, while Glebe Mtn. is visible looking upstream across the valley.

The trail crosses a brook to the right of a waterfall (1.4 mi.) and continues as a footpath through hardwood forest. After climbing a short, steep pitch, it takes a winding route through hemlocks atop a large rock outcrop, passes an Army Corps of Engineers benchmark on the left, then turns onto a woods road at a point above the West River (1.9 mi.).

Soon leaving the road to the right (2.2 mi.), the West River Trail crosses a brook in a dense hemlock stand. Emerging into a white pine forest, it descends to a clearing and reaches a junction at the end of a dirt road (2.4 mi.). To the right, a path leads a short distance to the West River. The stone abutments of Pratt's Bridge where the West River Railroad crossed the river, are visible to the left. Though the railroad was abandoned about 1937, the bridge remained until destroyed by ice in the 1970s.

The West River Trail turns left at the junction to follow the dirt road, which coincides with the railbed of the West River Railroad. The road passes through a mixture of open lands and trees, with a number of views to the West River on the right, finally arriving at the southern end of the Winhall Campground (4.1 mi.).

WINHALL CAMPGROUND TO SOUTH LONDONDERRY

Distance: 1.8 mi. (2.9 km)
Elevation Change: minor
Hiking Time: 2 hr. either direction

TO THE TRAIL: The start of this section of the West River Trail is separated from the northern end of the previous section (from Ball Mountain Dam) by a 1.5-mi. road walk through the Army Corps of Engineers' Winhall Campground. The campground, located in the town of Londonderry, is reached by turning east on the paved Winhall Station Road from Vt. 100, 2.4 mi. north of the junction of Vt. 30 and Vt. 100 in Rawsonville or 1.5 mi. south of the bridge in South Londonderry.

From a sign for the campground at the junction of Vt. 100 and Winhall Station Road (0.0 mi.), bear left almost immediately, then right at the next junction (0.2 mi.) to reach the campground gatehouse (0.9 mi.). Proceed a short distance to a fork.

To reach the northern trailhead for the previous section

of the West River Trail, turn right at the fork to cross a bridge over the Winhall River (1.0 mi.) and continue through the open camping areas along the West and Winhall Rivers. Parking is available at the end of the campgrounds where the road enters the woods (1.8 mi.), but vehicular traffic is permitted the next 1.7 mi. along the road to the site of Pratt's Bridge.

North of the Winhall Campground, the West River Trail is a dirt road extending toward the village of South Londonderry. The road is gated and uses the railbed of the West River Railroad. To reach the trailhead, go left at the fork beyond the gatehouse and follow the gravel road that parallels the north side of the river. Parking is available near the amphitheater in a mowed area (1.6 mi.). The trailhead is a short distance farther down the dirt road at a yellow gate at the edge of the woods.

DESCRIPTION: From the yellow gate (0.0 mi.), with the West River visible to the right, the roadbed eventually passes over the abutments of a stone culvert that permitted cattle to pass beneath the railroad (1.3 mi.) and reaches a second yellow gate (1.8 mi.). The trail then becomes a dirt road, passes posted properties, and ends in South Londonderry (2.7 mi.) where parking is available.

JAMAICA STATE PARK

Occupying 756 acres along a bend of the West River in the town of Jamaica, Jamaica State Park was recognized in 1996 as the best state park in Vermont. Semiannual water releases from Ball Mountain Dam, located upstream from the park, draw large numbers of whitewater paddling enthusiasts to the area in April and October.

The preceding description of the West River Trail contains information about access to the park and the trails described below.

OVERLOOK TRAIL

Distance: 3.0 mi. (4.8 km)
Elevation Change: 475 ft. ascent
Hiking Time: 1½ hr. either direction

This 2.0 mi. trail and 1.0 mi. of the West River Trail make a nice 3.0 mi. loop. One end of the trail departs the West River Trail and the other departs from a fence near the Hackberry Lean-to.

TO THE TRAIL: Follow the directions to Jamaica State Park on page 98. From the entrance to the park, walk 1.0 mi. north along the West River Trail.

DESCRIPTION: The blue-blazed Overlook Trail leaves right at a signed junction, across the river from a sheer rock wall. The trail's sometimes obscure, steep initial climb over tree roots and rocks is in stark contrast to the easy, flat roadbed of the West River Trail. The Overlook Trail passes right of a large meadow (0.4 mi.) before skirting the left side of the remains of a pond. This area may be wet depending on the season and rainfall. The trail soon reaches a junction with a sign pointing right. Here, a large boulder is visible near the summit ahead.

> **Junction:** A segment of trail forming a summit loop turns left, eventually rejoining the Overlook Trail below the summit.

Turning right, the Overlook Trail follows a series of switchbacks, beginning at a white birch with a triple trunk. It continues to climb to a rock outcrop at the summit of Little Ball Mtn. (1,164 ft.) where care should be taken near the steep ledges. The trail reaches a vista offering a marvelous view of the West River Valley, as well as the Green Mountains to the west. It now follows blue blazes painted on both trees and rocks to a second vantage point (1.0 mi.), which offers a view of the town of Jamaica. From this point, the trail continues along the summit ridge and passes the boulder that was visible from below. Here, the underside of the large rock is worn away, creating a small cave.

Junction: A sign pointing left indicates the direction back to the first junction, below the large boulder.

Turning right, the Overlook Trail descends, steeply in places, eventually reaching a sign pointing right (1.4 mi.). It then comes to and follows an old logging road, which gently descends to an opening in the park fence near the campground. Entering the camping area at the Hackberry Lean-to, the day-use parking lot is to the right along the access road.

2

HAMILTON FALLS

Distance: 1.1 mi. (1.8 km)
Elevation Change: 500 ft. ascent
Hiking Time: 1 hr. (reverse ½ hr.)

This obvious route departs the West River Trail, 1.9 mi. north of its trailhead in Jamaica State Park (page 98) and ascends to one of the highest and most spectacular water-falls in Vermont.

DESCRIPTION: Leaving the former West River Railroad bed right (0.0 mi.) at a sign indicating the falls, the trail to Hamilton Falls turns right and ascends steadily on an old road high above Cobb Brook, passing local views of the stream and its environs from increasing heights. The trail reaches the top of a ridge and an unmarked junction on the left (0.8 mi.) where a spur slabs downhill for about 325 ft. to the base of Hamilton Falls. From this vantage, there is an attractive view of the falls from the bottom. Caution: it is unsafe to attempt to climb the falls from this location.

The top of the falls is reached by following the main trail as it continues on the old road to a junction with a narrow public road (1.0 mi.). Here, the trail follows the road downhill left and soon turns left again onto a footpath that leads about 250 ft. to the top of Hamilton Falls (1.1 mi.). As noted by the prominent signs, these spectacular falls should be enjoyed with caution; at least ten people have died here in recent years.

•••••••••••••••••

WINDMILL HILL–PUTNEY MOUNTAIN

Located in eastern Windham County, the Windmill Hill–Putney Mountain ridge (USGS Newfane, Townshend) runs north and south, extending 16.0 mi. between Cambridgeport and Dummerston. The ridge is known as Windmill Hill or Windmill Mtn. in the north where it follows the town line between Athens and Westminster. In the south, along the town line between Putney and Brookline, it is referred to as Putney Mtn. The ridge rises steeply on the west side, then slopes gently east. At its highest point, in the Putney Mtn. section, it drops nearly 1,000 ft. into the town of Brookline.

The Windmill Hill–Pinnacle Association and the Putney Mountain Association were instrumental in developing a total of sixteen trails and protecting about 2,000 acres along the ridge. The two organizations continue to expand their interconnected trail systems and hope to protect wildlife habitat from Prospect Hill in Dummerston to Saxtons River.

These organizations are nonprofits dependent on membership support to protect land and maintain the trails. Both organizations publish maps and brochures for their trails. The Windmill Hill–Pinnacle Association can be contacted at 218 Barnes Road, Putney, Vermont 05346-9007. The Putney Mountain Association can be contacted at P.O. Box 953, Putney, Vermont 05346.

Hiking trails ascend to high points on either end of the ridge, at the summit of Putney Mtn. in the south and to the Pinnacle in the north. The following descriptions cover only a portion of the two trail systems. Display maps of the two systems are mounted at trailhead kiosks, which also provide leaflet maps. The systems use the same color-coding for trail marking, with the main north–south trail using various names but always marked with white disks, and the side trails are marked with yellow, blue, red, or orange disks.

2

Please note that dogs must be leashed; metal detectors are prohibited; and no artifacts may be removed. Groups larger than twelve and outdoor fires (allowed at the Pinnacle only, bring your own wood) require permits; call (802) 387-5737.

RIDGELINE TRAIL TO SUMMIT TRAIL

Distance: 0.6 mi. (0.9 km)
Elevation Change: 140 ft. ascent
Hiking Time: ⅓ hr. either direction

This trail, popular among area residents, follows the top of the Putney Mtn. ridge before ascending a short distance to the summit of Putney Mtn. From the summit there are good views west over the hills of the West River Valley to the Green Mountains, including Stratton Mtn., and east to New Hampshire's Mt. Monadnock. The summit is an excellent place to view hawks during the fall migration. The trail is in the Putney Town Forest or on lands protected by the Putney Mountain Association.

TO THE TRAIL: From U.S. 5 at the general store in the center of Putney Village (0.0 mi.), follow Westminster West Road (the portion of the road in the village is also known locally as Kimball Hill Road) northwest to a junction on the left with West Hill Road (1.1 mi.). Follow West Hill Road, keeping right at a fork (2.5 mi.) and bearing left at a sharp curve where Aiken Road leaves right (3.0 mi.).

Turn right on the unpaved Putney Mountain Road (3.4 mi.), immediately bear right at a fork and continue past a fork on the right to the parking lot for the trail (5.6 mi.), located on the right at the crest of the mountain ridge where the road curves sharply right.

DESCRIPTION: The white-blazed (white disks) trail begins at the far end of the parking lot (0.0 mi.) next to a sign reading "Welcome to Putney Mountain." Here, the yellow-marked West Cliff Trail leaves left.

> **Junction:** The West Cliff Trail is a slightly longer alternate route to the summit. It drops off the ridge and slabs the steep western side passing through tall hemlocks before reaching a junction (0.6 mi.). The blue-blazed Summit Trail leads right and climbs steeply 0.1 mi. to the summit of Putney Mtn. (0.7 mi.).

Bearing left from the same junction, the yellow-marked West Cliff Trail descends first west then north through open hemlocks and escarpments, passes a view (0.7 mi.), crosses a stream (1.3 mi.), briefly follows old woods road (1.7 mi.) and ends at a five-way trail junction called Five Corners (2.7 mi.). From there, the white-blazed Pinnacle Trail heads north 2.6 mi. to the Pinnacle (5.3 mi.).

The Ridgeline Trail immediately passes over a large outcrop of bedrock polished smooth by the continental glacier and meets a rutted road (0.1 mi.). The trail continues north through a mixed forest with an occasional red pine, a tree not commonly found in Vermont.

The trail splits and rejoins itself several times along its course. It passes a large ash tree, known as the Elephant Tree due to its peculiarly shaped limb (0.5 mi.), then forks. Bearing right, following white disks, the trail climbs past a stonewall to a junction (0.5 mi.). Here, the blue-marked Putney Trail leaves left for the summit of Putney Mountain (1,660 ft.) (0.6 mi.) and continues to the junction with the West Cliff Trail (0.7 mi.).

Looking west from the summit, Stratton Mtn. is dominant, while Mt. Snow and Haystack Mtn. are also visible. Looking east, the view encompasses much of southwestern New Hampshire, from Mt. Monadnock to Mt. Sunapee.

From the junction, the trail descends eastward to Banning Rd. (0.8 mi.), then follows white disks on Banning Road northward to the end of the town-maintained section (1.8 mi.) and continues on an old roadway northward to the five-way trail junction, Five Corners (2.6 mi.). From here, the white-marked Pinnacle Trail leads north to the Pinnacle (5.2).

2

THE PINNACLE

The Pinnacle is a high point on Windmill Hill located 2.0 mi. west of the village of Westminster West. Long held in private ownership, the Pinnacle was a popular destination for area residents. Purchase of lands along the ridge by the Windmill Hill–Pinnacle Association (WHPA) has secured public access. Three trails lead to the ridge: the white-marked Jamie Latham Trail from the north, the red-marked Holden Trail from the east, and the white-marked Pinnacle Trail (not described here) from the south.

JAMIE LATHAM TRAIL

Distance: 2.1 mi. (3.4 km)
Elevation Change: 430 ft. ascent
Hiking Time: 1¼ hr. (reverse 1 hr.)

This trail is named for Jamie Latham, who died in 1991, a young man from Westminster West who spent many hours visiting the Pinnacle. The route ascends the Pinnacle from the north and is marked with white disks.

TO THE TRAIL: From U.S. 5 at the general store in the center of Putney Village, follow the Westminster West Road north and west for 6.9 mi. to the village of Westminster

West. Reaching a junction at the end of an S curve in front of a church, turn left onto West Road, passing the white church on your left. From the north, the same junction may be reached by leaving Vt. 121 in the village of Saxtons River west of Bellows Falls and following the Westminster West Road south for 5.8 mi.

From the church (0.0 mi.), follow the gravel West Road to a junction and bear right onto Old Athens Road (0.6 mi.). At a white wooden gate with a road leading straight ahead to a private estate (1.5 mi.), the Old Athens Road turns sharply left. At an intersection at the bottom of a short downgrade (1.9 mi.), the Old Athens Road bears left. (From here, the road turns into a class 4 road with the condition of the road varying from season to season. It is generally passable by all but very low-clearance vehicles if caution is used.) In winter it is recommended to park here because the road to the trailhead is usually impassable and the parking area unplowed. A large parking lot and kiosk are on the left at 2.7 mi.

DESCRIPTION: From the kiosk (0.0 mi.), the white-marked trail leads briefly south, passes a field, then turns sharply right (0.1 mi.), followed by a sharp left into young woods. The trail crosses a swale on puncheon (0.3 mi.) and climbs to where an old road comes in from the left (0.4 mi.). After descending to cross a second swale and climbing briefly in a section where several overgrown roads branch off, the Jamie Latham Trail turns right (0.7 mi.) onto an old logging road now filling in with briars.

Climbing moderately, the trail follows the logging road to its end at a small clearing with a picnic table (0.9 mi.). Continuing as a footpath, the trail almost immediately reaches and briefly follows a stonewall right before turning left to cross the wall at a property corner. As the trail climbs moderately, it passes several hemlock groves before crossing another stonewall (1.3 mi.) near the top of the grade, then continues into a lovely, open hardwood forest.

The trail soon turns left onto a wider trail (1.5 mi.). As

the forest becomes a mixture of hardwoods and soft-woods, the trail reaches an intersection (1.8 mi.) with an older trail to the summit. Bearing right, the trail follows a wide, well-established path.

The footway turns to bedrock as the trail climbs toward the summit and an overgrown clearing. After passing a junction with the red-marked Holden Trail on the left, the Jamie Latham Trail continues straight to a clearing at the top of the Pinnacle (1,690 ft.) (2.1 mi.). A cabin, located here, is available for overnight camping. To reserve the cabin, contact the WHPA (see page 330). Views from the summit extend from Hedgehog Gulf at the base of the Pinnacle west to the Green Mountains.

HOLDEN TRAIL

Distance: 1.5 mi. (2.4 km)
Elevation Change: 458 ft. ascent
Hiking Time: ¾ hr. (reverse ¾ hr.)

This trail climbs the Pinnacle from the east on an old woods road.

TO THE TRAIL: From the church in Westminster West (see directions to the Jamie Latham Trail on page 109) (0.0 mi.), follow the gravel West Road passing the Old Athens Road on the right (0.6 mi.). Continue left on West Road to Windmill Hill Road North (1.0 mi.). Follow this road uphill until it turns to a class 4 road (1.8 mi.), then continue to a parking lot and the trailhead (2.1 mi.).

DESCRIPTION: This red-marked trail begins at a kiosk and elaborate gate (0.0 mi.). From the gate, the trail follows an old woods road climbing steadily to reach a trail sign (0.5 mi.). From here, it turns right onto another woods road. Following the woods road, the trail makes a gentle and variable climb, then descends slightly (0.9 mi.) to a moist area where short relocations and puncheon segments depart briefly from the road. A series of gentle switchbacks (1.2 mi.) bring the trail to the intersection (1.4 mi.) with the white-marked Jamie Latham Trail at the top of the ridge. Continuing left at this junction, it is a short flat distance to the summit clearing (1.5 mi.).

• • • • • • • • • • • • • • • •

NEWFANE TOWN FOREST

The trail system in the Newfane Town Forest was created by the Newfane Conservation System, starting in 2000, with subsequent assistance from the Vermont Youth Conservation Corps. A map including information on natural history, points of interest, and additional routes may be available at the trailhead or at the town office. Orange blazes mark the town forest boundaries.

WHITE FERN TRAIL

Distance: 2.3 mi. (3.7 km)
Elevation Change: 560 ft. ascent
Hiking Time: 1¼ hr. either direction

The White Fern Trail is a pleasant path that follows Schoolhouse Brook past a number of small cascades. The trail was cleared and blazed in 2000 by local volunteers. One main 2.0-mi. loop trail, with a 0.7-mi. alternate route, is accessed by a trail leading from a designated parking area.

TO THE TRAIL: From the village of Newfane (0.0 mi.), head south on Vt. 30. Pass the Newfane Elementary School on the left immediately before turning right onto Grimes Hill Road (2.5 mi.). Continue on this road to the stop sign in Williamsville (4.2 mi.) and turn left onto Depot Road. Cross a single-lane bridge and then climb for a short distance to a small cemetery on the right. Just after the cemetery is the entrance (4.8 mi.) to the Newfane town garage with a small trailhead parking area just within the entrance on the right.

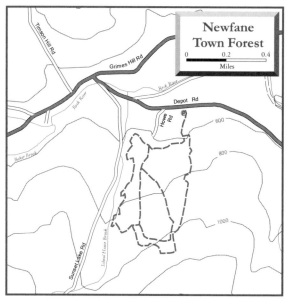

DESCRIPTION: From the parking lot, the trail begins 150 ft. down the gated town garage access road. The trail entrance is marked by a sign and arrow on the right side of the road, just before reaching a complex of buildings and sand piles. From the trailhead (0.0 mi.), the white-blazed trail leads through white pines interspersed with large apple trees. Soon entering a mix of successional woods, the trail crosses a few small streams and several old skidder ruts as it climbs easily to Chaos Junction (0.5 mi.).

A sign at the junction indicates that trails bear left to Mushroom Road and right to the waterfalls. Bearing left, the trail follows a gentle, mostly straight, even grade along an old woods road to the lower junction (0.6 mi.) where the Golden Gateway Trail, a yellow-blazed parallel route, bears left (see description following).

Mushroom Road climbs gradually to the upper junction (0.9 mi.) with the Golden Gateway Trail. The main white-blazed trail turns right off the logging road into the woods shortly before reaching the highest point of the loop. Large vines give this area its name, Tarzan's Forest. The trail begins to descend gradually, then moderately, (1.0 mi.) before reaching the edge of Town Brook (1.1 mi.). Along this bedrock stream, there are several miniature waterfalls, flumes, and pools. The trail climbs and descends along the slopes of the drainage cut before climbing out of the vale a final time (1.7 mi.) onto even ground and returning to Chaos Junction (1.8 mi.).

GOLDEN GATEWAY TRAIL

Distance: 1.3 mi. (2.1 km)
Elevation Change: 150 ft. ascent
Hiking Time: ⅔ hr. either direction

The Golden Gateway Trail was established in 2001 and was named by Newfane Elementary School students. It passes some impressive trees, many of which are yellow birches elevated on above-ground roots. It reaches Laura's Lookout, which has a good view across the Rock River Valley to Newfane Hill.

DESCRIPTION: The yellow-blazed Golden Gateway Trail bears left off Mushroom Road (0.0 mi.) and enters the woods along a flat stretch before crossing a small stream (0.7 mi.). It gradually climbs before veering right onto an old logging road (0.9 mi.). The trail climbs easily along a fairly straight course to the high point on the loop (1.0 mi.) where it bears right off the old road and begins a steady, easy descent through the woods. The trail reaches the extension of Mushroom Road (1.2 mi.), turns right onto it, and descends to the upper junction (1.3 mi.) with the white-blazed trail, which emerges from the woods on the left.

• • • • • • • • • • • • • • • •

BLACK MOUNTAIN

Distance: 3.2 mi. (5.2 km) loop
Elevation Change: 975 ft. ascent
Hiking Time: 2 hr. either direction

Located in the town of Dummerston, The Nature Conservancy's 374-acre Black Mountain Preserve supports extensive pitch pine and scrub oak communities and harbors several rare plant species. The plant communities are more like those of Massachusetts than Vermont due to the acidic nature of this granite mountain. The mountain rises quickly from the West River and has a rough horseshoe-shape, with the opening facing south (USGS Newfane). The old roads and trails in the preserve, not all of which are described here, are open to the public during daylight hours for foot travel only. Fires and overnight camping are not allowed. Although a blazed Nature Conservancy trail leads to the summit (1,280 ft.) from the west, many of the other routes on the mountain are unmarked, including a shorter route on private property from Black Mountain Road.

To the Trail: From Vt. 30 north of West Dummerston, cross the West River (0.0 mi.) on the Dummerston covered bridge and turn right onto Quarry Road. Follow this road south as it becomes Rice Farm Road and continue to an unmarked gravel road on the left (2.2 mi.) leading to the trailhead. Parking for three vehicles is available on the river side of Rice Farm Road.d.

Description: Leaving the public road (0.0 mi.) at a small nature trail sign, the Black Mountain Trail follows the old road uphill about 100 yds. to a cable gate and Nature Conservancy sign where the trail turns sharply right. It follows the road to the top of the hill where the first white blazes and a trail sign are found. Bearing right, the trail begins a gradual ascent, reaching a TNC register box and an older woods road on the right (0.3 mi.), which is the unmarked end of the return route. The blazed Black Mountain Trail continues straight ahead to cross a wetland on wooden planking.

After ascending and skirting the upper edge of an overgrown clearing, the trail enters the woods (0.5 mi.) and begins climbing along a series of switchbacks where care should be taken to follow the blazes. The trail reaches a ridge (1.1 mi.) below the true summit where it bears left for a distance before veering right and meandering through an extensive cluster of mountain laurel. The trail reaches its highest point a short distance below the summit, then begins an easy descent and emerges onto a large rock outcropping and vista (1.4 mi.), from which there are views south of the West River Valley, Connecticut River Valley, the Vermont Yankee nuclear station, and New Hampshire's Mt. Monadnock.

The trail continues along the rock outcropping, following painted blazes, and leaves the summit area to the north. At a woods road junction (1.6 mi.), the trail turns right onto the road and eventually leaves TNC property at a sign prohibiting campfires where the blazing ends (1.8 mi.). The now unblazed trail reaches an unmarked road junction in a sag (1.9 mi.).

Junction: This unmarked road leads left uphill about 0.5 mi. through old quarries to reach a T-junction. To the right, along a wide gravel path, it is about 0.4 mi. to a summit and view. Straight ahead, the trail leads to Black Mountain Road. These side trails are on private property, so please respect the land and buildings.

Turning sharply right from the junction, the trail descends south near a brook. After crossing a small tributary (2.3 mi.), it swings right of a beaver dam (2.5 mi.) and continues on easier grades to a woods road junction where it takes the more conspicuous right fork (2.7 mi.). The trail continues with minor elevation changes to the end of the trail loop (2.9 mi.) on the Black Mountain Trail. To the left, it is 0.3 mi. to the Rice Farm Road trailhead. Note: due to the lack of blazing on this descent route, careful observation is required most of the way to follow the sometimes indistinct path.

● ● ● ● ● ● ● ● ● ● ● ● ● ● ● ● ●

MOUNT OLGA

Distance: 2.0 mi. (3.1 km)
Elevation Change: 520 ft. ascent
Hiking Time: 1¼ hr. either direction

From the old, but maintained, fire tower on the summit of Mt. Olga (2,415 ft., USGS Wilmington), there are good views of southern Vermont, southwestern New Hampshire, and northern Massachusetts.

2

TO THE TRAIL: The two trails to the summit, which form a loop, begin in Molly Stark State Park. The park entrance is on the south side of Vt. 9, about 3.5 mi. east of Wilmington Village or 15.0 mi. west of Brattleboro. The park offers a variety of camping accommodations; a day-use fee is charged in season.

DESCRIPTION: Leaving the park road opposite the contact station (0.0 mi.), the blue-blazed main trail quickly crosses Beaver Brook on a wooden bridge and climbs gradually east through the woods. It reaches a junction of two stonewalls (0.1 mi.) where it turns left to follow the walls for about 100 ft. before bearing right. The trail then ascends a moderate grade before beginning an easier climb through evergreens. It reaches another stonewall (0.4 mi.), then begins a steep and winding climb to a junction with the summit trail (0.7 mi.).

Junction: The 0.1-mi. summit trail bears left and climbs to the crest of Mt. Olga at a fire tower. An old road that serviced the abandoned Hogback Mountain Ski Area leads several hundred feet east to the ski trails, from which there are good views northeast.

Mt. Olga became a fire lookout site in 1930 when a wooden tower with an octagonal cab was constructed on the summit. From 1949 to 1950, the wooden tower was removed and the present steel tower was moved to Mt. Olga from Bald Mtn. in Townshend. The tower was last used as a fire lookout in 1974. It was listed in the National Historic Lookout Register in 1996.

From the previously mentioned junction just below the summit (0.7 mi.), the blue-blazed Mt. Olga Trail follows a campground sign and descends through the woods on easy grades, eventually passing between two large rocks and crossing a small stream on a crude wooden bridge. The trail then bears left onto an old road (1.1 mi.), which it follows a short distance before bearing left again off the road and crossing a small stream on steppingstones. It reaches a stonewall on the right, which it follows to its end, passing a junction (1.5 mi.) with the Ghost Trail on the right.

Junction: The blue-blazed Ghost Trail provides an alternate route to the contact station. It leads south from the Mount Olga Trail to skirt the camping area on easy grades. The trail crosses over a small brook on a wooden bridge, passes two unused fireplaces, and crosses another brook before ending on a service road a short distance from the contact station.

The Mount Olga Trail continues straight ahead then crosses a small stream on a bridge, before reaching the loop road in the camping area (1.6 mi.). To the right, it is 0.2 mi. to the park headquarters and the contact station.

• • • • • • • • • • • • • • • •

RAMBLES

QUECHEE GORGE

Located in the Town of Hartford, this trail begins on a dike between Deweys Pond (or Deweys Mills Pond) and the Ottauquechee River, then parallels the river as it flows into Quechee Gorge. The land is part of 611 acres owned by the U.S. Army Corps of Engineers as part of the North

Hartland Dam flood control project and is leased to the Department of Forest, Parks and Recreation, which manages it for recreation.

TO THE TRAIL: From I-89 (Exit 1), proceed west on U.S. 4 about 3.0 mi. Just before the road crosses over Quechee Gorge, turn right onto Deweys Mills Road and follow it to its end at a T intersection (about 1.0 mile). Turn left at the intersection onto Quechee's Main Street (also called Clubhouse Road), then almost immediately left again, just past the Strong House Spa, into the Deweys Pond parking area. A sign here reads "Dewey's Landing."

DESCRIPTION: From the end of the parking area opposite the road, a blue-blazed trail leads south along the dike separating the Ottauquechee River from Deweys Pond. It follows along the river 0.4 mi. to a dam and waterfall that was once the site of the Dewey Woolen Mill. About 0.2 mi. beyond the dam the trail passes a small picnic area where rest rooms are available seasonally.

Continuing south, the trail proceeds along the rim of the gorge (separated from the cliff by a fence) to an overlook with a bench on the right, then passes under the U.S. 4 bridge, which is 165 ft. above the river. This bridge was built in 1911 for the Woodstock Railroad (1875–1933) to replace the original Howe Truss Bridge of wood timbers and iron. With the abandonment of the railroad, the bridge and rail bed became part of U.S. 4. Edward T. Mead's book *Over the Hills to Woodstock* tells the story of this railroad, of which some structures and roadbed remain visible.

Beyond the bridge the trail reaches an unmarked junction. Bearing right, it descends to the bottom of the gorge where the rushing waters become a placid river at the upstream end of the North Hartland Reservoir. Further exploration is possible along a footpath that continues downstream, but this eventually peters out. About two miles from Deweys Pond, a trail branches left off the above trail and eventually leads to the Quechee State Park campground on the south side of U.S. 4. Note: a trail map is available at Wilderness Trails, located behind the Quechee Inn at Marshland Farm across the road from the Deweys Pond parking area.

ESHQUA BOG

Located in the town of Hartland, Eshqua Bog is a 40-acre sanctuary jointly owned and managed by The Nature Conservancy and the New England Wild Flower Society. The site contains a variety of cold-climate holdover plants that largely disappeared from Vermont at the end of the last glacial period some 10,000 years ago. In late spring and early summer, a variety of wildflowers can be found, including several varieties of orchids and a spectacular vernal display of hundreds of lady's slippers in bloom. A 0.5-mi. white-blazed loop trail roughly circles the property, but the focal point of the preserve is a two-acre fen traversed by a boardwalk. A fen is a wetland where water comes principally from a local aquifer rather than rainfall or nearby streams or ponds.

TO THE TRAIL: From its junction with Vt. 12 in Woodstock Village, follow U.S. 4 east a short distance to the edge of the village where the main road makes a sharp left. Proceed straight on Hartland Hill Road (0.0 mi.), which soon turns southeast. Turn right on the unsigned Garvin Hill Road (1.1 mi.) and follow this gravel road to a small pull-off on the right (2.3 mi.) where limited parking is available. The entrance to the preserve is a short distance beyond the pullout.

DESCRIPTION: Past the entrance, the trail reaches a registration box and junction. While the boardwalk departs left and cuts across the center of the wetland, the loop trail goes right, skirting the edge of the bog in a mature hardwood forest. The trail climbs steeply up a bank at the northern end of the bog before meeting the western end of the boardwalk. The loop trail continues straight ahead on level ground around the south end of the bog and returns to Garvin Hill Road about 40 yds. south of the entrance.

The boardwalk crosses the center of the fen and offers an excellent opportunity to examine closely the wealth and variety of the wetland plant life. While cattails abound, more exotic species such as turtleheads, insectivorous pitcher plants, northern green orchids and tall white bog orchids are identified by small signs. Due to the fragile nature of the ecosystem, extreme care should be taken to remain on the boardwalk in the fen area. Also, dogs must be leashed.

2

Camp Plymouth State Park

Located along the east shore of Echo Lake in the town of Plymouth, the 295-acre Camp Plymouth State Park occupies the site of a former Boy Scout camp (USGS Ludlow). In 1855, gold was discovered along the banks of nearby Buffalo Brook resulting in mining operations that continued for some thirty years. Panning for gold remains a popular activity in the park to the present day. Camping is limited to a group camping area; obtain information at the park contact station. The park has a variety of day-use facilities, including a beach; a fee is charged in season. A short hiking loop heads north from the park entrance to a vista overlooking the lake.

To the Trail: Camp Plymouth State Park is located off Vt. 100, several miles south of Coolidge State Park. From the village of Tyson on Vt. 100 at the south end of Echo Lake, 5.2 mi. south of Vt. 100A in Plymouth Union and 5.5 mi. north of Vt. 103 in Ludlow Village, proceed east on Kingdom Road 0.5 mi. to a crossroads. Turn left on Scout Camp Road and continue 0.6 mi. to the park entrance on the left side of the road.

Description: The Echo Lake Vista Trail begins on a dirt road on the east side of Scout Camp Road, 200 ft. north of the park entrance (0.0 mi.). The trail follows the road 0.1 mi., then leaves it on the left along a footpath, which soon reaches an old cemetery. Continuing straight ahead, the trail climbs steadily, eventually reaching a vista (0.6 mi.) overlooking Echo Lake and the park. From the vista, the trail drops down the backside of the ridge and switches back, turning sharply south. It follows Buffalo Brook a short distance before crossing the brook and joining the dirt road the trail began on. Bearing right on the road, the route returns to the park (1.6 mi.). Note: there are no bridges at the stream crossings for the trail and the dirt road. Crossing on the large rocks may be tricky during high water or icy conditions.

WILGUS STATE PARK, THE PINNACLE

Located in Wilgus State Park with camping and picnic areas, this low hill offers good views of the New Hampshire hills to the east.

TO THE TRAIL: The blue-blazed loop trail begins on U.S. 5, opposite the entrance to the park, 1.1 mi. south of the junction of U.S. 5 and Vt. 131 in Ascutney village. Parking arrangements should be made with the park manager. There is adequate parking outside the gate during the snow-free off-season.

DESCRIPTION: From the highway (0.0 mi.), the trail climbs a bank and swings left, following a pleasant woods road on easy grades. Eventually turning right off the old road (0.3 mi.), the trail climbs to a lookout just below the wooded summit (0.5 mi.).

From the lookout, the trail passes over the summit (640 ft.) and makes a steep and winding descent through the woods to the highway (0.9 mi.). Following the park access road, it is 0.25 mi. south to the contact station and park entrance.

SPRINGWEATHER NATURE AREA

Located in the town of Weathersfield and encompassing nearly 70 acres of fields and forests, the Springweather Nature Area was developed by the Ascutney Mountain Audubon Society and the U.S. Army Corps of Engineers following construction of the North Springfield Flood Control Dam. Three blazed trails, totaling about 2.0 mi., wander through the site and offer a variety of moderate loop hikes.

To the Trail: From its intersection with Vt. 11 in Springfield (0.0 mi.), follow Vt. 106 north along the Black River. Turn right on Reservoir Road (1.9 mi.) and continue past the flood control dam to the signed nature area access road on the left (3.4 mi.). Bear right at the first intersection and proceed north a short distance to the main parking lot on the right (3.6 mi.). The trailhead for the Blue Trail and Red Trail is located across the gravel road at a bulletin board where a map of the site is posted. The access road continues north past this parking lot, ending at another parking area on the Black River where the Green Trail may be accessed.

The trail layout is intricate in places, sometimes with multiple loops and branches blazed the same color. To know your location at all times, pick up a trail map at the bulletin board. Because the area is not large and the terrain is not complex, an observant person should not get lost even without a map.

Description: The Blue Trail leaves the bulletin board left, crosses a small brook and climbs quickly to an open field. It crosses the field southward on a mowed path. A junction in the middle of the field offers two possibilities. Continuing straight ahead, the path leads to a small pond or marshy area, then bears east to the access road, a short distance south of the trailhead. To the right, the trail bears westward to another junction in the field. At this junction, both paths lead to a pair of loops on a forested hill. In circling the hill and paralleling the lake on a high bank, the trail offers views to the west and toward Mount Ascutney in the north.

The Red Trail departs the bulletin board right and soon reaches a series of junctions and small trail loops. Bearing left toward the lake, this trail also reaches the high bank above the water, which it follows north. At the farthest point on the loop from the trailhead, the Red Trail reaches a junction on the left with the Green Trail. Bearing right, the Red Trail curves southward to parallel the access road and return to the head of the loop.

The Green Trail, from its junction with the Red Trail, continues along the bank overlooking the lake before turning away and also heading toward the access road. The trail quickly reaches a junction where a spur right leads a short distance to the access road, north of the main parking lot. The more interesting route bears left and soon reaches a stream, near the site of Barretts Mill and an old bridge. The trail takes a short but steep route to cross the stream before continuing to a parking area at the trailhead at the north end of the access road.

FORT DUMMER STATE PARK

Fort Dummer State Park occupies 217 acres in the Connecticut River Valley just outside Brattleboro. Bordering the foothills of the eastern edge of the Green Mountains, the chestnut oak hardwood forest found in the park is more typical of southern New England than Vermont. The park contains a relatively short hiking loop (about 1.25 mi.) leading to two vistas overlooking the Connecticut River. A variety of camping facilities are available, and a day-use fee is charged in season.

TO THE TRAIL: Fort Dummer State Park is located a short distance south of Brattleboro. From I-91 exit 1, follow U.S. 5 north 0.25 mi. to the first traffic light and turn east (right) onto Fairground Road (0.0 mi.). Continue past the high school and town garage to an intersection near the bottom of a winding hill (0.5 mi.). Turn right to follow South Main Street and its continuation, Old Guilford Road, to a dead end at the park (1.6 mi.).

DESCRIPTION: From the park contact station, follow the paved road to its end at an intersection where dirt roads lead left and right to the two campgrounds. The trailhead is located a few yards north of the intersection at a sign for the Sunrise Trail. A blue-blazed trail leads a short distance to a junction marking the head of the loop. Bearing left at the junction onto a less-used red-blazed trail, the northern leg of the loop crosses over a small footbridge and continues an easy ascent, soon reaching another junction.

Junction: To the left, a yellow-blazed lookout spur leads a short distance to an opening with views from a granite ledge. While the original site of Fort Dummer was flooded when the Vernon Dam was constructed in 1908, its former location is visible on the western bank of the river at a point near the lumber company. From this overlook, there are also views southward to the Vermont Yankee nuclear station and beyond to Mt. Monadnock in New Hampshire and northern Massachusetts.

2

The main trail continues right at the junction, soon reaches another vista, then comes to a junction where a trail leaves right on a more direct route to the beginning of the loop. Continuing straight ahead, the southernmost leg of the loop follows marginally longer routing to reach the same spot.

Another loop can be made by heading south from the park gates on an old road paralleling I-91, then bearing left up a blazed trail to overlook Algiers Village of the Town of Guilford. The route then continues from the overlook back to the park's playground and the rest of Fort Dummer State Park.

SWEET POND STATE PARK

Once a private estate, Sweet Pond State Park (USGS Brattleboro) has a mile-long hiking trail that follows most of the undeveloped shoreline of the namesake pond. Several log benches at the ends of short spur trails offer pleasant sites for enjoying the pond and its surroundings from different angles. The park does not contain any developed facilities, nor is there any overnight camping. There is no entrance fee.

To the Trail: From U.S. 5 in Guilford (0.0 mi.), follow the paved Guilford Center Road west 1.7 mi. and turn left onto the paved Weatherhead Hollow Road. Opposite Weatherhead Hollow Pond, turn right on Baker Cross Road (5.6 mi.). Turn right again at the next intersection (6.1 mi.) and follow the gravel Sweet Pond Road uphill, past two forks to the right and a view of the outlet dam (7.4 mi.). At the Sweet Pond State Park sign (7.7 mi.), turn right, then quickly bear left to the parking area (7.8 mi.).

Description: From the parking area (0.0 mi.), the blue-blazed trail descends southwesterly a short distance before swinging sharply left and following an easy northward route through the woods parallel to the pond. The trail soon enters a Norway spruce plantation and passes a spur to the right (0.1 mi.) that leads a few feet to a bench on the shore. After passing another short spur (0.2 mi.), the trail crosses two tiny inlet brooks in a wet area and continues through a clearing to yet another spur (0.4 mi.). The trail then crosses the main inlet on an abandoned beaver dam.

From the inlet the trail enters an old hemlock forest and follows up and down routing above the east shore of the pond. After passing two spurs (0.8 mi. and 0.9 mi.) leading to views from the ledges, the trail reaches its terminus at the concrete outlet dam (1.0 mi.). Just beyond the dam is Sweet Pond Road, which can be followed uphill 0.3 mi. back to the park entrance road.

BLACK GUM SWAMP

Black Gum Swamp, located in J. Maynard Miller Municipal Forest in Vernon (USGS Bernardston), is the unlikely home of black gum trees (*Nyssa sylvatica*, known colloquially as tupelo, pepperidge, or buttonwood), some of which are more than 400 years old. Several other species of ferns and plant life that are normally found only in the southern United States flourish in this spot as well. Apparently established some 3,000 to 5,000 years ago when the region's climate was far warmer, these trees and plants have somehow managed to adapt to the present less-favorable environment.

A compact network of four color-coded trail loops provides access to two sections of the swamp, a scenic overlook and other areas within the municipal forest. There are no individual trail signs, but the generally well-defined trails are marked with diamond-shaped blazes. An interpretive bulletin board at the trailhead parking lot features a large map of the area and trail system, regulations governing use of the forest and interesting facts about its history and features. Trail maps, supplied by the Vernon Recreation Department, are in an adjacent mailbox. Note: Hikers are reminded of the requirement to remain on the trails when viewing the environmentally sensitive High Swamp and Lower Swamp.

To the Trail: From Vt. 142 in the Central Park area of Vernon, about 7.25 mi. south of U.S. 5 in Brattleboro, turn west on Pond Road. (This junction is 1.3 mi. south of the village of Vernon and several hundred feet north of a white church and the Vernon highway garage on Vt. 142.) From the highway (0.0 mi.), follow the paved Pond Road through the railroad underpass past a road on the right. Turn right on the paved Huckle Hill Road (1.2 mi.) and proceed uphill past several intersections before turning right on the paved Basin Road (2.5 mi.). The road ends (3.2 mi.) at the trailhead parking lot and a large sign for the Black Gum Swamp and J. Maynard Miller Municipal Forest.

Description: The red-blazed High Swamp Trail (0.5 mi. long) leaves the parking area to the west and ascends a narrow gravel roadway to a dead end opposite a private dwelling. Turning sharply right, it makes a brief and fairly steep ascent to meet the west end of the Overlook Trail, then ascends westerly on easier grades. After circling three sides of High Swamp, the trail descends easterly through the woods past a junction with the southern leg of the Lower Swamp Trail to complete its loop.

The green-blazed Overlook Trail (0.4 mi. in length) leaves the parking lot along a forest road that begins a few feet east of the municipal forest sign. After a moderately steep climb on the road, the trail reaches a clearing on the right (0.2 mi.) with two picnic tables and an excellent view across the Connecticut River Valley to Mt. Monadnock and its neighbors. Opposite the clearing, the trail turns left into the woods, climbs gradually a short distance to its highest point, then descends to meet the High Swamp Trail. Turning left this trail leads a short distance back to the parking lot.

The blue-blazed Mountain Laurel Trail (1.5 mi.) shares the forest road portion of the Overlook Trail as far as the clearing. Swinging off the road to the west, the trail climbs gradually through white birches and patches of mountain laurel, passes an old woods road to the right, then trends southwesterly to a woods road crossing at the edge of a large clearing. Here, the trail is joined by the Lower Swamp Trail at a sharp left turn, and both trails coincide over an up-and-down route through the woods to reach their end on the western side of the High Swamp Trail.

The silver-blazed Lower Swamp Trail (1.2 mi. long) begins and ends its triangular loop on the High Swamp Trail. From the southern side of the High Swamp, the Lower Swamp Trail leaves westerly through the woods on easy circuitous routing to avoid wet areas. After skirting the northern edge of the Lower Swamp (and the Massachusetts state line), the trail reaches a woods road junction. It turns sharply right to follow a woods road northerly to a junction with the Mountain Laurel Trail at the edge of a large clearing. The Lower Swamp Trail turns sharply right and follows up-and-down routing through the woods with the coinciding Mountain Laurel Trail to rejoin the High Swamp Trail on the western side of its namesake.

REGION 3
West Central Vermont

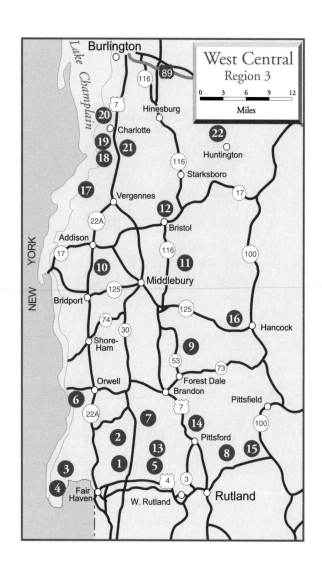

Lake Champlain

Burlington

NEW YORK

West Central
Region 3

0   3   6   9   12
Miles

116
89

7

20
19
18
21

Hinesburg

Charlotte

22

Huntington

116

Starksboro

17

Vergennes

22A

12

Bristol

116

11

100

Addison

17

10

Middlebury

125

Bridport

125

74

16

Hancock

30

Shore-Ham

9

53

73

Orwell

Forest Dale

6

Brandon

7

Pittsfield

22A

7

14

Pittsford

100

2

13

8

15

3

1

5

4

4

W. Rutland

3

Rutland

Fair Haven

West Central Vermont

RAMBLES

REGION 3
West Central Vermont

The Lake Champlain Valley plays a prominent role in this region. For the most part, the valley is gentle rolling country, but several steep escarpments and an intermittent series of hills along or near the shore stand out as landmarks. Many scenic trails travel near other lakes, including Lake Bomoseen and Lake Dunmore. Moosalamoo, a region of upland state and forest-service land, offers scenic walking and multiuse trails.

The eastern part of the west central region is dominated by the Green Mountains, which are well-defined ranges. The first range rises abruptly from the Champlain Valley as a steep front that includes the Hogback Mountains and West Mtn. of the Bristol-Monkton area and extends southward through Robert Frost Mtn. and Mt. Moosalamoo and to Blue Ridge Mtn. near Sherburne Pass. The second or main range of the Green Mountains lies somewhat farther east. Several scenic gaps, used for east-west highways, make prominent breaks in the otherwise generally even skyline of the main range.

North of the Rutland area, the Taconic Mountains and the Valley of Vermont gradually lose their identity, and north of Brandon, the Champlain lowlands, home to enormous swamps, become the major physiographic feature of the western portion of the state.

LAKE BOMOSEEN AREA

Situated at the northern end of the Taconic Mountain Range, Lake Bomoseen is the largest lake lying entirely within the boundaries of Vermont. The terrain is characterized by a series of north–south ridges heavily wooded with hemlock–white pine forest. Numerous smaller ponds are located throughout the area, but 202-acre Glen Lake, with its nearly undeveloped shoreline, offers the most spectacular scenery.

Within the 2,940-acre Bomoseen State Forest lie two state parks. Bomoseen State Park, in the southern part of the forest, offers picnicking, swimming and boating, as well as extensive camping accommodations and access to a pair of short trails. In the north, Half Moon State Park offers more secluded campsites and two short trails. Although it has no day-use area, hikers will not be turned away.

The two state parks are connected by the Glen Lake Trail, which extends along the shore of Glen Lake and over varied terrain.

BOMOSEEN STATE PARK

To the Trail: Located along the western shore of Lake Bomoseen in the town of Castleton, Bomoseen State Park is easily reached from exit 3 off U.S. 4 in Fair Haven by following the paved Scotch Hill Road (which becomes Glen Lake Drive at its northern end) north for 4.5 mi. through the hamlet of West Castleton. Alternatively, from Vt. 4A in the village of Hydeville, follow the paved Creek Road

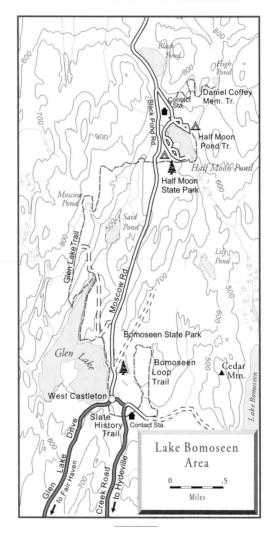

Black Pond

High Pond

Contact Sta.

Daniel Coffey Mem. Tr.

Half Moon Pond Tr.

Black Pond Rd.

Half Moon Pond

Half Moon State Park

Moscow Pond

Said Pond

Lily Pond

Glen Lake Trail

Moscow Rd.

Bomoseen State Park

Glen Lake

Bomoseen Loop Trail

Cedar Mtn.

Lake Bomoseen

West Castleton

Slate History Trail

Contact Sta.

Glen Lake Drive

to Fair Haven

Creek Road

to Hydeville

Lake Bomoseen Area

0   .5

Miles

north 4.0 mi., roughly following the west shore of Lake Bomoseen. Fees are charged in season.

BOMOSEEN LOOP TRAIL

Distance: 1.5 mi. (2.4 km)
Elevation Change: minor
Hiking Time: 1 hr. either direction

DESCRIPTION: This blue-blazed trail starts in a meadow behind the contact station and soon crosses Cedar Mountain Road. Proceeding through an old hayfield and past scattered rock walls, foundations, and apple trees at an old farm site, the trail crests a low hill where there is a good view of Glen Lake to the west. The trail continues through a mixed pine and hardwood forest with an open understory and returns to the starting point.

SLATE HISTORY TRAIL

Distance: 0.75 mi.(1.2 km)
Elevation Change: minor
Hiking Time: ½ hr. either direction

The story of the rise and fall of the local slate industry is told in a self-guided trail passing through a now-abandoned village of the West Castleton Slate Company. Sixty to seventy buildings once stood between Lake Bomoseen and Glen Lake where the West Castleton Mill operated between 1850 and 1929. A pamphlet describing the trail and its observation points is available at the park contact station and is recommended for exploration of the site.

TO THE TRAIL: Leave the Bomoseen State Park entrance, walk a short distance south on the public Creek Road, then turn right onto a mowed path. One of the three slate houses the route passes lies within the park and is open to the public on a limited basis.

GLEN LAKE TRAIL

Distance: 5.9 mi. (9.5 km)
Elevation Change: 500 ft. ascent
Hiking Time: 3½ hr. either direction

Constructed by the Vermont Youth Conservation Corps in 1987, this blue-blazed trail connects Bomoseen State Park with Half Moon State Park. The trail follows the shoreline of Glen Lake for some distance before swinging north through an area of beaver activity to its terminus at Half Moon State Park.

TO THE TRAIL: The trailhead is at the Glen Lake boat access in West Castleton. From Glen Lake Drive or Creek Road, a short distance west of the entrance to Bomoseen State Park, turn north on the unpaved Moscow Road and proceed a short distance to the boat access on the west. Parking is available on the east side of the road.

DESCRIPTION: From the boat access (0.0 mi.), the trail departs northwest and shortly reaches the shore of Glen Lake. Following the shore through a cedar-hemlock forest, the trail soon reaches the dirt Said Road (0.5 mi.), which it follows a short distance west around a marsh. Departing the road left (0.6 mi.), the trail heads back toward the water to a point jutting into the lake (0.9 mi.). Continuing north and again joining Said Road (1.6 mi.), the trail bears left along the road, passing through a gate and crossing a bridge, before departing the road again left. (At this point, hikers may encounter a temporary blue-blazed detour continuing up the road to the right until a timber-cutting operation is completed.) Continuing south along the lake's western shore, the main trail reaches a junction (2.4 mi.), where a short spur left leads to a vista overlooking Glen Lake and the hills to the east.

Past the spur, the trail leaves Glen Lake and climbs through the woods near a ridge. The trail passes a small pond or seep (3.3 mi.) in an area of beaver activity before reaching Moscow Pond (3.6 mi.) and following its margin around to the north. The trail continues north through beaver meadows and a logged area, reaching a vista overlooking another beaver pond (4.6 mi.). After crossing a stream on piles of slate (5.0 mi.), the trail reaches Moscow Road a short distance farther (5.5 mi.).

Junction: After a turn south onto Moscow Road, it is about 2.5 mi. back to the Glen Lake boat launch and the start of the Glen Lake Trail.

Continuing straight ahead, the trail soon ends at the Half Moon Pond Trail in Half Moon State Park (5.9 mi.). Via this trail, it is a short distance east or west to the state park campgrounds on either shore of the pond.

3

HALF MOON STATE PARK

Part of Bomoseen State Forest, Half Moon State Park is in the town of Hubbardton and occupies a small sheltered basin surrounding Half Moon Pond.
TO THE TRAIL: From the south, follow the unpaved Moscow Road north from Bomoseen State Park for about 3.0 mi. Alternatively, from exit 4 off U.S. 4 in Castleton, follow Vt. 30 north about 7.5 mi. and turn west on the paved Hortonville Road. Continue west for about 2.0 mi., then turn left on Black Pond Road. Follow this road south 1.5 mi. to the state park entrance.

DANIEL COFFEY MEMORIAL TRAIL

This blue-blazed trail leaves the north side of the park access road about halfway between the contact station and the camping area, roughly 0.1 mi. from each. The trail ascends easily for about 0.5 mi. on a winding woods road through open forest. The final 0.25 mi. of trail scrambles over a rocky ridge and descends to secluded High Pond, a small body of water rimmed by thick brush and sphagnum moss.

HALF MOON POND TRAIL

This path, marked with blue blazes and a sign reading "Nature Trail," is an easy 0.4-mi. lakeside walk around the eastern side of Half Moon Pond connecting the campgrounds on the north and south shores. Near the southwest end of the trail is a junction with the Glen Lake Trail, which crosses Moscow Road and proceeds south to Bomoseen State Park.

• • • • • • • • • • • • • • • • •

SHAW MOUNTAIN

Distance: 2.4 mi. (3.9 km) round trip
Elevation Change: 300 ft. ascent
Hiking Time: 1¾ hr.

Owned by The Nature Conservancy and located in the southwest corner of Benson, the Shaw Mountain Natural Area is notable for the presence of a great diversity of plant and animal life. The area is recognized for its ecological significance by the Vermont Non-Game and Natural Heritage Program and includes twenty-five rare plant species and seven distinct natural communities. A flyer available at the site identifies many plants found near the single hiking trail, which leads from the road access to a loop atop a limestone uplift forming the north summit (715 ft., USGS Benson).

TO THE TRAIL: From Vt. 22A in the town of Benson, about 7.0 mi. north of its junction with U.S. 4 in Fair Haven, turn west on Mill Pond Road (also known as Lake Road) (0.0 mi.), following signs for the villages of Benson and Benson Landing. Continue straight through a crossroads in the village of Benson (0.7 mi.) and proceed west along Benson Landing Road to a second four-way intersection (1.7 mi.). Turn left on Park Hill Road, and proceed south to a junction on the right (2.1 mi.) with Money Hole Road. Bear right and proceed past a road entering left (2.6 mi.). The trailhead, near a wooden sign on the left (3.7 mi.), is easy to miss. Parking is available for three cars.

DESCRIPTION: From the parking lot, the lightly used trail ascends steeply to a sign and register. Following white markings, the trail then descends to cross a marshy area on a footbridge before ascending moderately to reach a signed junction at the head of the summit trail loop. Turning right at the junction to make a counterclockwise circuit, the trail ascends gently west and passes through an open oak-hickory forest near the heavily forested, viewless north summit. Continuing around the south side of the ridge, the trail returns to the start of the summit loop.

3

● ● ● ● ● ● ● ● ● ● ● ● ● ● ● ●

HELEN W. BUCKNER MEMORIAL PRESERVE

The Buckner preserve in West Haven is one of a very few places in Vermont where hikers have a chance—albeit slim—of seeing an eastern timber rattlesnake. Two varieties of the reptile live among the rocky outcrops on the south face of Bald Mountain. They are among the eleven rare animal species, eighteen rare plants, and ten rare natural community types on this 3,500-acre property owned by The Nature Conservancy. The preserve is an outpost of Vermont nearly surrounded by New York State, occupying most of a peninsula bounded by the Poultney River and Lake Champlain. Its heights present sweeping views up the headwaters of the lake.

Because the area is home to rattlesnakes, visitors are cautioned to look before sitting down and to use a walking stick to part tall grass and brush. Rattlers will strike only if they are stepped on or harassed. Visitors are as likely to see a rattler stretched out on the sun-warmed gravel access road as on the hiking trails.

Two paths wind through this site. Tim's Trail is a 2.8-mile hike through fields and several types of forests. The Susan Bacher Memorial Trail is a 2.5-mile route that traverses a wooded ridge and skirts open fields near the former Galick farmstead whose lands are at the heart of the preserve. Each hike has an out-and-back portion that leads to a loop; a mile-long connector trail on private land links them. Brochures describing both hikes are available at the site.

TO THE TRAIL: From U.S. 4, 5.5 mi. west of the Vermont-New York border and about 0.3 mi. west of a railroad crossing, turn north on Vt. 9A (0.0 mi.). At a T intersection (0.9 mi.), turn left onto Vt. 9, then immediately right (1.1 mi.) on Vt. 10 (Doig Street), just after cresting a small hill. Turn left onto a dirt road (1.6 mi.) where the paved road curves right. Cross the bridge and bear left. Parking for Tim's Trail is down this dirt road on the right (2.3 mi.). Parking for the Susan Bacher Trail is a mile farther. This road is often flooded in the spring.

TIM'S TRAIL

Distance: 2.8 mi. (4.5 km) round trip
Elevation Change: 340 ft. ascent
Hiking Time: 1¾ hr.

DESCRIPTION: From the parking pullout (0.0 mi.), the well-marked trail follows the base of a cliff and talus slope eastward to an informational kiosk (0.2 mi.), passes a pond and views of Ward Marsh, then joins an old woods road at the second of two fence openings. It soon turns left to begin the loop (0.4 mi.) and ascends the ledges, from the top of which are views south and east (0.9 mi.). The trail descends quickly along rocky outcrops, crosses a small brook, and climbs again, eventually reaching a bench on the left (1.3 mi.) with expansive views. The path meets an old stonewall (1.5 mi.) at a junction where Tim's Trail turns sharply right. This intersection is easily missed from this direction, but a sign where the connector trail passes through an opening in the wall draws attention to the junction, now behind.

> **Junction:** The connector trail passes two small pools and ascends Austin Hill (elev. 641 feet). Here, the trail bends west and drops steeply to the Susan Bacher Trail (1.0 mi.)

3

From the junction, Tim's Trail doubles back to the right and follows the stonewall on a gentle descent, crossing several streams. It then winds back uphill and joins an old woods road. Just before this road crosses onto private property, the trail leaves it to the right and follows another stonewall. From here, it joins and leaves a series of woods roads on the descent back to the fields along Ward Marsh. It bears right at the edge of the field (2.4 mi.) to return to the start of the loop.

SUSAN BACHER MEMORIAL TRAIL

Distance: 2.5 mi. (4 km) round trip
Elevation Change: 340 ft. ascent
Hiking Time: 1½ hr.

DESCRIPTION: This well-marked trail climbs steeply from the parking area (0.0 mi.) past a view of the Galick farmstead where the family once raised mink and sheep to supplement their dairy operation. Turning sharply left and crossing an old field, the trail soon reaches the start of the loop (0.5 mi.). The left fork emerges into an open field and follows the fence line to a short spur leading to an information kiosk (0.65 mi.). Bald Mountain is visible ahead as the main route continues north along the perimeter of the hayfield, then turns right into the woods on an old logging road near a renovated barn. The trail leaves this road to the right (1.2 mi.) and climbs steeply to a hemlock grove before turning southward on more gentle terrain. After descending to cross a stream, it rises again and turns left along a ridge with winter views to the west. On descending from the ridge, the trail soon returns to the start of the loop (2.0 mi.).

• • • • • • • • • • • • • • • •

TACONIC MOUNTAINS TRAILS

This network of trails links some highly varied terrain in a relatively small area—sheer rock cliffs, waterfalls, deep forests, rolling meadows, high peaks with wide mountain views, and the most extensive oriental garden in Vermont, if not New England. The trails are on private property surrounding the owners' home, and they invite walkers to share the land on the understanding that there will be no smoking and no fires—ever.

TO THE TRAIL: From U.S. 4 west of Rutland, take exit 5 (0.0 mi.) north on the unmarked East Hubbardton Road (which becomes Monument Hill Road) toward the Hubbardton Battlefield. Just before reaching the battlefield, turn left on the unpaved St. John Road (6.0 mi.). Turn left (6.3 mi.) into a private drive, the first possible left turn from St. John Road. Continue to a parking area on the left (6.8 mi.), just beyond the second cattle guard and a short distance uphill from the house.

Trails are blazed in red except for two in yellow. Triple blazes indicate the beginning or end of a trail; double blazes mean a sharp change in direction.

JAPANESE GARDEN, MOUNT ZION MINOR, AND MOOT POINT

Distance: 1.2 mi. (1.9 km) round trip
Elevation Change: 115 ft. ascent
Hiking Time: ¾ hr. either direction

DESCRIPTION: From the parking area (0.0 mi.), the trail heads downhill and passes near the end of the house (where trail maps are available at no charge). From the field below the house, there are views southwest to the cliffs of Mt. Zion Minor, south to Bird Mtn. and the Herrick Mountains, and east to the central range of the Taconic Mountains. The trail continues downhill to an arched bridge and the Japanese Garden (0.2 mi.), with pools, waterfalls, stone lanterns, an island reached by another arched bridge, and views of the cliffs above.

At the north end of the garden is a large boulder with a ladder partway up it. Around the right side of this rock is the start of the red-blazed trail leading uphill. This trail weaves among massive boulders as it climbs to a junction (0.25 mi.) with the yellow-blazed Cave Trail.

Taking a sharp left, the trail ascends to a switchback, passes under a 20-ft. rock overhang, and climbs a short steep section leading to the top of the Mt. Zion Minor ridge. Farther south along this ridge is the best viewpoint from Mt. Zion Minor (0.3 mi.), overlooking the Japanese Garden 115 ft. below. There are also wide views of the Taconics from north to southeast.

At this point, the trail turns sharply west, crossing the ridge and reaching the red-blazed Moot Point Trail (0.4 mi.). It turns left to follow mossy ledges, crosses a small marsh on steppingstones, passes a woods road, and ascends to a ledgy ridge overlooking valleys on both sides. At Moot Point (0.6 mi.), there are fine views of the distant northeast to southeast, including Bird Mtn., and of the nearer southwest. Like the garden, this is an outstanding "carry in, carry out" picnic spot.

Returning to the junction with the Cave Trail on the right, the route continues past it on the red trail. It descends by two switchbacks to reach the yellow Cave Trail once again (1.0 mi.). Turning left on the Cave Trail, the route crosses a bridge, ascends among hardwoods along a ravine, and intercepts the red Springs Trail. This left continues up to Mt. Zion Major (see the following description). The trail turns right and crosses the stream to the parking area.

MOUNT ZION MAJOR AND BOULDER MAZE

Distance: 0.8 mi. (1.3 km) round trip
Elevation Change: 260 ft. ascent
Hiking Time: ¾ hr. either direction

DESCRIPTION: From the parking area (0.0 mi.) the route leads downhill toward the right-hand end of the house, turning right just before reaching a tool shed. The red-blazed Springs Trail starts at a blazed post in the field west of the shed. It enters the woods, crosses a stream, and passes the yellow Cave Trail on the left, as previously described (0.1 mi.). The trail ascends toward Mt. Zion Major through mixed hardwoods and conifers, with one switchback. At the second switchback, the yellow-blazed Cliff Trail branches right (0.3 mi.).

> **Junction:** The Cliff Trail presents an alternate route to Mt. Zion Major and offers many panoramic views. It is spectacular but challenging, for it follows the base of the cliffs through several steep ups and downs. It could be dangerous for children or inexperienced hikers and is impossible for dogs.

The red-blazed Springs Trail continues past this switchback and another above it, attaining a fairly level plateau. It soon emerges onto an open rocky ridge with sweeping views from northeast to southeast. The trail then dips slightly, traveling closer to the cliff edge, finally ending at the 1,220-ft. peak of Mt. Zion Major (0.5 mi.). This rock outcropping is an impressive lookout, with views northwest of the distant Adirondacks. Nearer are the Hubbardton Battlefield and the Taconic Mountains to the north, east, and southeast.

The return trip is on the Mickie Trail, also blazed in red, which starts near the edge of the peak plateau opposite the ending of the Springs Trail. It descends steeply through four switchbacks and reaches the base of the cliffs, soon passing the north end of the yellow Cliff Trail on the right. Continuing down, it winds through a maze of boulders (0.6 mi.) and enters the forest where grazing cows are occasionally seen. The trail crosses a stream on stepping-stones and shortly enters a field just north of the cattle guard beside the parking area (0.8 mi.).

NORTH WOODS TRAIL

This short red-blazed trail is almost completely level. In conjunction with various much longer loops through fields on both sides of Monument Hill Road, it makes a relaxed and scenic ski trail in winter, and in summer a quiet, undemanding amble. The trail starts near the point where the access road leaves the large field north of the house and enters the woods (0.0 mi.). The trail meanders in a roughly M-shaped course through an open, almost park-like stand of pines interspersed with small meadows and ends at the North Lookout (0.5 mi.), which is just left (east) of a lone pine. This spot offers perhaps the most panoramic mountain vistas on the property.

MEADOWS PATH

This path offers a leisurely stroll through gently rolling fields, with benches along the way. It also takes in some fairly spectacular distant views, as well as the Japanese Garden. (A special map is available for the Meadows Path.)

From the parking area, the route passes through a gate in the fence, then heads north to the start of the North Woods Trail, which it follows to the North Lookout before heading downhill (south) through another gate. Continuing down, past a bench in the meadow (a possible turnoff to the Japanese Garden) between two groups of trees, it crosses at the low point of Monument Hill Road.

Across the road in another large field, the trail continues east and slightly north to a small opening in the tree line. Going through, the trail heads gradually uphill and north, making a large loop through the upper meadow, then south to the high point. From here, it leads south again and west, to the same road crossing.

Instead of following the previous route on the other side, another path heads west and slightly north through another field, crosses a stream, and ascends northwest to the highest part of the field. From there a short woods road leads to the area below the Japanese Garden.

Leaving the garden and crossing the arched bridge to the north, avoiding the straight uphill, the path turns right to angle up the next ridge to the east. It passes through a grove of pines and joins the previously taken path at a bench in the field where the parking area is to the left.

FALLS AND CANYON TRAILS

Distance: 2.3 mi. (3.7 km) round trip
Elevation Change: 235 ft. ascent
Hiking Time: 1½ hr. either direction

Note: To shorten the walk to the waterfalls, use the alternate parking area. From the main parking area, drive out the access road, turn right on St. John Road and right again on Monument Hill Road. Pass several houses along a straight stretch, then one more house on the right. Turn right, then left. Just beyond is a low point in the road, with a turnoff into the alternate parking area on the right.

DESCRIPTION: From the main parking area (0.0 mi.), the trail leads downhill to the southeast, past the left end of the house. Descending between occasional pines to a brook crossing by a white birch on the opposite bank, it turns uphill a short distance, then continues southeast down an open field with wide mountain views. Passing between two groups of trees growing from old foundations, the trail reaches a crossing at the low point of Monument Hill Road (0.4 mi.).

Heading east across the paved road and entering another large field, it climbs uphill to the northeast, following a sometimes discernible farm track through an opening in the tree line (0.6 mi.). It continues in roughly the same direction to the high point of this field (360-degree view). The trail heads northeast to the tallest pine on the eastern edge of the field, roughly 175 ft. south of the northeast corner. The red-blazed Falls Trail starts beside this tree (0.7 mi.). It crosses two small brooks, ascends a grassy hill, and descends to the first of the waterfalls (1.0 mi.).

The trail climbs upstream along the left bank, past several other falls and a narrow gorge, finally crossing the stream above the highest cascade (1.1 mi.). It then heads downhill to the southwest and joins a woods road, at which point the red blazes end. Descending by the more used left fork, at 1.5 mi., it crosses a stream and reaches the Canyon Trail on the left.

This lengthy red trail turns several times before descending to the bottom of a deep canyon. Blazing ends at this point, but hiking can continue, often on the rock floor of the stream. (This surface may be extremely slippery and, without waterproof boots, wet feet are almost inevitable.) The route passes numerous waterfalls interspersed with level stretches to a long deep canyon with two high falls dropping into it at the far end, one from each side. Some distance farther, it ends at a series of low falls from very wide rock shelves stretching across the stream. At this point, the route turns left (north) to an unblazed woods road leading downhill to the start of the Canyon Trail.

The Canyon Trail follows the edge of a small field southwest beside a brook, crossing it (1.6 mi.) and continuing west across a larger field to the Monument Hill Road crossing used earlier (1.8 mi.). Departing at this point from the route previously taken, the trail leads west through another field, crosses a stream and ascends northwest to the highest point of land, entering a woods road on the narrow north edge of this field. Emerging below the Japanese Garden (2.1 mi.), it passes through the garden and proceeds uphill to the parking area.

●●●●●●●●●●●●●●●●

MOUNT INDEPENDENCE

Occupying a peninsula on the east shore of Lake Champlain in the town of Orwell, this low hill (306 ft.) has a commanding view of the narrow lake and nearby Fort Ticonderoga (USGS Ticonderoga). For this reason, the site was fortified by the Americans to bolster the weak defenses of Fort Ticonderoga after the fort's capture by the Green Mountain Boys in 1775.

A strong show of force at Independence and Ticonderoga plus the lateness of the season prompted the British to give up their plans for recapturing the fort in late 1776. The following spring, however, they made the American positions untenable by laboriously hauling their heavy artillery to the summit of Mt. Defiance, a craggy hill on the west shore, which the Americans had thought inaccessible. The hasty retreat from Fort Ticonderoga and Mt. Independence gave the British control of the lake again and set the stage for the battles of Hubbardton, Bennington, and Saratoga.

Most of Mt. Independence is owned by the Fort Ticonderoga Association and the state of Vermont and is open to the public between Memorial Day and mid-October. An admission fee is charged to hike the four scenic foot trails leading past the marked sites of the well-preserved remains of the fortifications. Hikers should respect these sites in particular, and the area in general, and leave them undisturbed. Collecting artifacts is prohibited by law. For more information, call (802) 759-2412, write to Site Administrator, 7305 Vt. Route 125, Addison, Vermont 05491 or log on to historicvermont.org/mountindependence.

To the Trail: Follow Vt. 73 west from Vt. 22A near Orwell. Take the first left on the paved Chipman Point Road, and after about 3.5 mi., turn right on Mount Independence Road. After the pavement ends, the road parallels Lake Champlain, eventually bears left at a fork and makes a sharp left turn uphill. Parking is in a designated area at the top of the hill; the museum and visitors center is on the right. A brochure and map are available at the center and are recommended.

Description: The trailheads are reached by passing through a gate near the visitor center, past a signboard with a map, and ascending northerly through a meadow for about 0.3 mi. to the trail information outpost where the four trails diverge.

The Orange Trail (2.5 mi. long) crosses the highest point of the mountain and continues to a junction at the northern tip of the peninsula where a short loop leads to the shore and back. Continuing straight ahead, the trail descends to the water along the slope of an old road, reaching the spot where a floating bridge led across the lake to Fort Ticonderoga. The trail makes a counterclockwise loop around the end of the peninsula, past a rock outcrop and a junction with the Blue Trail on the right. Continuing, the Orange Trail then returns toward the starting point via parallel routing along the eastern side of the peninsula, at one point passing through a large area of black chert, a toolmaking stone.

The Blue Trail (2.2 mi. long) is slightly more difficult, leaving the information outpost to follow the route of a Revolutionary War supply road along the west side of the peninsula and ending at the Orange Trail near its tip. Some of the original stonework, built by American troops, remains visible along the roadbed. A quarry site along this trail was used by the French for stone that was hauled across the ice to build Fort Carillon, later renamed Ticonderoga by the British.

The Red Trail (0.6 mi. long) departs west to a lookout where there are fine views. Mt. Defiance lies directly across the lake to the west and to the north the red roofs of Fort Ticonderoga are clearly visible.

The White Trail (0.8 mi. long) loops east from the information outpost to the site of a battery position, which affords a view over East Creek toward Orwell and up the lake toward Larabees Point.

•••••••••••••••••

HIGH POND

Distance: 1.6 mi. (2.6 km)
Elevation Change: 170 ft. ascent
Hiking Time: 40 min. (reverse 50 min.)

Despite its name, the hike to this deep, pristine pond in Sudbury is almost entirely downhill. The pond is part of a roughly 2,800-acre preserve owned by The Nature Conservancy and notable for having one of the state's finest virgin stands of eastern hemlock. The land also once supported cross-country trails connected to a ski area called High Pond Mountain that operated from around 1940 until the early 1980s. Remnants of the trails and directional signs can still be found.

TO THE TRAIL: From Vt. 30 about 6 mi. south of Sudbury village or 7.5 mi. north of U.S. 4, turn east on Monument Hill Road. Follow it uphill 3.4 mi. and turn north on Ganson Hill Road where a large house stands on the corner. Alternatively, from U.S. 4 at exit 5, travel north on the un-

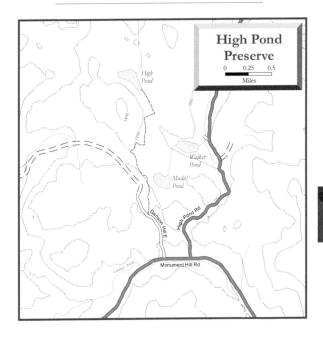

High Pond Preserve

0   0.25   0.5
Miles

High Pond

Walker Pond

Mudd Pond

Ganson Hill E

High Pond Rd

Monument Hill Rd

3

marked East Hubbardton Road (which becomes Monument Hill Road) about 10 miles to Ganson Hill Road. The parking lot is 0.6 mi. up Ganson Hill Road on the left, surrounded by "No Trespassing" signs and 0.2 mi. below a house at the end of the road. The trail begins across the road about 75 feet farther.

DESCRIPTION: From the road (0.0 mi.), the trail follows a small stream uphill and crosses a low ridge before turning right onto an old road at the end of a clearing (0.3 mi.). After descending briefly, it again turns right, leaving this woods road for another one (0.4 mi.), and enters an older hemlock forest. The trail reaches an intersection where there is a weathered wooden sign that once pointed the way on cross-country ski trails (1.1 mi.). Following the modern green and yellow markers to the left, it resumes its descent. At the bottom of the hill, it bears left onto another old road, then another that soon reaches one end of the narrow pond (1.6 mi.).

• • • • • • • • • • • • • • • •

BLUE RIDGE MOUNTAIN

Distance: 2.4 mi. (3.9 km)
Elevation Change: 1,490 ft. ascent
Hiking Time: 2 hr. (reverse 1¼ hr.)

Located in the towns of Mendon and Chittenden, Blue Ridge Mtn. has a number of peaks. The highest and southernmost summit (3,278 ft., USGS Chittenden) is reached by the blue-blazed Canty Trail, which is maintained by the Killington Section of the Green Mountain Club.

TO THE TRAIL: Take U.S. 4 east 6.2 mi. from U.S. 7 in Rutland or west 2.9 mi. from Sherburne Pass and turn north on the paved Old Turnpike Road. The trailhead is 0.7 mi. up this road on the left, marked by a small "Blue Ridge" sign at a gated private lane. Limited parking is available on the shoulder of the public road, legal only when all four wheels are off the pavement. Care also should be taken not to block the private lane.

DESCRIPTION: From Old Turnpike Road (0.0 mi.), the Canty Trail passes around the gate and follows the lane northwest. It tends right (0.1 mi.) to pass the derelict buildings of Tall Timbers Camp, then follows the footpath down into a small ravine (0.2 mi.) where a brook runs.

Climbing steeply up the north bank, the trail passes a possible glacial kettle hole and, entering the Green Mountain National Forest, descends from the low ridge onto a woods road. The trail soon dips to cross Sawyer Brook (0.8 mi.) and climbs steeply up the west bank to join

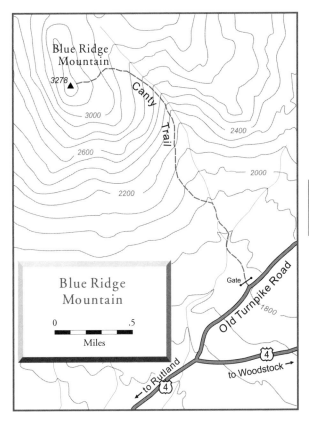

Blue Ridge
Mountain

3278

Canty Trail

3000

2400

2600

2000

2200

Gate

Old Turnpike Road

1800

Blue Ridge
Mountain

0 .5
Miles

to Rutland

4

4

to Woodstock →

another woods road through recently logged forest. From here the route parallels the west side of the brook for a mile; special care must be taken to follow the blazes and remain near the brook, ignoring several skid roads.

The trail ascends gradually, then begins a steady climb to a spur on the right (1.6 mi.), marked by a small sign, that leads 100 ft. to a large cascade. Continuing on easier grades, the trail trends away from the brook to the west (1.7 mi.) and enters a mixed hardwood and evergreen forest. The woods road peters out and the trail makes a sharp left turn (2.1 mi.) to climb steeply through mossy woods before entering a stand of paper birch at a junction 50 ft. south of the summit (2.4 mi.). Following the right branch, there is a view from the summit ledge to the east and northeast that encompasses Spruce Mtn. in Plainfield and the peaks of Groton State Forest. More extensive views may be found by following the left spur to Rutland Lookout, a rock outcrop southwest of the main summit. Here, the view extends from the Coolidge Range in the southeast to Mt. Equinox in the southwest, Dorset Peak, the Taconics as far north as Grandpa's Knob, and west into the Adirondacks. The city of Rutland lies in the valley below.

• • • • • • • • • • • • • • • •

MOOSALAMOO

The 20,000-acre Moosalamoo region includes a large network of hiking, biking, cross-country skiing, and snowmobile trails on Green Mountain National Forest and Branbury State Park lands. Silver Lake, the cliffs at Rattlesnake Point, and the Falls of Lana are natural highlights in this area (USGS East Middlebury), which is bounded on the north by Vt. 125, on the west by Lake Dunmore, on the south by Vt. 73, and on the east by the Long Trail. The name Moosalamoo is derived from an Abenaki word meaning moose call.

Moosalamoo is roughly bisected by USFS Road 32 (also known as the Goshen-Ripton Road or the North Goshen Road). The majority of the summertime day-use destinations lie west of this road. A free map printed by the Moosalamoo Partnership is widely available and is invaluable for

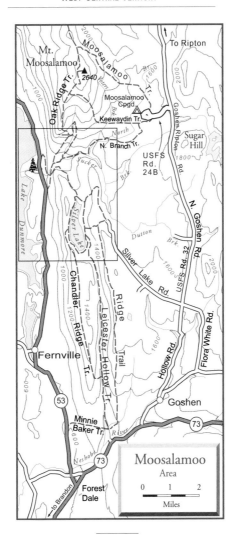

Mt. Moosalamoo

Moosalamoo Tr.

To Ripton

▲ 2640

Oak Ridge Tr.

Moosalamoo Cpgd

Keewaydin Tr.

Goshen Ripton Rd.

Sugar Hill

N. Branch Tr.

USFS Rd. 24B

N. Goshen Rd.

Lake Dunmore

Silver Lake

Dutton

Silver Lake Rd.

USFS Rd. 32

Chandler Ridge Tr.

Ridge

Leicester Hollow Trail

Flora White Rd.

Hollow Rd.

Fernville

53

Goshen

73

Minnie Baker Tr.

River

73

Forest Dale

Neshobe

To Brandon

Moosalamoo
Area

0   1   2

Miles

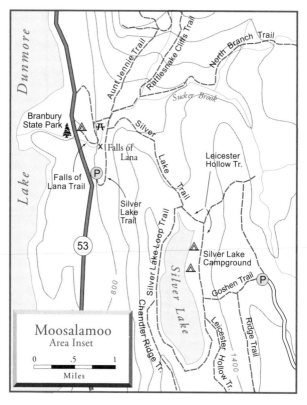

Moosalamoo
Area Inset

0   .5   1
Miles

year-round exploration of this broad area. Contact the Green Mountain National Forest, Branbury State Park, or the Green Mountain Club for a copy of the brochure.

Branbury State Park is on the eastern shore of Lake Dunmore and is transected by Vt. 53. The park site at the foot of Mt. Moosalamoo was formerly a farm, then a summer camp for boys before becoming the 69-acre Branbury

State Park in 1945. Named for its location in Brandon and Salisbury, the park offers a variety of camping accommodations. Day-use facilities include a large sandy beach on Lake Dunmore. A park access fee is charged in season.

On the eastern shore of Silver Lake, in the northwest corner of Leicester, is the U.S. Forest Service Silver Lake Campground. The area is accessible only by two nonmotorized multiuse trails and a foot trail. Primitive camping without charge at fifteen established sites is available on a first-come, first-served basis.

The USFS Moosalamoo Campground is in the northeast corner of the town of Goshen, west of USFS Road 32. The campground lies on USFS Road 24B and is accessible to motor vehicles during the summer camping season, when a fee is charged.

BRANBURY STATE PARK NATURE TRAIL

TO THE TRAIL: Follow Vt. 53 north about 6.0 mi. from Vt. 73 at Forest Dale, or from the junction of U.S. 7 and Vt. 53 south of Middlebury, follow Vt. 53 south 3.5 mi. Branbury State Park is on the east side of Lake Dunmore.

DESCRIPTION: About 0.3 mi. long, the nature trail begins and ends on the east side of Vt. 53 about 0.1 mi. north of the park entrance. It climbs the hillside and makes a short loop before returning by the same route. A nature trail guide is available at the park where naturalists are on duty during the camping season.

FALLS OF LANA TRAIL

Distance: 0.7 mi. (1.1 km)
Elevation Change: 200 ft. ascent
Hiking Time: ½ hr. either direction

ABOUT THE TRAIL: This trail provides access to the Falls of Lana picnic area, an important way point for reaching other trails in the western portion of the Moosalamoo area. Hikers not staying in Branbury State Park where the trail starts, will find ample free parking a short distance south at the head of the Silver Lake Trail, which also ascends to the picnic area. Used in combination, these two trails provide interesting loop possibilities.

TO THE TRAIL: The Falls of Lana Trail starts in the Branbury State Park camping area on the east side of Vt. 53, opposite the main state park entrance.

DESCRIPTION: The blue-blazed trail departs the paved road in the rear of the campground between sites 22 and 23 (0.0 mi.) and zigzags up the ridge to a softwood plateau. Bearing right to scramble up the rocks, the trail reaches a spur on the right (0.3 mi.) that leads to a pool below the falls. After again ascending steeply and trending left, the trail reaches an overlook with views of Lake Dunmore (0.4 mi.). Bearing right and descending slightly, the trail soon reaches a junction with another blue-blazed trail on the left, which descends over rocky and sometimes steep terrain to the nature trail. The Falls of Lana Trail climbs moderately to the right to pass through the Falls of Lana Picnic Area (0.5 mi.) to a signed trail junction.

Junction: To the left, the Rattlesnake Cliffs Trail provides access to Rattlesnake Point, other trails leading to Mt. Moosalamoo and the USFS Moosalamoo Campground. Doubling back to the right, the Falls of Lana Trail crosses Sucker Brook on a bridge and follows a woods road downstream to its terminus at the Silver Lake Trail (0.7 mi.).

Junction: From this junction, it is a 0.5 mi. descent along the Silver Lake Trail to Vt. 53, from which point it is 0.4 mi. north via the highway to the park. The Falls of Lana are located a short distance downhill and can be viewed from above via unmarked spurs off the Silver Lake Trail.

In this area, Sucker Brook has carved a deep gorge in the solid rock. When U.S. Army General Wool visited the site in 1850, his fellow travelers decided that Sucker Brook Falls was too prosaic a name. During his tour of duty in Mexico, the general had become known as General Llana, the Spanish word for wool. In tribute to the general, the party christened the site the Falls of Lana.

RATTLESNAKE CLIFFS TRAIL

Distance: 1.6 mi. (2.6 km)
Elevation Change: 870 ft. ascent
Hiking Time: 1¼ hr. (reverse ¾ hr.)

This blue-blazed U.S. Forest Service trail links the Falls of Lana Picnic Area and Rattlesnake Point

TO THE TRAIL: The trail begins at the north end of the Falls of Lana Picnic Area, which is easily accessed by the Falls of Lana Trail or the Silver Lake Trail about 0.5 mi. from their trailheads.

DESCRIPTION: From the trail junction where the Rattlesnake Cliffs Trail departs the Falls of Lana Trail (0.0 mi.), the Rattlesnake Cliffs Trail follows a woods road. The Aunt Jennie Trail soon leaves left, while the Rattlesnake Cliffs Trail continues straight ahead to a junction (0.3 mi.) with the North Branch Trail on the right. Taking the left fork, the Rattlesnake Cliffs Trail follows a woods road across a small stream.

After climbing steadily for some distance, the trail crosses the brook again (0.9 mi.) and swings south. Slabbing the east slope of the ridge, the trail eventually reaches a junction (1.5 mi.) where the upper end of the Aunt Jennie Trail rejoins from the left. Continuing straight ahead a short distance, the Rattlesnake Cliffs Trail reaches a second junction where the Oak Ridge Trail leaves right to ascend to the summit of Mt. Moosalamoo. Taking the left fork, the trail leads a short distance to Rattlesnake Cliffs (1.6 mi.) where separate overlooks south and west provide spectacular views of Lake Dunmore, the Otter Creek watershed, and the Adirondacks.

3

AUNT JENNIE TRAIL

Distance: 1.2 mi. (1.9 km)
Elevation Change: 850 ft. ascent
Hiking Time: 1 hr. (reverse ¾ hr.)

TO THE TRAIL: This blue-blazed U.S. Forest Service trail departs the Rattlesnake Cliffs Trail to the left 0.1 mi. north of the Falls of Lana Picnic Area.

DESCRIPTION: From the Rattlesnake Cliffs Trail, the Aunt Jennie Trail ascends steadily on an old woods road through a mixed hardwood-softwood forest until it levels briefly before swinging north. The trail climbs more steeply to the base of Rattlesnake Cliffs and passes through a huge boulder field. It then swings east and continues to climb steeply using switchbacks, eventually crossing an old woods road. The trail then begins a more moderate ascent before reaching its terminus on the Rattlesnake Cliffs Trail a short distance east of the lookout.

OAK RIDGE TRAIL

Distance: 8.0 mi. (12.9 km)
Elevation Change: 1,200 ft. ascent
Hiking Time: 4¾ hr. (reverse 5¼ hr.)

The Oak Ridge Trail extends from the Rattlesnake Cliffs Trail north to Vt. 125 west of Ripton. The southern portion of the trail provides an ascent to the summit of Mt. Moosalamoo from the western side of the Moosalamoo area. The lesser-used northern section of the trail continues past the summit and makes a long descent to Vt. 125. Hikers may see occasional orange "Cross Moosalamoo Trail" markers on this section.

TO THE TRAIL: This U.S. Forest Service trail leaves the Rattlesnake Cliffs Trail to the north at a junction just west of the northern terminus of the Aunt Jennie Trail.

DESCRIPTION (NORTHBOUND): From the junction (0.0 mi.), the blue-blazed Oak Ridge Trail climbs north and follows the flat but narrow top of a ledge, which drops precipitously to the west. Continuing on easy grades past limited views of Lake Dunmore to the west and south toward Silver Lake, the trail soon reaches a junction where the Keewaydin Trail enters on the left from private land. The two trails coincide for a short distance, climbing to the top of a knoll (0.9 mi.) where the Keewaydin Trail departs right.

The Oak Ridge Trail dips into a shallow sag, then makes a steep and winding climb to the southern end of the Mt. Moosalamoo summit ridge (1.2 mi.) where there is a fine view east of the main range of the Green Mountains from Middlebury Gap south to Brandon Gap. The trail continues north along the ridge, soon reaching a signed junction (1.4 mi.). To the right, a spur trail leads a short distance past the signed summit of Mt. Moosalamoo (2,640 ft.) and drops to an open ledge where there is another fine vista. From this spot, the view of the spine of the main range extends from Middlebury Gap, northward along the Vermont Presidential Range and past the peaks of Lincoln Mtn. to Camel's Hump and Mt. Mansfield.

Descending northerly past the summit spur, the Oak Ridge Trail passes an overlook on the right (1.5 mi.) where there are wide views east and south. After passing another view east, the trail reaches a junction (1.8 mi.) on the right with the Moosalamoo Trail, which descends 2.3 mi. to the USFS Moosalamoo Campground west of the Goshen-Ripton Road (USFS Road 32). The Oak Ridge Trail ends its descent in a shallow sag, just beyond which is another view east (2.0 mi.). The trail then follows up-and-down routing on or near the ridgeline past views to the east and west (2.6 mi.), just below the northernmost summit (2,310 ft.) of the ridge.

After passing over the summit (2.7 mi.), the trail makes a winding descent away from the ridge and continues generally easterly on easier grades over routing that includes portions of old woods roads. Shortly after ending its descent and resuming a northerly direction, the trail rises to cross USFS Road 92 (4.3 mi.). To the right, the road leads

3

0.75 mi. east to Goshen-Ripton Road (USFS Road 32), from which point it is 0.8 mi. north to Vt. 125 just east of Ripton Village and 2.6 mi. south to the USFS Moosalamoo Campground entrance.

The Oak Ridge Trail continues north, crossing Hale Brook, then USFS Road 92A (4.5 mi.). Ascending easily, the trail swings northwest near a brook crossing (5.2 mi.), crosses another small stream (5.8 mi.), then swings around a hill (1,641 ft.) to cross a low ridge (6.0 mi.) a short distance below the summit. The trail then descends to a junction with an old road and a utility line (6.7 mi.). It follows the road downhill to the west, bears right at another junction (7.9 mi.), and continues a short distance to reach its terminus at a parking area adjacent to Vt. 125 (8.0 mi.).

MOOSALAMOO TRAIL

Distance: 2.3 mi. (3.7 km)
Elevation Change: 800 ft. ascent
Hiking Time: 1½ hr. (reverse 1 hr.)

This trail climbs to the summit of Mt. Moosalamoo from the east. It departs the USFS Moosalamoo Campground and ascends to meet the Oak Ridge Trail a short distance north of the summit. Via this latter trail it is a short climb to the summit of Mt. Moosalamoo.

TO THE TRAIL: To reach the USFS Moosalamoo Campground from the north, turn south off Vt. 125 on the Goshen-Ripton Road (USFS Road 32) at a junction 5.2 mi. east of U.S. 7 in East Middlebury. Continue south on USFS Road 32 for 3.4 mi., to the signed campground access road on the right. The same point is reached from the south by following USFS Road 32 north for about 6.2 mi. from Vt. 73 east of Forest Dale. Continue west along the access road for 0.7 mi. to reach the campground. The trailhead is at the rear of a parking lot on the north side of the access road just before the gated campground entrance. Parking is available for twelve cars.

DESCRIPTION: The Moosalamoo Trail, blazed in blue and marked with occasional orange diamonds reading "Cross Moosalamoo Trail," climbs around and over a knoll, makes a brief jog onto and off a woods road, and shortly crosses the north branch of Voter Brook on a footbridge (0.5 mi.). From this point, the trail begins a gradual and steady ascent, eventually swinging sharply left and ascending more steeply to end at a signed junction with the Oak Ridge Trail (2.3 mi.). Following this trail left, it is 0.25 mi. to the Mt. Moosalamoo summit (2,640 ft.) where there are views east and north from two overlooks.

NORTH BRANCH TRAIL

Distance: 2.2 mi. (3.5 km)
Elevation Change: 650 ft. descent
Hiking Time: 1 hr. (reverse 1½ hr.)

The North Branch Trail connects the USFS Moosalamoo Campground with the Falls of Lana Picnic Area and provides possibilities for loop hikes across Mt. Moosalamoo.

TO THE TRAIL: The North Branch Trail starts at the Moosalamoo Campground directly across the road from the parking area for the Moosalamoo Trail.

DESCRIPTION: From the Moosalamoo Campground (0.0 mi.), the blue-blazed North Branch Trail, also marked occasionally with orange "Cross Moosalamoo Trail" diamonds, follows easy grades on high ground and soon crosses USFS Road 24B. The trail then descends for a short distance to reach a junction with the Keewaydin Trail on the right (0.3 mi.). Continuing straight ahead, the North Branch Trail eventually makes a short, steep descent to cross the north branch of Voter Brook (1.1 mi.). The trail follows the brook downstream, keeping generally to high ground and passing interesting cascades. The trail continues, in sight of Sucker Brook, to reach its terminus at the Rattlesnake Cliffs Trail (2.2 mi.). Straight ahead, it is 0.3 mi. to the Falls of Lana Picnic Area.

SILVER LAKE TRAIL

Distance: 1.5 mi. (2.4 km)
Elevation Change: 520 ft. ascent
Hiking Time: 1 hr. (reverse ¾ hr.)

Silver Lake and the USFS Silver Lake Recreation Area are reached by this unblazed but obvious multiuse trail.

TO THE TRAIL: A paved parking lot for this trail is on the east side of Vt. 53, 0.4 mi. south of the entrance to Branbury State Park. Overnight parking is strongly discouraged here because of recurrent vandalism.

DESCRIPTION: Leaving the parking lot (0.0 mi.) and rising quickly to a woods road, the trail climbs a short distance east, soon swings north and ascends on easy grades. Passing under the penstock that brings water from Silver Lake Dam to the power plant on Vt. 53 (0.3 mi.), the trail continues past unmarked spurs on the left overlooking the Falls of Lana and reaches a junction (0.5 mi.).

> **Junction:** Straight ahead, the Falls of Lana Trail continues a short distance across Sucker Brook to a junction where there are trails to the picnic area, Branbury State Park, Rattlesnake Cliffs, Mt. Moosalamoo, and Moosalamoo Campground.

Turning sharply right at the junction, the Silver Lake Trail continues on the woods road and ascends east for a short distance before resuming its northerly direction (0.6 mi.). Following easy grades, the trail passes a beaver meadow on the left (1.2 mi.) and ascends to a power line clearing (1.4 mi.). After following the power line a short distance, the trail turns right (1.5 mi.) and reaches a junction a few feet northeast of the Silver Lake Dam (1.5 mi.). Leaving right and continuing across the dam is the Silver Lake Loop Trail, while straight ahead the Leicester Hollow Trail leads around the east shore of Silver Lake.

SILVER LAKE LOOP TRAIL

Distance: 1.7 mi. (2.7 km)
Elevation Change: minor
Hiking Time: 1 hr. either direction

Also known as the Rocky Point Trail, this trail loops part way around Silver Lake; however, it joins with the Leicester Hollow Trail and the Goshen Trail to complete the loop.

To the Trail: This USFS trail begins just east of the Silver Lake Dam at the terminus of the Silver Lake Trail.

Description: From the junction (0.0 mi.), this blue-blazed trail crosses the dam and follows the west shore of the lake, occasionally clambering onto the rocky slopes of Chandler Ridge. To the north, there are frequent views of Mt. Moosalamoo. After crossing a point and passing a junction with the Chandler Ridge Trail (0.5 mi.), the trail crosses a small inlet brook at the southwest corner of the lake (1.3 mi.). It continues through the woods to the southeast corner (1.5 mi.), crosses an inlet brook on a bridge (1.6 mi.), and swings north. After following the east shore a short distance, the trail swings right and ends at a junction with the Leicester Hollow Trail (1.7 mi.).

> **Junction:** Following the Leicester Hollow Trail north, it is 0.2 mi. to the Goshen Trail and 0.8 mi. back to the dam, making a total loop distance of 2.5 mi.

MINNIE BAKER TRAIL

Distance: 1.2 mi. (1.9 km)
Elevation Change: 450 ft. ascent
Hiking Time: ¾ hr. (reverse ½ hr.)

To the Trail: This multipurpose U.S. Forest Service trail starts at a parking area on the east side of Vt. 53, 1.7 mi. north of its junction with Vt. 73 in Forest Dale.

DESCRIPTION: From the parking area gate (0.0 mi.), the Minnie Baker Trail follows a woods road northeasterly, bears right at a woods road junction (0.2 mi.), and ascends to cross the ridge (0.8 mi.). It then descends to reach its terminus (1.2 mi.) at the Leicester Hollow Trail, just north of that trail's southern end and a short distance south of the start of the Chandler Ridge Trail.

LEICESTER HOLLOW TRAIL

Distance: 4.6 mi. (7.4 km)
Elevation Change: 450 ft. ascent
Hiking Time: 2½ hr. (reverse 2¼ hr.)

Cyclists, hikers, and skiers use this multiuse trail. Lying in a hollow parallel to the Chandler Ridge Trail and the Ridge Trail, it leads to primitive camping on the eastern side of Silver Lake.

TO THE TRAIL: The southern end of the trail is reached via the Minnie Baker Trail and the northern end via the Goshen and Silver Lake trails. Churchill Road (USFS Road 40) no longer provides parking or access to the Leicester Hollow Trail because of a bridge closure, and it should not be used.

DESCRIPTION: The Leicester Hollow Trail follows an old road north from a USFS gate (0.0 mi.) and immediately reaches an unsigned intersection where the Ridge Trail leaves right. Continuing on the road, the trail reaches a signed junction on the left (0.2 mi.) with the Minnie Baker Trail, then a second signed junction on the left, this time with the Chandler Ridge Trail. The Leicester Hollow Trail remains on the well-defined old road on the valley floor and ascends northerly on easy grades, eventually making the first of numerous crossings of Leicester Hollow Brook (0.9 mi.).

Ascending deeper into the hollow past old rock slides and mossy boulders, the trail passes a gorge and pool on the left (2.9 mi.) and continues its gradual climb to a junction with the Silver Lake Loop Trail on the left (3.8 mi.). The trail then continues past a junction on the right with the Goshen Trail (4.0 mi.) and passes several campsite spurs on the left (4.2 mi.). After crossing an inlet stream on a bridge, the trail passes through the picnic area and ends at the Silver Lake Trail near the dam (4.6 mi.).

CHANDLER RIDGE TRAIL

Distance: 4.3 mi. (6.9 km)
Elevation Change: 800 ft. ascent
Hiking Time: 2½ hr. (reverse 2 hr.)

Traversing Chandler Ridge, this trail has nice views of the Green Mountains and the Adirondacks.

To the Trail: This blue-blazed USFS trail leaves the Leicester Hollow Trail at a signed junction 0.25 mi. north of its southern terminus.

Description: From the junction, the trail ascends southwesterly a short distance, then swings northwesterly to slab the west slope of the ridge. After reaching the ridgeline (0.6 mi.), the trail passes views to the east of the Green Mountains (0.8 mi.) and continues past westerly views of the lower end of Lake Dunmore and the Adirondacks beyond (1.0 mi.). After passing over a bump, the trail turns to the right into a gully (1.2 mi.) and continues northerly on the east slope of the ridge.

The trail returns to the ridge (1.8 mi.), crosses a minor bump (2.0 mi.), and follows easy up-and-down routing west of the ridgeline before eventually reaching several limited views west (3.4 mi.). After passing another view (3.9 mi.), the trail returns to the ridge, then descends to reach its terminus at a junction with the Silver Lake Loop Trail (4.3 mi.) on the west shore of the lake.

Junction: To the left, it is 0.5 mi. to the Silver Lake dam and northern terminus of the Leicester Hollow Trail. To the right, via the Silver Lake Loop Trail, it is 1.2 mi. to the

3

Leicester Hollow Trail. Or, via the Silver Lake Loop Trail, Leicester Hollow Trail and the Goshen Trail, it is 1.8 mi. to the Ridge Trail.

RIDGE TRAIL

Distance: 3.9 mi. (6.3 km)
Elevation Change: 700 ft. ascent
Hiking Time: 2¼ hr. (reverse 2 hr.)

Maintained on national forest land by the Churchill House Inn, this ski trail is marked with blue diamonds and generally parallels the Leicester Hollow Trail but follows higher ground to the east.

TO THE TRAIL: The trail leaves the Leicester Hollow Trail about 50 ft. north of the U.S. Forest Service gate at the southern end of the Leicester Hollow Trail.

DESCRIPTION: From the unsigned junction (0.0 mi.), the trail ascends southerly on an old woods road for some distance, then assumes a more easterly direction. Eventually swinging sharply north (0.5 mi.), the trail crosses a wide, grassy forest service road (0.6 mi.) and continues its ascent toward the ridge, but does not cross it. Bearing left at all junctions and briefly following reddish-orange blazes beyond the Glade Trail junction (1.8 mi.), the trail eventually reaches a junction with the Goshen Trail (3.9 mi.), 0.4 mi. east of its junction with the northern end of the Leicester Hollow Trail.

GOSHEN TRAIL

Distance: 0.6 mi. (0.9 km)
Elevation Change: 270 ft. descent
Hiking Time: 20 min. (reverse ½ hr.)

TO THE TRAIL: Marked with blue blazes, this USFS trail begins at a parking area at the end of USFS Road 27. From Vt. 73, 1.6 mi. east of Forest Dale, follow the Goshen-Ripton Road (USFS Road 32) north for 2.3 mi. to a crossroads. Turn left on USFS Road 27 and continue north to the end of the road (4.3 mi.) and the parking area.

DESCRIPTION: From the parking area (0.0 mi.), the trail crests a low ridge and crosses a power line (0.1 mi.). Descending through the woods, it reaches a junction on the left with the Ridge Trail (0.2 mi.), crosses a small stream in a hollow (0.3 mi.), and rises to join an old road (0.4 mi.). The trail then descends to its terminus near the northern end of the Leicester Hollow Trail (0.6 mi.).

ROBERT FROST INTERPRETIVE TRAIL

Distance: 1.0 mi. (1.6 km)
Elevation Change: minor
Hiking Time: ½ hr. either direction

The first part of this loop trail is handicap-accessible, while the remainder uses boardwalks, gravel paths, and an unimproved dirt footbed. Several of Robert Frost's poems are posted along the trail so they can be enjoyed in appropriate settings.

TO THE TRAIL: This USFS trail loop begins at a parking area on the south side of Vt. 125, 2.0 mi. east of Ripton and 3.8 mi. west of Middlebury Gap (USGS East Middlebury).

DESCRIPTION: From the parking area, the trail passes through woods and old clearings. A spur trail from the loop connects to the Water Tower Trails. The U.S. Forest Service maintains all the old fields along this trail with prescribed fire to preserve the scenic open appearance.

WATER TOWER TRAILS

Distance: 2.3 mi. (3.7 km) round trip
Elevation Change: 375 ft. ascent
Hiking Time: 1¾ hr.

The Water Tower Trails form a loop around a small wooded hill, with two shortcuts offering steeper options bisecting the loop. The namesake water tower, which can't be

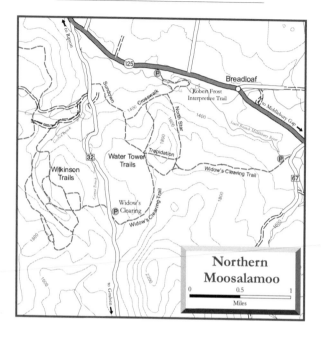

Northern Moosalamoo

0   0.5   1

Miles

seen from the trails, stands off USFS Road 32 near the former site of a Job Corps center run by the Forest Service in the 1960s. It lent its name to a timber sale in the area and subsequently to the trail system established on the skid roads that remained. The description below follows a counterclockwise circuit of the hill on wide, fairly smooth trails.

To the Trail: A short spur trail leads from the Robert Frost Interpretive Trail to the start of this well-signed USFS loop.

Description: From the point where the spur trail leaves the Robert Frost Interpretive Trail (0.0), the path climbs slightly to a T intersection marked with the number 5. This is the start of the loop. Turning right onto the Crosswalk Trail the route climbs gently through mixed woods to a junction on the left with the Afternoon Delight Trail.

Junction: To the left, the Afternoon Delight Trail cuts across the hillside on steeper grades for 0.5 mi. and rejoins this loop hike.

Continuing straight, the trail descends slightly and crosses a narrow stream. In a small clearing immediately beyond the stream, it turns sharply left onto the Sundown Trail (0.4 mi.), which climbs steadily as it winds toward the south slope of the hill and a junction with the other end of the Afternoon Delight Trail and a trail called Trepidation (0.8 mi.).

Junction: Bearing slightly left, the Trepidation Trail presents a short, steep climb to the south end of the wooded summit plateau. From here, there are winter views through the trees before the trail drops more gently to rejoin the loop hike after 0.3 mi.

About 75 yards beyond this multiway intersection, the route joins the Widow's Clearing Trail, which comes in from the right.

Junction: To the right, the Widow's Clearing Trail rolls and dips gently through open understory westward to a parking area on USFS Road 32, 1.9 mi. south of Vt. 125. Across the road is the Wilkinson Trails network, described below.

This hike continues straight ahead, following the base of the hill until the Widow's Clearing Trail departs again right (1.2 mi.). Bearing left, the main trail almost immediately passes the end of the Trepidation Trail on the left and begins a gentle descent, on what's now called the North Star Trail. Here, there may be glimpses through the trees of the Breadloaf Range north of Vt. 125.

Soon the trail bends slightly right and begins a steadier descent. Rocks and numerous rivulets make this next section the roughest portion of the trail. At the end of the loop (2.2 mi.), the trail turns right onto the spur trail to return to the Robert Frost Interpretive Trail. The most direct route back to the parking area from there is to the left.

WILKINSON TRAILS

This warren of short interconnected USFS trails totals 5.2 miles, presenting many possible routes and a maximum elevation change of 400 ft. Some of the trails follow a brook and beavers are active in the area.

TO THE TRAIL: The trail system begins across from the Widow's Clearing parking area on USFS Road 32, 1.9 miles south of its intersection with Vt. 125 just east of Ripton village.

• • • • • • • • • • • • • • • •

SNAKE MOUNTAIN

Distance: 1.8 mi. (2.9 km)
Elevation Change: 900 ft. ascent
Hiking Time: 1½ hr. (reverse 1 hr.)

Snake Mtn. is on the Addison-Weybridge town line (USGS Port Henry) and derives its name from the serpentine shape of its long ridge. When a hotel was established near the summit sometime after 1870, the name changed to Grand View Mtn. The new name, however, lasted only slightly longer than the hotel. A large concrete foundation remains, offering excellent views of the Champlain Valley and the Adirondacks. The summit and most of the mountain are part of the 1,215-acre Snake Mountain Wildlife Management Area and the western cliffs have sometimes been closed because of nesting peregrine falcons. The lower end of the trail is on private property. The path to the summit is part of an extensive network of logging

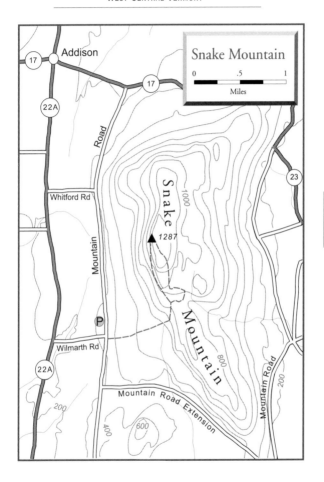

Snake Mountain

0   .5   1
Miles

3

roads on the mountain, and hikers should stay on this well-traveled route.

TO THE TRAIL: From the junction of Vt. 22A and Vt. 17 at Addison Four Corners (0.0 mi.), follow Vt. 17 east to a junction on the right with Mountain Road (0.8 mi.). Follow this road south past Whitford Road to a parking lot on the right, about 500 ft. north of the junction with Wilmarth Road (3.5 mi.). Alternatively, from Vt. 22A about 2.7 mi. south of Vt. 17, turn east on Wilmarth Road and follow it to Mountain Road and the parking area. The trailhead is on the east side of this road junction.

DESCRIPTION: The route passes through a gate (0.0 mi.) and follows a wide, often muddy woods road east to a T junction (0.7 mi.). Turning left and continuing more steeply north, the trail swings east onto the ridge to another junction (0.9 mi.), where it takes the right fork and continues up the old blue-blazed carriage road.

> **Junction:** To the left, a narrower and sparsely orange-blazed trail ascends gently, then moderately, to reach the south shore of tiny Red Rocks Pond (1.5 mi.), where there are views west. The trail follows a ledge along the pond's western shore, then reenters the woods on the right and climbs gently to rejoin the carriage road.

The main route continues its winding climb, eventually passing the spur trail from the pond (1.7 mi.) and reaching the concrete foundation (1.8 mi.) just southwest of the true summit (1,287 ft.). Although a snowmobile trail blazed with orange diamonds continues past the hotel site, it does not present any loop-hike possibilities.

• • • • • • • • • • • • • • • • •

ABBEY POND

Distance: 2.3 mi. (3.7 km)
Elevation Change: 1,260 ft. ascent
Hiking Time: 1¾ hr. (reverse 1¼ hr.)

Located in the northwest corner of Ripton, this attractive wilderness pond is reached by a blue-blazed USFS trail, which follows old woods roads along or near the outlet brook (USGS South Mtn.). From the pond, there is a view of the twin peaks of Robert Frost Mtn. The trail has sometimes been closed to protect nesting great blue herons.

TO THE TRAIL: Follow Vt. 116 north 4.4 mi. from its intersection with Vt. 125 in East Middlebury or 6.9 mi. south from Vt. 17 outside Bristol village. Turn east on a gravel road next to the USFS Abbey Pond Trail sign and follow the right spur 0.3 mi. to the parking area. The land next to the road and parking lot is private property; please be respectful of the owner.

DESCRIPTION: From the parking area (0.0 mi.), the trail enters the woods and climbs moderately to a bridge (0.2 mi.). It continues beside the stream to a second crossing,

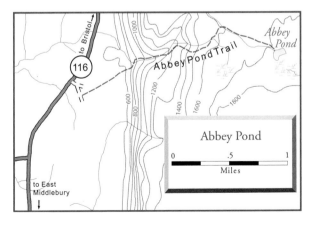

this time on rocks, then ascends steadily to a third stream crossing (1.6 mi.), after which the terrain is gentler. The trail reaches the pond near its outlet (2.1 mi.).

• • • • • • • • • • • • • • • • •

BRISTOL LEDGES

Distance: 1.0 mi. (1.6 km)
Elevation Change: 960 ft. ascent
Hiking Time: 1 hr. (reverse ¾ hr.)

From the ledges on the southwest side of Hogback Mtn. (USGS Bristol), there are good views of Bristol Village and the lower Champlain Valley. The ledges are reached by following an unmarked woods road westward from the Bristol reservoir.

To the Trail: From Main Street (Vt. 116 and 17), a short distance east of the shopping district in Bristol Village, turn north on Mountain Street. Turn right almost immediately on Mountain Terrace, then bear right again at the next fork and continue to the end of the street. Parking is discouraged along this narrow residential street; obey all signs and be sure not to block driveways or the gate. Hikers are encouraged to park a short distance away in the shopping district or at the town green.

Description: From the end of the street (0.0 mi.), the route climbs a winding jeep road generally eastward, curving left at a fork, toward the Bristol reservoir (0.2 mi.). Just before reaching the clearing where the reservoir structure stands, it bears left on an eroded woods road and continues straight ahead uphill. Soon turning sharply left (0.3 mi.), the trail ascends easily in a northerly direction, passing a narrow trail on the right, then a rough path on the left leading back downhill (0.6 mi.). From here, the trail climbs steadily on the rough jeep road to the rock ledges (1.0 mi.).

• • • • • • • • • • • • • • • • •

RAMBLES

HUBBARDTON BATTLEFIELD

In the summer of 1777, after a British force captured Mt. Independence and Fort Ticonderoga, the American army hastily retreated through Hubbardton. The only Revolutionary War battle fought in Vermont occurred here on July 7, 1777, when Seth Warner's Green Mountain Boys staged a rearguard action against General Burgoyne, checking the British advance and allowing the main American force time to escape. A small visitors center, with a diorama and period artifacts, gives a good overview of the battle and the terrain. An easy path encircles Monument Hill, the site of the Battle of Hubbardton.

TO THE TRAIL: Leave U.S. 4 at exit 5 near Castleton, and turn north on the paved East Hubbardton Road. The visitors center is on the left, about 7.0 mi. north of U.S. 4.

DESCRIPTION: The trail begins at the visitors center parking lot (0.0 mi.) and follows a mowed strip through open fields. Turning right at a fork (0.1 mi.) and then left, the trail follows the northern edge of the field and reaches a small hill. Passing to the west of a small slate house, it descends easterly to a junction at a small bridge (0.4 mi.). The trail follows the right fork to a small loop around the Selleck Cabin Site (0.5 mi.), before recrossing the bridge and gently ascending Monument Hill. Passing south of the visitors center, the trail reaches the monument dedicated to the battle before returning to the parking lot (0.7 mi.).

PITTSFORD RECREATION AREA

This system of trails is located in the town-owned Pittsford Recreation Area and consists of a half-dozen interconnecting paths, blazed in different colors and totaling about 3.0 mi. The 200-acre recreation area lies north and east of U.S. 7 and is roughly bounded on the northwest by Plains Road, which leaves U.S. 7 about 0.25 mi. north of the Pittsford village green, and on the southeast by Furnace Road, which leaves U.S. 7 about 0.75 mi. south of the village green.

The trail network, designated for foot travel only, is open to the public year-round without charge and leads through abandoned pastures, woodlands, and wetlands. A flyer, containing a map of the trails as well as brief descriptions, is available at the town offices on Plains Road, about 0.75 mi. from the junction with U.S. 7.

TO THE TRAIL: The main entrance to the recreation area is on Furnace Road, about 0.5 mi. from U.S. 7 and adjacent to the Vermont Police Academy. This entrance is near the day-use facilities, which include picnic areas and a swimming pond (a fee is charged in season).

DESCRIPTION: Convenient access to the network may be gained from two of the trails. The Blue Trail traverses most of the recreation area and starts behind the Pittsford town offices. The trail leads south and east to the main entrance of the Pittsford Recreation Area on Furnace Road. The White Trail starts behind the Pittsford Congregational Church near the village green and leads into the recreation area and a junction with the Blue Trail.

GIFFORD WOODS STATE PARK

Camping facilities are available and a day-use fee is charged in season. The Appalachian Trail passes through the park about 2.0 mi. east of its departure from the Long Trail at Maine Junction in Willard Gap. These trail systems are described in the GMC's *Long Trail Guide* and in a brochure available at the park contact station.

Across Vt. 100 from the park gates lies Gifford Woods Natural Area, a seven-acre, old-growth virgin hardwood stand containing many grand trees with an understory of native wildflowers. The area contains no formal trails nor development of any kind and is designated both as a National Natural Landmark and a State Fragile Area.

To the Trail: Gifford Woods State Park is on Vt. 100, 0.6 mi. north of its junction with U.S. 4 in Killington.

Description: Within the park, the Kent Brook Trail follows fairly gentle terrain to make a counterclockwise loop of the camping area through a northern hardwood forest. Starting just inside the park entrance, the yellow-blazed trail follows a well-defined footpath north through the day-use area. The hiking trail crosses a cross-country ski trail and climbs the hillside before descending slightly to cross the Appalachian Trail west of the campground. It crosses a woods road and briefly follows Kent Brook before doubling back left and ending on a road at the south end of the park (0.7 mi.). The park entrance is to the right on this road.

3

TEXAS FALLS NATURE TRAIL

Texas Falls lies in a dramatic ravine; several observation points and a bridge overlook the ravine.

To the Trail: From Vt. 125, 3.2 mi. east of Middlebury Gap and 3.1 mi. west of Vt. 100 in Hancock, a paved road leads north 0.5 mi. to a parking area on the left.

Description: From the parking area, a self-guided nature trail (descriptive brochure available at the site) crosses a rustic bridge over Texas Falls and follows Hancock Brook upstream 0.3 mi. toward the Texas Falls Picnic Area. Bearing right just before the paved road at the picnic area, it reaches the upper section of the nature trail, which leads 0.9 mi. back to the falls. The complete loop is 1.2 mi. (1.9 km) and will take about ½ hr. to hike.

BUTTON BAY STATE PARK

Located in Vergennes, Button Bay State Park occupies a 253-acre former farm site on a bluff overlooking Lake Champlain. The park is named for the buttonlike concretions formed by clay deposits that are found along the shoreline. Overnight camping and day-use facilities are available, with a fee charged in season. Button Point Natural Area, a 13-acre peninsula forming the western end of the park, contains fossils, an old-growth forest stand, and several rare or endangered plant species.

To the Trail: From the traffic light in the city of Vergennes, continue south about 0.5 mi. on Vt. 22A then turn west on Panton Road. Follow the state park signs about 6.5 mi. northwest, then south over local roads to the state park entrance.

Description: A 0.5-mi. gated gravel road (no motor vehicles) leads west from the park picnic area to the natural area and the nature center where a guide and pamphlet describing the interesting geology of this area are available. In season, a park naturalist runs daily nature programs for adults and children; information is available by calling: (802) 475-2377. From the center, the 0.5-mi. Champlain Nature Trail explores the hardwood forest and bluffs above the lake.

KINGSLAND BAY STATE PARK

Located in the town of Ferrisburg, Kingsland Bay State Park currently offers only day-use facilities. Occupying 264 acres along the shores of Lake Champlain that was formerly the site of an exclusive girls camp, this striking area was also home to one of the earliest settlements in Ferrisburg.

To the Trail: From its junction with Vt. 22A near Vergennes, proceed north on U.S. 7 about 0.5 mi. and turn west on Tuppers Crossing Road (0.0 mi.), just past a sign for Kingsland Bay State Park. Turn right on Botsford Road as indicated by a second state park sign and continue straight through a crossroads (1.1 mi.) on Hawkins Road. Follow this road along Little Otter Creek to Kingsland Bay State Park Road and the entrance to the state park on the right (4.5 mi.).

DESCRIPTION: A level trail, about 1.0 mi. long, leaves the northern end of the parking area and parallels the shoreline around the peninsula. The trail follows a wooded route before breaking onto the shoreline, offering intimate lake views of sailboats on Kingsland Bay and more sweeping vistas across the lake to the Adirondacks

WILLIAMS WOODS

3

In 1996, The Nature Conservancy acquired this 63-acre wooded tract in the town of Charlotte. It is an exceptional example of mature Vermont bottomland. Within its gently rolling terrain, unlogged stands of hemlock and oak closely resemble the forest seen by the first settlers of the Champlain Valley. The nature preserve is open to the public for foot travel over a 1.6-mi. trail loop marked by green and yellow plastic diamonds, wooden arrow signs, and white blazes.

TO THE TRAIL: From its junction with U.S. 7 (0.0 mi.), follow Ferry Road west to Charlotte and a four-way intersection (0.3 mi.). Turn south on Greenbush Road and proceed straight through a staggered intersection (2.3 mi.) where roads leave right, then left. The trailhead is soon reached on the right at a sign (3.2 mi.). Limited parking is available on the shoulder of the road, and care should be taken to park vehicles off the traveled surface.

DESCRIPTION: From the entrance sign (0.0 mi.), an access trail leads west a few hundred feet to a register box usually containing copies of an interpretive brochure. The access trail then winds along and crosses two wooden bridges to reach a junction with the trail loop (0.4 mi.). Following an arrow to the right, this trail makes a counterclockwise circuit around the preserve, returning to the junction with the access trail (1.2 mi.). From here, the entrance is to the right (1.6 mi.).

A conspicuous feature of the preserve's forest is the profusion of downed trees, many blown down because only a shallow layer of topsoil covers the impermeable clay. The trail is challenging due to many protruding roots and occasional wet areas.

CHARLOTTE PARK AND WILDLIFE REFUGE

This town park's 290 acres encompass active cropland, pastures, abandoned orchards, meadows in various stages of succession, woodlands, and wetlands. A nature trail with ten stations winds through the site, and an interpretive brochure available at the parking area describes the flora, fauna, and evidence of history that can be observed here. Dogs are not allowed.

TO THE TRAIL: From its junction with U.S. 7 (0.0 mi.), follow Ferry Road west to Charlotte and a four-way intersection (0.3 mi.). Turn north on Greenbush Road and proceed to the park entrance marked with stone pillars (1.8 mi.), just south of a railroad overpass. Ample parking is available here, and a signboard describes the site and the code of conduct for visitors.

DESCRIPTION: From the parking area (0.0 mi.), the trail crosses a stream and reaches an overlook (0.4 mi.) before traversing pasture and woodlands to the final stop at an overlook of Lake Champlain (1.0 mi.). From here a longer loop circumnavigates another pasture, or a shorter loop returns directly to the parking area.

MOUNT PHILO STATE PARK

Occupying 168 acres in the town of Charlotte, Mount Philo State Park was established in 1924 and is the oldest park in the state system. A limited number of campsites are available atop the mountain and on its north side. Some very fine views of the Adirondacks and nearly the entire length of Lake Champlain can be seen from the north- and west-ledge lookouts of this 980-ft. mountain (USGS Mt. Philo).

To the Trail: From the junction of U.S. 7 and Ferry Road, follow U.S. 7 south 3.0 mi. to a junction on the left with State Park Road. The same point may be reached from the south by following U.S. 7 north for about 7.5 mi. from its junction with Vt. 22A near Vergennes. Turn east on State Park Road and continue 0.6 mi. to the park entrance at a four-way intersection. A paved state park road ascends to the summit area.

Description: A blue-blazed trail starts at a bulletin board next to the parking lot (0.0 mi.) and ascends the northwest side of the mountain. After crossing a park road (0.4 mi.), the trail soon reaches a junction at the base of a rocky outcrop.

> **Junction:** Here, a blue-blazed trail departs right and skirts an interesting area along the base of the cliffs, leading south and eventually ending on the park access road (0.5 mi.). From this point, it is 0.7 mi. downhill along the road back to the park entrance or about 0.3 mi. up the road to the contact station atop the mountain.

Bearing left at the junction, the main trail climbs to the top of the ledges and soon arrives at a second junction (0.5 mi.) where a blue-blazed trail departs left and leads 0.25 mi. to a camping area low on the mountain's north flank. The main trail continues straight ahead and reaches the first of several outstanding vistas atop the mountain (0.6 mi.). Near the top of the cliff, the blazes soon end, and the trail skirts the summit picnic area before following an old carriage road through the woods (0.7 mi.). The trail ends on the summit access road on the western side of the mountain (1.0 mi.), a short distance below the contact station.

In 1924 to 1926, the summit of Mt. Philo became a fire lookout station. In 1938 to 1940, the CCC constructed a steel tower on the mountain, which remained an active outpost until the 1950s. During the 1970s, the tower was removed.

GREEN MOUNTAIN AUDUBON NATURE CENTER

Owned by the Green Mountain Audubon Society, the Green Mountain Audubon Nature Center is a 255-acre sanctuary that includes a great diversity of natural habitats, a working sugarbush, and a butterfly garden. There is no admission fee, but contributions are accepted. Green Mountain Audubon also offers a variety of natural history programs for adults and children. For information, Contact Green Mountain Audubon at 255 Sherman Hollow Road, Huntington, Vermont 05462; (802) 434-3068; vt.audubon.org/centers.html.

TO THE TRAIL: The nature center is on the Richmond-Huntington Road, about 5.0 mi. south of Richmond village and about 1.5 mi. north of Huntington village. There is a visitors center with parking on Sherman Hollow Road about 0.25 mi. west of the highway and a parking lot near the sugarhouse on the main highway 0.1 mi. north of Sherman Hollow Road.

A 5.0-mi. network of trails, open every day from dawn to dusk, crisscrosses the property. These trails lead to a variety of wildlife habitats and offer views of the neighboring mountains, with Camel's Hump the most spectacular. A map, available at the nature center, is invaluable for locating and identifying the numerous trails found on both sides of Sherman Hollow Road.

East Central Vermont

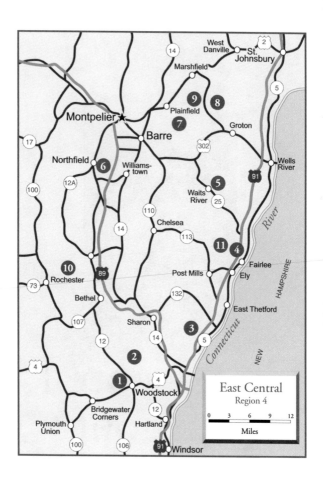

West
Danville
St.
Johnsbury
14
Marshfield
2
5
9 8
Plainfield
7
Groton
Montpelier ★
Barre
302
Wells
River
17
91
Northfield 6
Williams-
town
100
12A
5
Waits
River
25
110
Chelsea
14
113
11 4
Fairlee
10
89
Post Mills
Ely
73
Rochester
132
HAMPSHIRE
Bethel
East Thetford
107
3
Sharon
14
5
12
2
Connecticut
NEW
4
1
Woodstock
4
Bridgewater
Corners
12
Plymouth
Union
Hartland
100
106
91 Windsor

East Central
Region 4

0   3   6   9   12

Miles

REGION 4
East Central Vermont

REGION 4
East Central Vermont

Most of the hiking trails in this region are dispersed as single trails up prominent peaks. Along the western edge, the easternmost of three ranges of the Green Mountains runs from the Braintree Mountains in the south northward to the Northfield Mountains.

The Marsh-Billings-Rockefeller National Historic Park in Woodstock, Vermont's only national park, is popular for its historic significance and its network of walking trails and old carriage roads.

East of Barre is a discontinuous range sometimes called the Granite Hills that extends north. This area of the state is similar geologically to New Hampshire. Several peaks reach elevations in excess of 3,000 ft. in the Orange-Groton area where Vermont's largest state forest is located. With 25,000 acres, Groton State Forest includes lakes, bogs, inspiring summits, and plenty of land for hiking and camping.

WOODSTOCK AREA

R ising above the village of Woodstock northwest of the Ottauquechee Valley, Mt. Tom (USGS Woodstock North, Woodstock South) has more than 20 mi. of foot trails, cross-country ski trails, logging roads, and carriage roads. The main natural features in the area are Mt. Tom, Mt. Peg, Eshqua Bog (see Region 2), and Quechee Gorge (see Region 2).

The Billings Museum, the Rockefeller home, and the Mt. Tom lands were incorporated in the Marsh-Billings-Rockefeller National Historic Park in 1998. George Perkins Marsh (1801–1882), an early conservationist, first owned the farmlands, later purchased by Frederick Billings (1823–1890). Billings developed his farm as a model of wise agricultural stewardship. The property has numerous "reforestation plantation" areas, clearly identified on the official park map, available at the Prosper Road Trailhead kiosk or the visitors center. Especially interesting is the stand of European larch planted in 1887, found off the carriage road between the Pogue and the South Peak of Mt. Tom. After his death, his wife Julia and their three daughters sustained Billing's plan. Later, his granddaughter, Mary French, and her husband, Laurence S. Rockefeller, continued this commitment to stewardship, eventually gifting the farm to establish Vermont's first national park.

The park includes the Billings Farm and Museum, a working dairy farm with a museum of agricultural and rural life, as well as carriage roads, walking trails, and a visitors center with displays in the Carriage House. A trail map issued by the national park is invaluable for exploring the area. During winter, the Woodstock Ski Touring Center grooms the trails for cross-country skiing; walking on the trails is not allowed. For more information, contact the national park at Marsh-Billings-Rockefeller National

Historic Park, P.O. Box 178, Woodstock, Vermont 05091; (802) 457-3368; or online at nps.gov/mabi. Access to the trails is via Prosper Road, the National Park visitors center, Faulkner Park on Mountain Avenue, or the River Street Cemetery.

MOUNT TOM VIA FAULKNER TRAIL

Distance: 1.6 mi. (2.6 km)
Elevation Change: 550 ft. ascent
Hiking Time: 1 hr. (reverse ¾ hr.)

The graded pathway, long and winding switchbacks, and park benches along the route make this a Vermont rarity. The unblazed but obvious trail begins in Faulkner Park.

TO THE TRAIL: From the Woodstock village green, cross U.S. 4 to Mountain Avenue and drive or walk through the covered bridge across the Ottauquechee River. Bear left on Mountain Avenue where it crosses River Street and continue a short distance west to Faulkner Park on the right. Roadside parking is available.

DESCRIPTION: Follow the asphalt path along the stonewall, which forms the eastern boundary of the park, to where the trail enters the woods just below a large boulder (0.0 mi.). The path promptly begins a gradual zigzag climb, and hikers should avoid the temptation to follow rogue paths between the switchbacks. The path reaches a junction (0.5 mi.) on the right with the Lower Link Trail, which follows easy grades for 0.2 mi. to a terminus on the Precipice Trail. Past this junction, the Faulkner Trail continues a zigzag climb to another junction (1.2 mi.) on the right, this time with the Upper Link Trail, which also leads 0.2 mi. to the Precipice Trail. From this junction, the Faulkner Trail leads straight ahead to ascend to a knoll (1.5 mi.) where there are views to the south and east.

The trail then drops into a shallow sag before beginning a short, difficult climb, aided by steel cable handrails

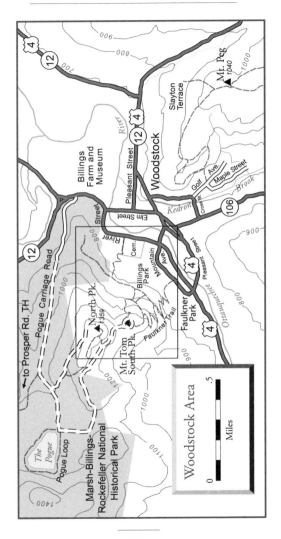

Woodstock Area

Miles

0 .5

over slippery ledge rocks, and meeting the end of a carriage road on the South Peak (1,250 ft.) of Mt. Tom (1.6 mi.). Here, there are fine views south of Woodstock and Okemo Mtn. (Ludlow Mtn.) and east to the Ottauquechee River.

About 125 ft. to the right, at the communication poles, the Precipice Trail descends a short distance to a rock lookout where there are impressive views. The carriage road atop the south peak forms a short circular loop, which affords views in all directions and also leads northwest to the Pogue. To reach the North Peak (1,359 ft.) from the South Peak, descend the carriage road and take a short side trail right.

ALTERNATE ROUTE: The Precipice Trail is a more challenging route to the south summit of Mt. Tom. Starting near the horse shed behind the visitors center on Vt. 12, the trail is narrower and steeper, with handrails and drop-offs, which can be slippery and dangerous when wet or icy.

THE POGUE

Distance: 1.1 mi. (1.8 km)
Elevation Change: 80 ft. descent
Hiking Time: 35 min. either direction

This small pond, located northwest of Mt. Tom, is reached by following a carriage road on easy grades. There are several ways to reach the Pogue: from Prosper Street, from the Billings Farm and Museum, or from one of the trails at the summit of Mt. Tom (described earlier). Only the description from the South Peak of Mt. Tom is described here. The other routes are described in the national park brochure.

TO THE TRAIL: From Faulkner Park, follow the directions to the south peak of Mt. Tom via the Faulkner Trail, described on page 190.

DESCRIPTION: Leaving the Faulkner Trail at the south peak of Mt. Tom (0.0 mi.), an unblazed carriage road ascends

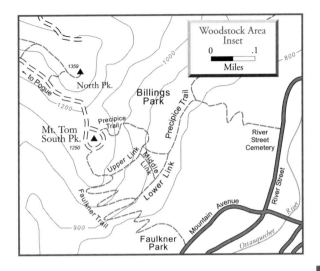

northwest, passes two signs for the North Peak Trail (0.3 mi.), and bears left at a junction where an unmarked trail turns right (0.5 mi.). Continuing through the woods for some distance, the road bears right in a large clearing (0.8 mi.) where there are extensive views west. The road then descends to a large meadow and turns right to follow its margin, shortly reaching a four-way junction (1.0 mi.).

Junction: The road left reaches the southeast corner of the Pogue in about 400 ft. and continues to circle the small pond, making a loop about 0.75 mi. long and returning via the path straight ahead. To the right at the four-way junction, another carriage road makes a very gradual descent, eventually reaching a fork. To the right at this junction, a ski trail leads back to the North Peak Trail near the River Street Cemetery; on the left, a steeper trail descends to Vt. 12 at the Billings Farm and Museum about 0.5 mi. north of the village green.

UNNAMED HIGH POINT

Distance: 0.5 mi. (0.8 km)
Elevation Change: 400 ft. ascent
Hiking Time: 2 hr. (one way)

From the Billings Farm and Museum parking area, travel 2.7 mi. north on Vt. 12. Turn left on Prosper Road for 0.7 mi. to the trailhead parking area on the left.

DESCRIPTION: From the Prosper Road trailhead of the Marsh-Billings-Rockefeller National Historic Park, the route follows a woods path to the carriage road, then takes the first right off the carriage road onto a trail. At the next junction, the left fork switchbacks to an overlook at 1,421 ft. The right fork eventually ends on the carriage road to the South Peak of Mt. Tom or at the Pogue. The National Historic Park map, which is available at the trailhead, is useful for following this trail.

MOUNT PEG

Distance: 0.5 mi. (0.8 km)
Elevation Change: 320 ft. ascent
Hiking Time: ½ hr. (reverse ¼ hr.)

This pleasant walk, especially good for children, up Mt. Peg has a nice view. For a longer return hike, take the alternate route described. In winter, this trail is a good snowshoe outing.

TO THE TRAIL: Located in the southern part of the village, the blazed, graded path to the summit (1,080 ft.) begins at the intersection of Golf Avenue and Maple Street (USGS Woodstock South). From the village green, follow South Street (Vt. 106) south for about 0.1 mi., past the Woodstock Inn. Turn left on Cross Street, continue past Court Street on the left to cross Kedron Brook, then turn right onto Golf Avenue at the next intersection. Continue a short distance to another intersection with Maple Street.

Just before the Maple Street sign is a three-car parking lot on the left. The trail enters the woods from a driveway behind the parking lot on the left side of Golf Avenue. An informal sign marks the beginning of the trail.

DESCRIPTION: From the sign (0.0 mi.), the trail climbs on switchbacks through the woods, branching and rejoining itself several times. Bearing left at each fork makes for a longer hike and bearing right for a shorter one.

The trail continues to a junction with a small loop trail that leads around the summit. It turns left into the loop, then immediately right at a junction where a spur trail leads north to Slayton Terrace. The summit loop climbs southward to a small picnic area on the summit of Mt. Peg (0.5 mi.) before reaching a junction where a side trail departs left (description follows). The summit loop then swings north and descends to rejoin the start of the circuit.

ALTERNATE RETURN ROUTE: From the southeastern corner of the summit loop (0.0 mi.), a side trail departs south and is marked first by red arrows on trees, then diamond-shaped metal markers or red blazes. The trail passes through a wooded area, crosses a power line on private property, and reaches the end of an old field. Turning left, the trail ascends steadily in the open past extensive views east, north and west. After reaching the woods on a ridge (0.4 mi.), cross-country ski trails and bridle paths lead south to the Woodstock Country Club/Ski Touring Area. While hiking is encouraged along the trails in warmer weather, during the winter these trails are maintained for skiing only, and an access fee must be paid at the touring center. The red-blazed trail continues past the Woodstock Country Club's golf course and eventually leads to a field at the Health and Fitness Center. A bicycle path nearby along the shoulder of Vt. 106 leads north about 1.5 mi. back to Woodstock. A return to Mt. Peg may also be made via other ski trails or paths, using the map issued by the touring center.

• • • • • • • • • • • • • • • •

AMITY POND NATURAL AREA

Distance: 2.9 mi. (4.7 km) loop
Elevation Change: 660 ft. ascent
Hiking Time: 1¾ hr. either direction

Located in the northwest corner of Pomfret, the Amity Pond Natural Area (USGS Woodstock North) consists of woodlands and upland pastures donated to the state for nonmotorized and nonwheeled outdoor recreation. The area is circled by a loop trail that coincides for a distance with the Sky Line cross-country ski trail. The ski trail, which travels between Woodstock and Pomfret, is marked with blue and orange markers. It is possible to walk a shorter 1.4-mi. loop using the Crossover Trail. The longer 2.9-mi. loop described involves a pleasant 0.3-mi. walk on the gravel Broad Brook Road.

TO THE TRAIL: From U.S. 4 in Woodstock, follow Vt. 12 north 1.2 mi. to a fork and turn right on South Pomfret Road. At the South Pomfret post office (3.3 mi.), bear right at a fork and continue north through the village of Pomfret to the hamlet of Hewetts Corners (7.9 mi.). Reaching a junction, bear right, staying on the paved road, then take an immediate left onto another paved road where signs point to I-89 and Sharon. Continue a short distance to a gravel road on the left (8.5 mi.). Bear left onto the gravel Allen Hill Road and continue uphill to a wide spot at a height of land (10.8 mi.). On the right side of the road is a small parking area for five cars.

DESCRIPTION: Across the road to the west is the signed entrance to the Amity Pond Natural Area. Two trails leave from here. The most obvious is a side trail that leads from the sign straight ahead a short distance to Amity Pond Shelter. From the shelter, this trail passes right of a small pond, ascends a bank, and crosses a field to join the main trail just below Amity Pond.

The beginning of the main trail is more difficult to spot. From the sign (0.0 mi.), the Amity Pond Trail de-

parts right and parallels the road a short distance before ascending through a wooded area. The trail breaks into the
open to a height of land (0.2 mi.) where there are views to
Mt. Ascutney, Killington, and Pico Peak. Amity Pond,
named to commemorate the lifelong friendship of two area
women who met frequently at this spot, is located in the
meadow west of the trail. The small pond has all but disappeared behind trees growing near the trail at the height
of land.

The trail begins a gentle descent and, near a large rock,
is joined on the left by the side trail from Amity Pond Shelter. Descending to a well-marked junction at the head of a
large loop (0.3 mi.), the trail bears right and crosses the
rest of the open field before reentering the woods. After
crossing a stonewall, the trail descends to a junction (0.6
mi.) with the north end of the Crossover Trail.

Junction: To the left, this trail leads a short distance to
Sugar Arch Shelter, then continues a short distance beyond to rejoin the Amity Pond Trail on its return leg to the
parking lot.

4

Bearing right at the junction, the Amity Pond Trail
passes through a small clearing (0.7 mi.) and descends
through the woods to cross a power line (0.8 mi.). After
descending steadily on an abandoned road, the trail turns
right just before a fenced field (0.9 mi.) and follows the
fence line along the edge of the woods. The trail keeps to
the right of a fenced horse pasture and barn. It then
crosses a small footbridge just above the house and traverses a field to Allen Hill Road, a gravel-surfaced town
road. Turning left, it follows this road to its intersection
with Broad Brook Road (1.1 mi.) by the East Barnard
Cemetery.

The Amity Pond Trail turns left onto Broad Brook
Road and crosses the Broad Brook on a concrete bridge
(1.4 mi.). Immediately after this bridge, it turns off the
town road to the left, fords the brook (be prepared for wet

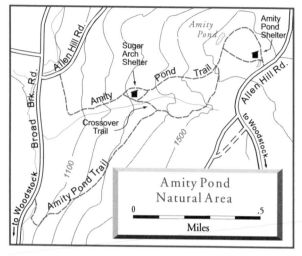

Amity Pond
Natural Area

0 ————————— .5

Miles

feet), and follows an old woods road along Broad Brook. The trail then makes a sharp left turn (1.5 mi.), begins a winding climb, and crosses a small brook (1.7 mi.). Near an old moss-covered stonewall (2.0 mi.), it makes another sharp left turn to parallel the orange-marked boundary line and crosses a small drainage on a log bridge.

Ascending, the Amity Pond Trail reaches a junction on the left with the south end of the Crossover Trail (2.2 mi.), leading from Sugar Arch Shelter, then crosses a power line (2.4 mi.). The trail drops down to a brook crossing (2.5 mi.) and, after climbing steadily a short distance, leaves the woods to continue uphill through a field. The trail quickly reaches the junction marking the beginning of the loop and turns right to pass Amity Pond again before returning to the parking area (2.9 mi.).

• • • • • • • • • • • • • • • • •

GILE MOUNTAIN

Distance: 0.7 mi. (1.1 km)
Elevation Change: 390 ft. ascent
Hiking Time: ½ hr. (reverse 20 min.)

Located in a municipal forest in the northwest corner of the town of Norwich, Gile Mtn. (USGS South Strafford) boasts a well-maintained fire tower on its summit (1,873 ft.), from which there are panoramic views. An easy ascent along an obvious, well-trodden trail makes this a good hike for young children.

To the Trail: From the junction in the village of Norwich where U.S. 5 turns east off Main Street (0.0 mi.), continue north along Main Street a short distance before turning left on Turnpike Road (0.6 mi.). Continue past the end of the pavement (2.5 mi.) and ascend through a sheltered valley to the signed parking area on the left (5.2 mi.), just before a farmhouse on the right.

Description: From the back of the parking lot (0.0 mi.), the trail follows the tower trail sign to a logging road (0.1 mi.) on the left, which it follows along blue blazes. The trail soon leaves the road right (0.2 mi.), crosses a log bridge, and ascends to cross an open swath beneath a power line (0.3 mi.) where there is a fine view of the neighboring New Hampshire hills. Entering the woods again at a stand of old birches, the trail follows easy switchbacks to ascend to a cabin (0.7 mi.), just below the fire tower where from the observation platform there are spectacular views in all directions. To the east, over the nearby Connecticut River Valley, lie the White Mountains, while Mt. Ascutney's bulk dominates the southern horizon. To the west, the spine of the Green Mountains is visible in the distance.

●●●●●●●●●●●●●●●

THE PALISADES

Distance: 1.1 mi. (1.8 km)
Elevation Change: 350 ft. ascent
Hiking Time: ½ hr. either direction

Rising dramatically west of the Connecticut River, the Palisades are a series of cliffs along the east side of Morey Mtn. A trail created by the Lake Morey Trails Association ascends to the edge of the precipice from the west. In recent years, the rocky outcrops have become a nesting site for peregrine falcons, which are legally protected from human disturbance during the breeding season. A clearly marked area near the cliff top is off-limits to hikers between March 15 and August 1. Since the ascent to the edge of the nesting area is fairly short, it is recommended this hike be reserved for the fall season when the cliff top is accessible.

TO THE TRAIL: From I-91 exit 15, a short distance west of U.S. 5, turn west onto Lake Morey Road. Turn right almost immediately at a four-way intersection, then turn right again into the parking lot of the Fairlee Fire Department across from the Lake Morey Country Club. Ample parking is available, but care should be taken to leave vehicles on the right side of the lot as far from the fire station entrance as possible.

DESCRIPTION: Although there are a few remaining yellow "Lake Morey Trails" metal squares, the trail is marked with white blazes, the first one being on one of the I-91 signposts. From the south end of the parking lot at the corner nearest the interstate (0.0 mi.), the trail goes between the chain-link fence and the I-91 exit ramp and passes to the right of several old crab apple trees before making abrupt turns left then right. Now an obvious path in the woods, the trail winds steeply for a few hundred feet, still heading north, parallel to the interstate. Passing through a mixed hardwood-softwood forest, the trail follows a fence on the left and soon arrives at a sign warning of the peregrine falcon nesting area ahead.

The trail levels off briefly (0.1 mi.), then resumes its climb, but less steeply. It passes through an opening in the fence, levels off, then ascends gradually before making jogs left, then right (0.2 mi.). Passing another trail on the left, the path crosses a seasonal stream and reaches a power line. There is no trespassing past this point during the peregrine falcon nesting season from March 15 to August 1; the area is regularly patrolled. From this cut, there are views south to Fairlee, the Connecticut River, and Mt. Ascutney. The trail continues straight across the swath cut by the power line and reenters the woods, winding along ledges to a level ridge that leads to the open area above the Palisades (0.7 mi.) where there are pastoral views of farms, church steeples, and white clapboard houses on the river at Orford, New Hampshire, and views of Mt. Cube and Smarts Mtn. to the east. The trail continues north and ends (1.1 mi.) at another partially open area with views south and east.

● ● ● ● ● ● ● ● ● ● ● ● ● ● ●

4

WRIGHT'S MOUNTAIN/DEVIL'S DEN

Distance: 1.0 mi. (1.6 km)
Elevation Change: 415 ft. ascent
Hiking Time: ¾ hr. (½ reverse)

Located in the northeast corner of Bradford, Wright's Mtn. offers good views north, west, and southwest from a rock lookout west of the summit (USGS East Corinth). Because of the efforts of the Bradford Conservation Commission and local volunteers, many improvements have recently been made to the Wright's Mtn. trail system, a 278-acre forest with scenic overlooks. A second trailhead was established off Chase Hollow Road. Parking lots and kiosks were constructed at both trailheads, and the trail network was expanded to include the cave known as Devil's Den

TO THE TRAIL: The trail begins on Wright's Mountain Road, 2.3 mi. from its junction with Vt. 25. From Vt. 25 (0.0 mi.), follow Wright's Mountain Road north. Stay on the main road past the fork intersection with Fulton Road (2.1 mi.) and park in the lot at the trailhead on the right (2.3 mi.).

ALTERNATE TRAILHEAD: From Vt. 25, take Chase Hollow Road north for 1.3 mi. Parking and the trailhead are on the left.

DESCRIPTION: WRIGHT'S MOUNTAIN TRAIL (1.6 MI.): From the Wright's Mountain Road parking area, the distance to the summit lookout via the Wright's Mountain Trail is 0.8 mi., about half the trail's total length. This north section of the Wright's Mountain Trail, as well as Sylvia's Trail and Ernie's Trail, are all unblazed woods roads, but all the junctions have signs.

Leaving the summit to the south, the newer section of the Wright's Mountain Trail is marked with yellow blazes. It shortly comes to another view of Mt. Ascutney, Winslow Ledges, and Smarts Mtn. The trail gradually levels out in hardwoods before meeting Ernie's Trail.

SYLVIA'S TRAIL (0.4 MI.): Climbing steeply at first, this trail gets easier and rejoins the Wright's Mountain Trail below the summit.

CHASE HOLLOW TRAIL (0.6 MI. IN, 0.7 MI. OUT): This yellow-blazed trail starts at the Chase Hollow Road parking area. It begins with a steep climb through the forest and a small stream crossing, following the "Best Way In" and "Best Way Out" signs. The trail follows an old logging road for a short distance before turning left and leading between a rock ledge and a stream. Crossing the stream, it arrives at the junction of Ernie's Trail and the Devil's Den Spur Trail.

DEVIL'S DEN SPUR TRAIL (0.2 MI.): The Devil's Den Spur Trail is a primitive, unblazed trail over rough terrain.

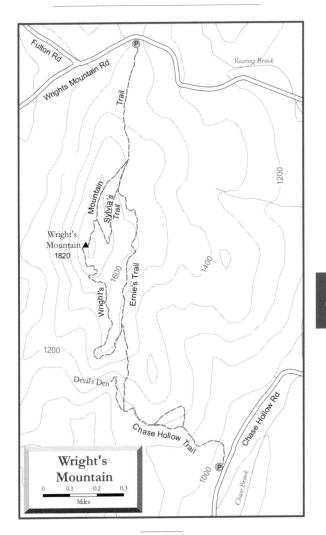

Fulton Rd

Wrights Mountain Rd

Roaring Brook

Trail

1200

Mountain

Sylvia's
Trail

Wright's
Mountain
1820

Wright's

1600

Ernie's Trail

1400

1200

Devil's Den

Chase Hollow Trail

Chase Hollow Rd

1000

Chase Brook

Wright's
Mountain

0   0.1   0.2   0.3
Miles

4

Anyone wanting to explore the two-room stand-up cave chamber should bring a flashlight.

ERNIE'S TRAIL: (0.9 mi.): Ernie's Trail switchbacks uphill from the Chase Hollow Trail, then follows an old logging road. At 0.4 mi., the trail meets the Wright's Mountain Trail, with a vernal pool just north of the intersection. From here, the trail is gradual until its intersection with Sylvia's Trail.

• • • • • • • • • • • • • • • •

PAINE MOUNTAIN

Distance: 2.8 mi. (4.5 km)
Elevation Change: 1,198 ft. ascent
Hiking Time: 2½ hr. (reverse 1½ hr.)

Paine Mtn. (2,411 ft., USGS Barre West, Brookfield, Northfield, Roxbury) is the southernmost extremity of a range of hills rising east of the Dog River Valley in the town of Northfield. The area was largely cleared of forest in the last century to provide fuel for the new Central Vermont Railway, but like much of the rest of Vermont, it has now mostly reverted to woodland. There remains much evidence of human activity, including a network of old roads and many rusted and broken pipes that once carried water west to Northfield. The ascent described, known informally as the Clark Route, follows old town roads that now form a multiuse trail system on the lands of the town of Northfield, Norwich University, and the Northfield Telephone Company. An alternate descent route is given in the description. Additional trails on the mountain, as well as the natural and cultural history of the area, are described in the *Paine Mountain Guidebook*, written by GMC member Bill Osgood. The book is available from the GMC.

TO THE TRAIL: From the common in the village of Northfield (0.0 mi.), proceed south on Vt. 12 and turn left onto Vt. 64

(2.1 mi.). Proceed eastward on Vt. 64, ascending to reach an intersection on the left with Barrows Road (3.4 mi.). Turning north onto this road and ignoring a dead-end fork to the left, there is parking for eight to ten vehicles along the roadside at the junction. Note: Although it is tempting to drive on Barrows Road beyond this point, there is no parking further along the road and cars will be towed.

DESCRIPTION: From the parking area (0.0 mi.), the route follows Barrows Road easterly to a junction near a house (0.3 mi.) where an old town road forks left and the Barrows Road curves right. Bearing left along the eroded roadway, the unblazed but obvious trail ascends north, eventually reaching an open meadow (0.9 mi.) where there are views back down the Robinson Brook Valley. The Clark family, for whom this route is named, formerly operated a hill farm in this area.

While still in the meadow, the trail crosses a snowmobile trail. Bearing left out of the meadow and climbing steeply at first, the trail continues on more moderate grades through a dense growth of young sugar maple trees. Slightly farther along, the trail passes through an old apple orchard and descends to a brook crossing (1.7 mi.) before reaching a conifer plantation established in the 1930s as part of the Norwich Town Forest. At a fork (1.8 mi.), the trail bears right and continues uphill, then follows a sharp switchback, which veers south. After the grade moderates, the trail reaches another junction (2.3 mi.). Here, it turns sharply left and ascends a spur to a bronze survey marker at the wooded summit (2.8 mi.) of Paine Mtn. At the summit, evidence of the severe damage caused by the 1998 ice storm is apparent. The storm broke off the crowns of the trees, opening the understory to sunlight.

ALTERNATE RETURN ROUTE: A slightly different route offers substantial views of the two mountain ranges to the west. At the junction below the summit (0.0 mi.), proceed straight, past the trail on the right used for the ascent. Known informally as the Hawk Watch Trail, this route

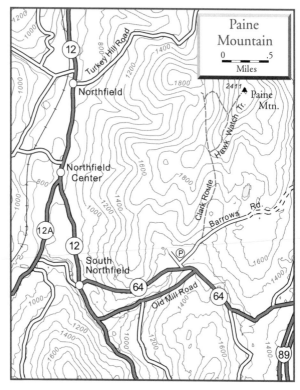

soon reaches a semiopen pasture with a shelter (0.1 mi.) where there are excellent views west over the Dog River Valley. By moving about the clearing, it is possible to gain views over the closer third range of the Green Mountains (known as the Northfield Mountains south of the Winooski River) to the more distant main range of the Green Mountains. The view extends almost unbroken from Camel's Hump south to Lincoln Gap, with Killington and Pico visible to the southwest. To the south, stands the monadnock of Mt. Ascutney. Hawk watches are staged in this clearing in spring and fall, as Paine Mtn. is in the line of a major migratory route. A footpath, indistinct at times, leads south from the clearing, then veers west through a young hardwood forest and raspberry canes to rejoin the Clark Route (0.4 mi.) in the old apple orchard described in the ascent route.

• • • • • • • • • • • • • • • •

SPRUCE MOUNTAIN

HIKING TIME: 2.2 mi. (3.5 km)
ELEVATION CHANGE: 1,180 ft. ascent
HIKING TIME: 1¾ hr. (reverse 1 hr.)

Located in the town of Plainfield, the summit of Spruce Mtn. (3,037 ft., USGS Barre East, Knox Mtn.) is the site of a preserved fire tower, from which there is a panoramic view of north central Vermont and western New Hampshire. The occasionally blue-blazed but obvious trail to the summit is partly in the L. R. Jones State Forest and partly in Groton State Forest.

TO THE TRAIL: From its junction with Vt. 110 in East Barre, follow U.S. 302 east 1.1 mi. and turn north onto Reservoir Road (0.0 mi., called Brook Road when it enters Plainfield). After reaching the end of the pavement (4.9 mi.), continue to a junction (5.6 mi.) and turn right onto East Hill Road. Proceed uphill and turn right again onto Spruce Mountain Road (6.5 mi.). At the next junction (6.8 mi.), turn left as indicated by signs reading "Summit Trail ½ M" and follow the narrow and winding road to a parking area at the start of the trail (7.5 mi.).

DESCRIPTION: From the parking area, the trail passes through a set of gateposts before following a wide woods road southeast. It follows the old road on easy grades for

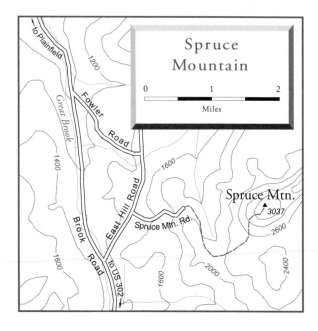

some distance before beginning a gradual ascent, offering occasional views to the summit tower on the left. Gradually swinging east, the trail reaches the end of the well-defined road at a clearing (1.0 mi.). Continuing straight ahead, it passes through several wet areas where long-ago fire tower lookouts placed steppingstones and built up the footbed with gravel fill. The trail soon crosses a small stream bridged by a pair of cut logs (1.3 mi.) before continuing along more raised trail bed.

Following a northeasterly course in deep woods, the trail begins a moderately steep climb (1.5 mi.), bearing north through spruce forest. Passing two large boulders split from the bedrock (1.6 mi.), the trail climbs somewhat less steeply over granite slabs for some distance. Resuming a steady ascent (1.9 mi.), it passes through a fern-filled clearing, then continues on easier grades to the summit and the tower (2.2 mi.). The cellar hole from the care-taker's cabin is nearby.

Spruce Mtn. was first used as a fire lookout in about 1919, when a summit trail, cabin, telephone line, and tower were built. In 1931, the original tower was replaced, then in 1943 to 1944, the tower from Bellevue Hill in St. Albans was transferred to the summit. The site was aban-doned as a fire lookout in 1974. In 1994, the tower was placed on the National Historic Lookout Register.

●●●●●●●●●●●●●●●●

GROTON STATE FOREST

With 25,000 acres, Groton State Forest is the second-largest contiguous block of land owned by the state of Vermont. Located in the towns of Groton, Peacham, Marshfield, Orange, and Topsham (USGS Groton, Barnet, Marshfield), the forest is generally bounded on the north by U.S. 2, north of Marshfield, and on the south by U.S. 302, west of Groton. Vt. 232 bisects it. Along this road lie five state park campgrounds; from south to north, they are Ricker, Stillwater, Big Deer, Kettle Pond, and New Discov-ery. Day-use facilities are available on Lake Groton.

The campgrounds and many of the area's bodies of water and mountains are linked by a network of hiking and multiuse trails, which are shown in the Department of Forests, Parks and Recreation's "Groton State Forest Guide," available free at various contact stations. A second department pamphlet, the "Groton State Forest History Guide," may be obtained in season at the Groton Nature Center, located near the north end of Lake Groton on the Boulder Beach access road. Groton's geology is more sim-ilar to the White Mountains of New Hampshire than

4

Vermont's Green Mountains. The exposed granite bedrock makes for a rocky, rough topography.

Logging is common in Groton State Forest and may disrupt portions of the trail system, so hikers should obtain current trail information from park personnel. In some cases, trees have been marked for cutting with blue paint. Be especially careful to follow the trail in these areas. Primitive camping is allowed within designated areas of the forest, including many backcountry lean-tos. Check with park personnel before camping away from the established campgrounds.

BIG DEER MOUNTAIN

Distance: 1.4 mi. (2.3 km)
Elevation Change: 380 ft. ascent
Hiking Time: 50 min. (reverse 40 min.)

TO THE TRAIL: The New Discovery Campground is on the east side of Vt. 232, 4.4 mi. south of its junction with U.S. 2 east of Marshfield. From the entrance to the campground, follow the access road 0.2 mi. to a junction at Campsite 40 and bear left. Go through a gate toward Peacham Pond. Limited roadside parking is available just before and after the trailhead, which is on the right side of the road, 0.5 mi. from the campground entrance.

DESCRIPTION: Leaving the road (0.0 mi.), the blue-blazed Big Deer Mountain Trail descends through a red pine plantation and a logged area to a CCC-era lean-to (0.7 mi.). Passing left of the shelter, the trail then ascends gently to a junction (1.1 mi.) with the Osmore Pond/Big Deer Mountain Trail. Bearing left at the junction, the trail begins a steeper ascent to reach the crest of Big Deer Mtn. (1,992 ft.) (1.3 mi.), then follows the ridge on gentle grades among giant boulders to reach a rock outcrop with a stunning view south to Lake Groton (1.4 mi.).

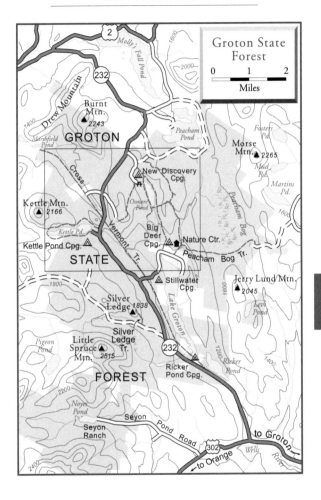

Groton State
Forest

0   1   2
Miles

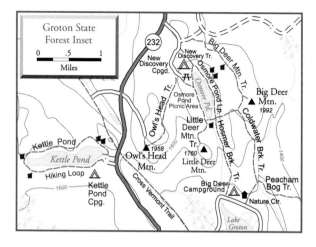

NEW DISCOVERY/OSMORE POND TRAIL

TO THE TRAIL: From the entrance to the New Discovery Campground where some parking is available, follow the access road 0.2 mi. to a junction.

DESCRIPTION: The blue-blazed New Discovery/Osmore Pond Trail begins at the junction left of the bathhouse and descends steadily through a spruce-fir stand to cross a logging road (0.3 mi.). The trail then passes through an old firewood cutting area before arriving at its terminus on the north shore of Osmore Pond at a junction with the Osmore Pond Hiking Loop.

OSMORE POND HIKING LOOP

Distance: 1.8 mi. (2.9 km)
Elevation Change: 150 ft. ascent
Hiking Time: 1 hr. either direction

TO THE TRAIL: This blue-blazed trail begins at the Osmore

Pond picnic shelter, accessed through the New Discovery Campground off Vt. 232.

DESCRIPTION: From the shelter (0.0 mi.), the trail descends to the shore and continues southerly through the picnic area. After following the shore for some distance and passing views across the pond to Big Deer Mtn., the trail bears away from the pond and reaches a junction on the right (0.4 mi.) with the Little Deer Trail. Continuing straight ahead, the trail first crosses the outlet of Osmore Pond on a plank bridge, passing a spur path left that leads to a shoreline lean-to. The trail then passes through a wet area on puncheon built by the Vermont Youth Conservation Corps in 1997, before reaching a four-way junction (0.5 mi.).

> **Junction:** From this junction, the Osmore Pond/Big Deer Mountain Trail leads straight ahead 1.0 mi. to a vista near the summit of Big Deer Mtn. The Hosmer Brook Trail departs right, leading about 1.3 mi. south to the Boulder Beach access road at the north end of Lake Groton.

Turning left at the junction, the Osmore Pond Loop passes through open forest for some distance before entering deep woods and passing two lean-tos (1.0 mi., 1.4 mi.). At the north end of the pond, the trail reaches a junction on the right (1.5 mi.) with the New Discovery Campground/Osmore Pond Trail before following the shoreline back to the picnic shelter (1.8 mi.).

LITTLE DEER MOUNTAIN

Distance: 0.5 mi. (0.8 km)
Elevation Change: 280 ft. ascent
Hiking Time: 25 min. (reverse 20 min.)

TO THE TRAIL: This blue-blazed trail leaves the Osmore Pond Hiking Loop, 0.4 mi. south of the picnic shelter.

DESCRIPTION: From the junction (0.0 mi.), the trail climbs easily through the woods. At a sharp left turn (0.2 mi.), it begins a steady climb to the wooded summit of Little Deer

Mtn. (1,760 ft.) (0.5 mi.). The trail then continues 50 yds. farther to a rock outcrop where there is a good view south over Lake Groton.

OSMORE POND/ BIG DEER MOUNTAIN TRAIL

Distance: 1.0 mi. (1.6 km)
Elevation Change: 510 ft. ascent
Hiking Time: ¾ hr. (reverse ½ hr.)

DESCRIPTION: Marked with blue blazes, this trail leaves a four-way junction with the Osmore Pond Hiking Loop and Hosmer Brook Trail at the south end of Osmore Pond (0.0 mi.). The trail climbs steadily to a low ridge (0.2 mi.), crosses a wet sag on puncheon, and reaches a junction on the right (0.4 mi.) with the Coldwater Brook Trail from Lake Groton. It then slabs northerly up the mountain to arrive at its terminus at a junction (0.7 mi.) with the New Discovery/Big Deer Mountain Trail. To the right, it is a short steep climb over Big Deer Mtn. to the scenic vista south of the summit (1.0 mi.).

HOSMER BROOK TRAIL

Distance: 1.3 mi. (2.1 km)
Elevation Change: 370 ft. ascent
Hiking Time: 1 hr. (reverse ½ hr.)

This trail provides a link between the Big Deer Campground at the north end of Lake Groton and Osmore Pond, near the New Discovery Campground. The southern trailhead is found on the Boulder Beach access road, which leaves the east side of Vt. 232 near the north end of Lake Groton, about 5.5 mi. north of U.S. 302 and 0.3 mi. north of the entrance to the Stillwater Campground.

TO THE TRAIL: From Vt. 232 (0.0 mi.) follow the Boulder

Beach access road east past the trailhead (1.3 mi.) to the Groton Nature Center (1.6 mi.) and parking.

DESCRIPTION: From the trailhead on the Boulder Beach access road (0.0 mi.), this blue-blazed trail bears north and gradually ascends through open forest on a woods road. Upon reaching Hosmer Brook (0.5 mi.), the trail follows its east bank upstream to a four-way junction (1.3 mi.).

> **Junction:** From this junction, the Osmore Pond/Big Deer Mountain Trail departs right and leads 1.0 mi. to a vista near the summit of Big Deer Mtn. To the left, the west branch of the Osmore Pond Hiking Loop leads about 0.5 mi. to the Osmore Pond Picnic Area. Straight ahead, the east branch of this trail leads 1.3 mi. around the north end of the pond to reach the same spot.

COLDWATER BROOK TRAIL

Distance: 2.0 mi. (3.2 km)
Elevation Change: 489 ft. ascent
Hiking Time: 1¼ hr. (reverse 1 hr.)

4

This trail follows Coldwater Brook north and links the north end of Lake Groton and the south end of Osmore Pond near Big Deer Mtn. The trailhead is at the Groton Nature Center.

TO THE TRAIL: The Groton Nature Center is a short distance past Big Deer Campground on the Boulder Beach access road, which leaves Vt. 232 near the north end of Lake Groton, about 5.5 mi. north of U.S. 302. The area provides access to the Coldwater Brook Trail, Hosmer Brook Trail, and Peacham Bog Trail. In addition, the center has two short loop trails, the 0.6-mi. Nature Trail and the 0.9-mi. Little Loop Trail.

DESCRIPTION: The blue-blazed Coldwater Brook Trail initially coincides with the Peacham Bog Trail, beginning at a signpost in the northeast corner of the nature center parking lot (0.0 mi.). At a junction (0.4 mi.), the Peacham

Bog Trail bears right, while the Coldwater Brook Trail bears left to slab around a low knoll before passing two large boulders on the left (0.6 mi.). The trail ascends gradually through several boggy areas (0.7 mi.) and crosses a stream before reaching the stonework of an old sawmill (1.1 mi.), one of several that once used the waters of Coldwater Brook.

From the sawmill site, the trail ascends to a junction (1.2 mi.) where an unmaintained spur leads right. Bearing left at the sign for Big Deer Mtn. and ascending on easy grades over occasional wet areas and rough footing, the trail reaches its terminus (2.0 mi.) on the Osmore Pond/ Big Deer Mountain Trail.

Junction: To the right, the Osmore Pond/Big Deer Mountain Trail leads about 0.6 mi. to a vista near the summit of Big Deer Mtn., while to the left, it leads 0.4 mi. to a junction with the Hosmer Brook Trail. By this trail, it is 1.3 mi. south to the Boulder Beach access road and a short distance east to the nature center.

OWL'S HEAD MOUNTAIN

Distance: 1.9 mi. (3.1 km)
Elevation Change: 360 ft. ascent
Hiking Time: 1¼ hr. (reverse 1 hr.)

Although not high, this mountain with its rocky summit offers outstanding panoramic views. A 1.9-mi. foot trail leads to the summit, while a 1.0-mi. auto road, open to cars only in summer, leads to a parking area and summit trail 0.25 mi. from the top. A drive up the road and the short walk to the summit make a perfect hike for children. Alternatively, a loop a little longer than 4.5 mi. may be hiked using the trail described, the auto road, and a 1.5-mi. walk on Vt. 232 and the trailhead access road.

TO THE TRAIL: This blue-blazed trail begins on the road to the Osmore Pond picnic shelter. From the entrance to the New Discovery Campground on Vt. 232, continue south on the highway a short distance to the second left-hand turn. Follow the dirt road east, bearing right at a fork after 0.25 mi., before reaching the trailhead on the right, about 0.5 mi. from Vt. 232. Limited roadside parking is available.

DESCRIPTION: From the access road (0.0 mi.), the trail follows an old road that links the picnic shelter with the maintenance area to the north and turns left (0.1 mi.) into the woods just before the maintenance area. The trail then follows a level path under a power line (0.3 mi.) before starting a gentle ascent. Climbing steadily, then more steeply to attain the ridgeline (1.2 mi.), the trail passes over a rock ledge, descends west into a small dip, then ascends to the Owl's Head picnic area parking lot (1.6 mi.). The trail climbs rock stairs on steep terrain to the open summit (1,958 ft.) (1.9 mi.) with its airy stone shelter. From the summit, there are good views of Lake Groton, Kettle Pond, the White Mountains, and the Green Mountains. No camping is allowed on Owl's Head.

KETTLE POND HIKING LOOP

Distance: 3.2 mi. (5.2 km)
Elevation Change: minor
Hiking Time: 1½ hr. either direction

TO THE TRAIL: This trail begins at the large Kettle Pond parking area on the west side of Vt. 232, 7.1 mi. north of U.S. 302 and 4.0 mi. south of U.S. 2. Although there is a sign for the parking area, no sign indicates the presence of the trailhead.

DESCRIPTION: This blue-blazed trail begins at the northwest corner of the parking lot (0.0 mi.). Following a level grade, it divides (0.2 mi.) a short distance before reaching the pond. At the junction, a spur left leads to the pond's edge. Bearing right at the junction, the trail follows the north side of the pond, passes two lean-tos, and continues through the woods to a left turn (0.5 mi.). It then passes through a wet area to the shore where it continues along the shoreline, traversing an area with large boulders at the site of an old camp (0.8 mi.) and former lean-to (1.2 mi.).

The trail then bears right and shortly passes another lean-to (1.7 mi.). Circling the west end of Kettle Pond, it traverses some wet and rocky areas. After passing a private camp, the trail climbs over and around some large boulders to another lean-to. The trail remains near the shoreline for a distance, before reaching its terminus at the Kettle Pond Group Camping Area (3.0 mi.). Straight ahead via the access road, it is a short distance back to Vt. 232, then a short distance north to the Kettle Pond parking area.

PEACHAM BOG

Distance: 2.8 mi. (4.5 km)
Elevation Change: 433 ft. ascent
Hiking Time: 1 hr. 40 min. (reverse 1 hr. 25 min.)

The Peacham Bog natural area contains a 125-acre peat bog, the second largest in the state and one of two documented raised (or domed) bogs in Vermont. Because of the fragile bog environment, to say nothing of the possibility of getting lost, it is important to remain on the trail in the bog. Follow directions to the Groton Nature Center described in the Coldwater Brook Trail on page 215.

DESCRIPTION: Marked with blue blazes, the Peacham Bog Trail begins at a signpost in the northeast corner of the nature center parking area and coincides with the Coldwater Brook Trail for a short distance. From the sign (0.0 mi.), the trail climbs a steep embankment, then descends gradually through the woods to a junction (0.4 mi.) where the Coldwater Brook Trail departs left.

Bearing right at the junction, the Peacham Bog Trail soon crosses Coldwater Brook on a bridge, before following it downstream a short distance. Resuming an easterly direction, the trail begins an easy ascent, crosses a logging road (0.7 mi.), and continues along on variously rocky and wet footing. After crossing a small stream (1.5 mi.) and cresting a low ridge, the trail descends on easy grades into a shallow sag (2.4 mi.). It then passes by a leg of the bog, which has been dammed by beavers (2.6 mi.), and returns to the woods briefly before reaching the bog itself (2.8 mi.). The trail crosses the southeast corner of the bog on a boardwalk and bridge for about 250 yds. before entering the woods again and reaching its terminus at a junction with a multipurpose trail. This trail, not maintained for hiking, leads about 1.5 mi. east to exit Groton State Forest and ends on a public road near Martin's Pond, south of the hamlet of Green Bay.

SILVER LEDGE TRAIL

Distance: 0.6 mi. (0.9 km)
Elevation Change: 500 ft. ascent
Hiking Time: ¾ hr. (reverse ½ hr.)

Marked with blue blazes, the trail begins on a logging road marked Beaver Brook Road Trail that leaves the west side of Vt. 232, 1.0 mi. north of the Ricker Pond Camping Area and 3.5 mi. south of the Kettle Pond parking area. The trailhead is on the right side of the logging road, 0.7 mi. from Vt. 232. A grassy pull-off can accommodate two vehicles, while additional parking is available along the roadside.

DESCRIPTION: From the logging road (0.0 mi.), the Silver Ledge Trail bears right into the woods, quickly crosses Beaver Brook, then begins a winding climb through a mixed hardwood-softwood forest. After passing a ledge (0.5 mi.) with a vista of Lake Groton and with the White Mountains in the distance, the trail quickly reaches the summit of Silver Ledge (1,838 ft.) (0.6 mi.). Two large boulders are found nearby, and there is a limited view of Lake Groton through the trees.

• • • • • • • • • • • • • • • •

CROSS VERMONT TRAIL

When completed, the Cross Vermont Trail (CVT) will be Vermont's first west-to-east, long-distance, multiuse trail—spanning 75 mi. from Lake Champlain in Burlington to the Connecticut River in Wells River. Trail founders envision the trail as a safe, scenic link between villages, public places, schools, playgrounds, and state parks.

West of Montpelier, the trail will follow existing and future bike and recreation paths as well as on-road routes. Portions of the former Montpelier and Wells River Railroad bed will be used to develop the trail east of Montpelier.

The ten-year-old Cross Vermont Trail Association, a grassroots, nonprofit organization, has completed and designated 28 mi. of the trail. The three best sections for walking are outlined here. For more information, contact the Cross Vermont Trail Coordinator, c/o Cross Vermont Trail Association, 81 East Hill Road, Plainfield, Vermont 05667; georges@together.net.

EAST MONTPELIER

This signed and designated 1.6-mi. section of the CVT passes through land the Montpelier–Wells River Railroad once traveled. Walkers, cyclists, horseback riders, nordic skiers, snowshoers, and snowmobilers enjoy the trail. Trail users should yield to snowmobiles and horseback riders. The trailhead is on the east side of Vt. 14, 0.8 mi. south of its junction with U.S. 2 in East Montpelier. The trail ends at the East Montpelier/Plainfield town line where there is a gate with no trespassing signs.

GROTON STATE FOREST

This 9.2-mi. section of the CVT can be accessed from several places in Groton State Forest. Parking areas are at

Ricker Pond and Kettle Pond, found on the east and west sides of Vt. 232, respectively.

The trail is shown as a class 4 road on USGS quads and in *DeLorme's Vermont Atlas & Gazetteer*. The signed and designated segment of the trail reverts to private ownership at either end of the state forest where the boundaries are clearly marked. Walkers, cyclists, horseback riders, nordic skiers, snowshoers, and snowmobilers enjoy the trail. During winter, trail users should yield to snowmobiles; during summer, trail users should yield to horseback riders.

As it travels through the state forest, the trail passes by historic railroad markers, through a boreal-transitional forest, and along glacial ponds and lakes, including Marshfield Pond, Kettle Pond, Lake Groton, and Ricker Pond. The Lake Groton Nature Center can be accessed via a side road. One of the highlights of the trail is a view of Big Deer Mtn. with its sheer granite cliffs.

Southeast of the state forest boundary, the trail continues as a bicycling route south on Vt. 232, then east on U.S. 302. After passing the Upper Valley Grill, the trail leaves the highway at Little Italy Road where the route rejoins the old rail bed. For the next 3.0 mi., the Cross Vermont Trail passes through a mixed spruce, birch, and beech forest, with views of farms, ponds, and bogs. The route ends at the Mills Memorial Ballfield in South Ryegate where there is ample parking.

WELLS RIVER

Newbury and Wells River host 1.75 mi. of the CVT. Two points on U.S. 302 provide access to the trail. A western (recommended) trailhead with ample parking is on the Ryegate-Newbury town line on the north side of U.S. 302, next to the Curious Cow, Too gift shop. Eastern access is just west of the state fishing access where the Wells River comes closest to U.S. 302.

The Wells River CVT is remarkably diverse along its short length, passing through a large white pine and eastern hemlock stand, as well as wetlands and bogs with viewing benches and wildlife habitat boxes. The trail segment is divided in the middle by the I-91 bridge over the Wells River. Travel under the bridge is rough going (similar to a steep talus slope), but a path suitable for bicycles is scheduled for construction.

Two trails in the area intersect with the CVT. West of the I-91 bridge is the Boltonville Nature Trail, approximately 1.0 mi. long. It explores the upland slopes and riparian floodplain of the Wells River. This trail makes a junction with the CVT at two points from the north. East of the I-91 bridge is the Blue Mountain Nature Trail, which is also approximately 1.0 mi. long and joins the CVT from the north. This trail passes through upland hemlock and spruce-fir forest and offers beautiful views of the Wells River from cliffs and ledges.

• • • • • • • • • • • • • • • •

MOUNT CUSHMAN

Distance: 2.3 mi. (3.7 km)
Elevation Change: 1,254 ft. ascent
Hiking Time: 1½ hr. (reverse 1 hr.)

This hike follows a class 4 road built through the saddle between Rochester Mtn. and Mt. Cushman, which both lie in the town of Rochester. It leads along a ridge to the former location of a fire tower near the summit of 2,750-ft. Mt. Cushman. Clearings along the route offer views both east toward Randolph and the Upper Connecticut River Valley and west toward the spine of the Green Mountains.

TO THE TRAIL: From Exit 4 of I-89 (0.0 mi.), take Vt. 66 West down the hill to Randolph. Turn left on Vt. 12 South,

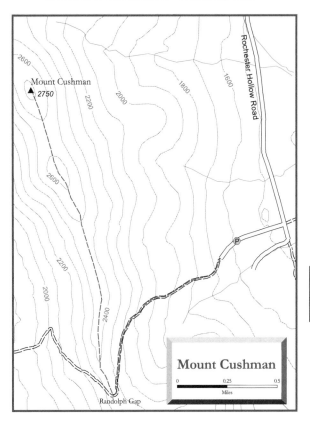

Main Street (2.6 mi.), then right on School Street (2.7 mi.). At a Y intersection (3.4 mi.), bear left and go over the railroad tracks. Continue on Thayer Brook Road to a T intersection (7.4 mi.). Turn left on Rochester Hollow Road and continue to a four-way intersection (10.3 mi.), marked with a VAST trail sign on the left. At this junction, turn right and continue 0.2 mi. to the end of the road and the trailhead where there is parking for several vehicles. The road from the VAST sign to the trailhead is not plowed in winter and is used by snowmobiles. Limited winter parking is available along Rochester Hollow Road.

DESCRIPTION: From the parking area (0.0), the trail follows the class 4 road until reaching the height of land (0.8 mi.) where there is an unmarked but obvious four-way intersection. The trail to the left leads to the summit of Rochester Mtn. At the intersection, take the woods road right; this runs along the ridge to Mt. Cushman. The road comes to a clearing with views east (1.9 mi). The cement footings of the former fire tower can still be seen. Past this point, the trail continues to the summit (2.3 mi.) and a west-facing clearing.

• • • • • • • • • • • • • • • •

BALD TOP MOUNTAIN VIA CROSS RIVENDELL TRAIL

Distance: 3.3 mi. (5.3 km)
Elevation Change: 1,350 ft. ascent
Hiking Time: 3 hr. (reverse 2 hr.)

The Cross Rivendell Trail is a project of the Rivendell Interstate School District and community members from the four towns of Rivendell (Vershire, West Fairlee, and Fairlee, Vermont, and Orford, New Hampshire.) The trail, which will span the four towns from Flagpole Hill in Vershire to Mt. Cube in Orford, is largely complete, though the section on the west side of Bald Top is not expected to be finished until 2007. For more information, please contact the Rivendell Trails Association, P.O. Box 202, Fairlee, Vermont 05045.

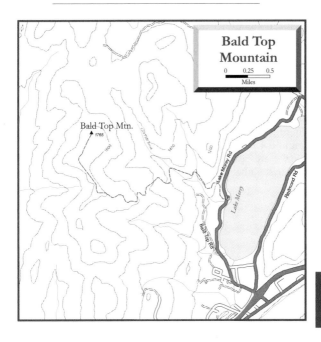

Bald Top Mountain

0   0.25   0.5
Miles

Bald Top Mtn.
▲ 1765

4

TO THE TRAIL: From exit 15 of I-91 in Fairlee, turn west on Lake Morey Westside Road. Trailhead parking is at the Lake Morey boat ramp approximately 1.4 mi. from I-91.

DESCRIPTION: The blue-blazed trail begins across the road from the parking area and turns right at the signboard (0.0) to climb moderately. At 0.3 mi., it reaches the top of the gravel pit where there is a view and a junction with the Glen Falls Trail on the left before passing above Glen Falls Gorge. This is a scenic, but very steep trail.

At 0.5 mi., the Echo Mountain Trail leaves right. The main trail crosses a stream, then the Howdy's Trail (0.7 mi.).

It bears right on Bald Top Road (0.9 mi.), then leaves the road left on a woods road. At 1.1 mi., it turns left onto a trail; a private driveway continues ahead. The Cross Rivendell Trail ascends past a viewpoint at the ridge crest.

At 1.6 mi., the trail crosses a woods road and passes through the "hurricane (1938) area." At 2.3 mi., it bears right on the Bald Top Trail, which is a woods road. Following the ridge, it turns right at two intersections, reaching the summit clearing at 3.2 mi. The 1,776-ft. summit is right 0.1 mi. farther. Many trails leave the summit, and the views are spectacular in all directions. To the east are Smarts, Cube, and Moosilauke Mtns., to name a few.

Northwest Vermont

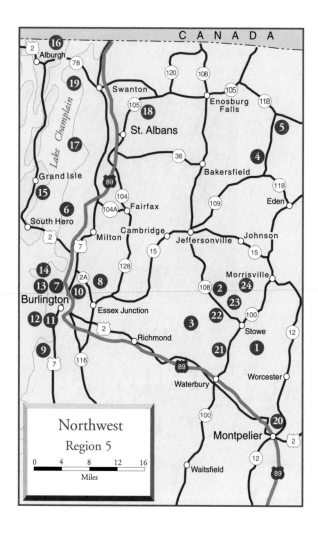

CANADA

2 Alburgh
16
78
19
Swanton
120
108
105
105
18
Enosburg
Falls
118
St. Albans
5
36
4
Bakersfield
17
118
Lake Champlain
89
Eden
104
109
Grand Isle
104A Fairfax
15
6
Johnson
South Hero
Cambridge
Jeffersonville
15
2
Milton
7
15
128
Morrisville
14
2A
24
13 7 8
108 2
10
23
Burlington
3
22
Essex Junction
100
12 11
2
21
Stowe
1
Richmond
9
12
7
116
89
Waterbury
Worcester
100
20
Northwest
Montpelier
Region 5
2
0   4   8   12   16
Miles
12
Waitsfield
89

Region 5
Northwest Vermont

This region is a land of contrasts, featuring Lake Champlain in the west and the Worcester Range in the east. Lake Champlain, with its scenic shoreline and islands, reaches its greatest width in northern Vermont. Along or near the shore are numerous low hills where fossil remains and traces of old shorelines are reminders of glacial times when a deeper and wider Lake Champlain was an arm of an inland sea. Farther east, along the valley floor, is a fragmented chain of low mountains, which were once part of the Green Mountains. To the south, in Addison County, these hills become more organized and form the first range of the Green Mountains.

The northern Green Mountains run south to north near the eastern margin of the region. In approximately 20 mi., they rise from their lowest point (326 ft.) at a water gap cut by the Winooski River to their highest elevation (4,395 ft.) at the Chin of Mt. Mansfield. In the northern part of the region, the main range continues from the Lamoille River northward into Quebec, becoming the Sutton Mountains. A significant subrange, called the Cold Hollow Mountains, parallels the main range on the west from the Waterville area northward for several miles.

The third range of the Green Mountains lies east of Vt. 100. After originating in the Sherburne-Stockbridge area, the range is known as the Northfield Mountains south of the Winooski River, continues as the Worcester Mountain Range north of the Winooski, and is known as the Lowell Mountains north of the Lamoille River.

WORCESTER MOUNTAINS

The Worcester Mountain Range is a prominent ridge rising east of the main range of the Green Mountains. Geographically, it is the third range of the Green Mountains (USGS Montpelier, Middlesex, Stowe, Mt. Worcester, Morrisville). Of the dozen or so prominent peaks in the range, Mt. Hunger (3,586 ft.) is the most conspicuous and best known—perhaps because of its bald south summit. However, the highest point (3,642 ft.) is a nameless peak sometimes referred to as Mt. Putnam, about 2.8 mi. north of Mt. Hunger's south summit.

From White Rock Mtn. north, much of the range is included in Putnam State Forest, while the northernmost peak, Elmore Mtn., is in Elmore State Park. The Department of Forests, Parks and Recreation along with the Vermont Youth Conservation Corps have made major improvements and additions to the Worcester Range hiking trails in recent years, linking the Mt. Hunger summits with Stowe Pinnacle and Worcester Mtn. to the north.

Once a well-kept secret, the range now is almost as popular as the more prominent peaks in the Green Mountain Range. To minimize erosion along the fragile high-elevation terrain of the range, the Worcester Mountain Range trail system is closed by the state of Vermont between mid-April and Memorial Day.

5

ELMORE MOUNTAIN

Distance: 2.1 mi. (3.4 km)
Elevation Change: 1,450 ft. ascent
Hiking Time: 1¾ hr. (reverse 1 hr.)

Although it is one of the lowest peaks in the Worcester Mountains, Elmore Mtn. (USGS Morrisville) may offer the most varied and interesting views, due to its isolated location at the north end of the range and its commanding view of the pastoral Lamoille River valley. A trail to the summit and its well-maintained fire tower begins in Elmore State Park, which has camping and day-use facilities (including a beach for an after-hike swim), with a fee charged in season.

TO THE TRAIL: The entrance to Elmore State Park is on the west side of Vt. 12, a short distance north of the village of Lake Elmore. Enter the state park and continue straight ahead and uphill on an old CCC road. Parking for the trail is at a chained gate near a picnic shelter where the blue blazes for the trail begin.

DESCRIPTION: The trail begins on the road through the gate (0.0mi.) and ascends to the south, passing near some beaver ponds. Near the end of the road, the trail turns sharply right (0.5 mi.) at a blue arrow and sign on a tree. Following a well-worn path through open woods and climbing steadily in places, the trail reaches a grassy clearing, a short distance below the ridge (1.4 mi.). The cellar hole is from the old fire lookout's cabin. There is a good view east overlooking Lake Elmore.

To the right, on the west side of the clearing, the trail begins a steep and winding climb over rocks and ledges, soon reaching a level area and junction where, on the right, the Balanced Rock Trail leaves to the north. To the left, the Elmore Mountain Trail continues about 100 ft. to the old fire tower on the summit (2,608 ft.) (1.6 mi.).

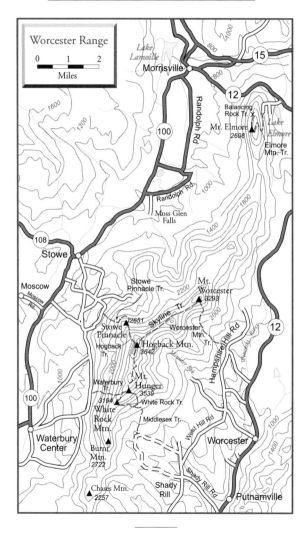

Worcester Range

0   1   2
Miles

Lake
Lamoille

Morrisville

15

12

1600

100

1200

Balancing
Rock Tr. X

Mt. Elmore
2608

Lake
Elmore

Elmore
Mtn. Tr.

Randolph Rd

Randolph Rd

Moss Glen
Falls

1000

1400

1800

108

Stowe

Moscow

Moscow
Rd

Stowe
Pinnacle Tr.

2200

Mt.
Worcester
3293

2000

Skyline Tr.

2651

Stowe
Pinnacle

Worcester
Mtn.
Tr.

12

Hogback
Tr.

Hogback Mtn.
3642

Hampshire Hill Rd

Waterbury Tr.

Mt.
Hunger
3539

3194

White
Rock
Mtn.

White Rock Tr.

Middlesex Tr.

West Hill Rd

Worcester

100

Waterbury
Center

Burnt
Mtn.
2722

Chases Mtn.
2257

Shady
Rill

Shady Rill Rd

Puthamville

5

From the tower or, to a lesser extent, from the open rocks to the south, there are impressive views of the main range of the Green Mountains from the Jay Peak area south to the Lincoln Ridge. The high ridge of the Worcester Range may be seen extending southward, with Waterbury Reservoir lying in the valley to the west. To the north lies the Lamoille River Valley; Burke Mtn. and various peaks in the Northeast Kingdom may be seen to the east.

A fire lookout station was established atop Elmore Mtn. in 1938 to 1940, with the construction of a telephone line, cabin, and the existing 60-ft. enclosed cab Aermotor steel tower. The station remained active until 1974. In 1983, the lookout's cabin fell victim to arson. The tower was repaired and repainted in 1987 and added to the National Historic Lookout Register in 1995.

BALANCED ROCK TRAIL

DESCRIPTION: The blue-blazed Balanced Rock Trail begins at a junction with the Elmore Mountain Trail just north of the Elmore Mtn. fire tower. From the junction (0.0 mi.), the trail follows easy grades just east of the ridgeline to a cleared view east (0.1 mi.). Continuing in the woods for some distance, the trail crosses to the west side of the ridge (0.3 mi.) and reaches open rock (0.4 mi.), where there is an excellent view of the Stowe Valley and the Mt. Mansfield area. Quickly returning to the east side of the ridge, the trail descends through the woods to another vantage point overlooking Lake Elmore. The trail continues a short distance further to the cigar-shaped Balanced Rock (0.5 mi.), a boulder left perched on the ridge by a long-ago glacier.

STOWE PINNACLE

STOWE PINNACLE TRAIL

Distance: 1.4 mi. (2.3 km)
Elevation Change: 1,520 ft. ascent
Hiking Time: 1½ hr. (reverse 1 hr.)

From this prominent spur (2,651 ft.) on the northwest side of Hogback Mtn. (USGS Stowe), there are excellent views of Mt. Mansfield and other peaks in the main range of the Green Mountains, as well as of the Stowe Valley. The trail also provides links to the Hogback Trail, which ascends to the ridge of the Worcester Range.

TO THE TRAIL: From Vt. 100, about 1.5 mi. south of the village of Stowe and 8.1 mi. from I-89, turn east on Gold Brook Road just north and opposite the Nichols Farm Lodge and Gold Brook Campground (0.0 mi.). Bear left at the first fork (0.3 mi.) and follow Gold Brook upstream through an intersection at Covered Bridge Road (1.2 mi.). Continue on the road to a T intersection (1.9 mi.), and turn right on Upper Hollow Road. Continue to a small parking area on the left (2.5 mi.) and the signed trailhead.

DESCRIPTION: From the rear of the parking area (0.0 mi.), the blue-blazed and well-worn trail passes from an abandoned pasture into a mixed hardwood forest and crosses a stream (0.5 mi.). It begins a steeper climb over a series of wide switchbacks before reaching a junction, from which an unmarked spur trail leads left for 100 ft. to a ledge and view of the valley below. Continuing straight at the junction, the trail reaches a notch just below Stowe Pinnacle (0.9 mi.), then follows the contour of the mountain to the south side of the summit. Here, the trail reaches a junction with the Hogback Trail (description follows), which departs left to ascend 1.0 mi. to the Skyline Trail and the ridgeline of the Worcester Range. Continuing to the right on easy grades over rocky outcrops and through scrub growth, the Stowe Pinnacle Trail reaches the open summit (1.4 mi.).

5

HOGBACK TRAIL

Distance: 1.0 mi. (1.6 km)
Elevation Change: 920 ft. ascent
Hiking Time: ¾ hr. (reverse ½ hr.)

Originally, this blue-blazed trail was the northern leg of the Skyline Trail until the lengthy ridge-top section from Hogback Mtn. north to Mt. Worcester was completed. The trail provides access to the ridgeline from the northwest.a signed junction on the Stowe Pinnacle Trail, about 1.0 mi. from the Stowe Pinnacle trailhead on Upper Hollow Road (page 235).

TO THE TRAIL: The Hogback Trail starts at a signed junction on the Stowe Pinnacle Trail, about 1.0 mi. from the Stowe Pinnacle trailhead on Upper Hollow Road (page 235).

DESCRIPTION: The Hogback Trail departs the junction (0.0 mi.) southeast, passing through stands of hemlock and large birch to make a relatively flat approach to the high northwestern flank of Hogback Mtn. The trail then makes a steep ascent, using many switchbacks that wind between large trees and scrambles across ledges to eventually level out in a spruce-fir transition zone atop a western spur of the mountain (0.5 mi.). Resuming a steep ascent over the rocks, the trail passes limited views toward Mt. Mansfield before reaching the summit of Hogback Mtn. (0.9 mi.) and its terminus at a signed junction with the Skyline Trail (1.0 m.). From the junction, it is about 3.0 mi. south to Mt. Hunger's southern summit and 6.0 mi. north to Mt. Worcester.

MOUNT HUNGER

Although the north summit (3,586 ft.) of this popular mountain (USGS Stowe) is heavily wooded, the bald south summit (3,539 ft.) is famous for its excellent views of the Green Mountains and the White Mountains. There are direct routes to the south summit from the west (Waterbury Trail) and east (Middlesex Trail) and indirect routes from the north (Skyline Trail) and south (White Rock Trail). The Worcester Trail, which ascended from the northeast, has been abandoned and is no longer included in this guide.

As a result of a long-ago forest fire, the south summit has been left an exposed and barren outcrop, similar to the higher summits found to the west in the main range of the Green Mountains. Although large black spruce and balsam fir trees engulf the north summit, these same species are dwarfed on the south summit from wind exposure, in a state known as krummholz or crooked wood.

From the summit, nearly every peak in the main range of the Green Mountains is visible, from Whiteface Mtn. in the north to Killington Peak in the south. A number of Adirondack peaks are visible to the west beyond Lake Champlain. To the east, Mt. Washington and the Presidential Range, Mt. Moosilauke, and Franconia Ridge can be seen in the distance; Burke Mtn. and Bald Mtn. are among the numerous northeast Vermont mountains nearer at hand. Directly south are most of the other peaks in the Worcester Range.

WATERBURY TRAIL

Distance: 2.2 mi. (3.5 km)
Elevation Change: 2,290 ft. ascent
Hiking Time: 2¼ hr. (reverse 1¼ hr.)

This blue-blazed trail starts north of Waterbury Center and ascends the western flank of the mountain to its south summit.

TO THE TRAIL: From I-89 exit 10, take Vt. 100 north (0.0 mi.) and turn right on Howard Avenue (2.9 mi.). Continue straight through a four-way intersection with a stop sign (3.2 mi.) to another stop sign. Turn left on Maple Street then right on Loomis Hill Road (3.4 mi.). Continue uphill. Just after the pavement ends (5.3 mi.), the road

5

forks. Bear left onto Sweet Road and continue to the signed trailhead and a parking lot on the right (6.7 mi.). Howard Avenue leaves Vt. 100, 6.8 mi. from the Vt. 100/Vt. 108 junction in Stowe.

Description: From the trailhead at the back of the parking area (0.0 mi.), the trail begins a moderate climb through a mixed hardwood forest, passing around and over interesting rock formations. It passes near a stream (0.6 mi.), then continues its climb along steep grades, aided by stretches of rock stairs. The trail enters a birch forest and levels off, following the contour of the mountain to reach a series of waterfalls (1.0 mi.). It makes a short ascent left of the falls before turning to cross the stream and continue its steep climb along a series of switchbacks. Care should be taken when walking along the exposed rock surfaces, which can be slippery in wet weather. Eventually, the trail crosses a stream on a primitive log bridge (1.8 mi.) before entering the spruce-fir transition zone where scrambles over rocky ledges become more common.

The trail reaches a signed junction (2.0 mi.) where the White Rock Trail, which leads 1.0 mi. to the summit of White Rock Mtn., branches right. From the junction, the Waterbury Trail continues straight ahead, ascending steeply on open rocks to the south summit (2.2 mi.) and a junction with the Skyline and Middlesex Trails.

MIDDLESEX TRAIL

Distance: 2.8 mi. (4.5 km)
Elevation Change: 1,900 ft. ascent
Hiking Time: 2½ hr. (reverse 1½ hr.)

Most of this blue-blazed trail follows the route of a carriage road built in 1877 by the proprietors of the Pavilion Hotel in Montpelier to transport guests up the mountain. A short trail, complete with wooden stairways to ease the steep climb over the ledges, connected the end of the road and the summit. This trail ascends the mountain from the east.

TO THE TRAIL: From Montpelier, follow Vt. 12 north past the Wrightsville Dam to a junction on the left with Shady Rill Road (0.0 mi.). Follow this road westerly up a long hill and straight through a junction, passing the Shady Rill Baptist Church (1.2 mi.). Continue to an offset four corners (2.2 mi.) and turn right on Story Road. Bear left on Chase Road (2.6 mi.) and left again on North Bear Swamp Road (3.4 mi.). After passing a private driveway through a broad field on the right (4.3 mi.) and a second small road to the right (4.7 mi.), look for a small sign pointing to a large parking area on the right (4.8 mi.).

DESCRIPTION: From the parking area (0.0 mi.), the trail leads into the woods for a short distance before joining a woods road and passing through an iron gate. It then bears left and narrows as it passes a sign-in box. Ascending on easy grades through a birch forest, the trail turns left (west) and begins a moderate ascent. It climbs to a marked junction on the left with the White Rock Trail (1.6 mi.).

> **Junction:** This trail leads to a spur to the summit cone of White Rock Mtn. and to the Waterbury Trail 0.2 mi. below the Mt. Hunger summit.

At the junction, the Middlesex Trail swings right and ascends more steeply to an outlook (2.3 mi.). Continuing at the base of a series of ledges and coming to an apparent dead end, the trail suddenly swings sharply left and up a ledge (2.5 mi.). It then climbs steeply in the open to the south summit of Mt. Hunger, following blue blazes on rocks and trees to a signed junction with the Waterbury Trail and Skyline Trail (2.8 mi.). Care should be taken to note where the trail comes out on the summit because blazing is sometimes obscure.

5

WHITE ROCK MOUNTAIN

Distance: 1.5 mi. (2.4 km)
Elevation Change: 630 ft. ascent
Hiking Time: 1 hr. (reverse ¾ hr.)

The blue-blazed Bob Kemp Trail leads to the summit of White Rock Mtn. (3,194 ft.) from both the Middlesex Trail (ascending the ridge from the east) and the Waterbury Trail (ascending from the west). Using these trails, it is possible to make a loop hike of Mt. Hunger. The White Rock Trail traverses a variety of terrain and can be challenging.

DESCRIPTION (FROM THE EAST): The White Rock Trail turns left off the Middlesex Trail 1.6. mi. from the Middlesex Trail parking lot. From the junction (0.0 mi.), the White Rock Trail ascends steeply through the woods past several views to a signed junction (0.7 mi.).

> **Junction:** To the left, a blue-blazed spur trail leads 0.15 mi. around the south side of the peak before climbing through a short steep notch to the crown of White Rock Mtn. The elevation gain from the Middlesex Trail junction to the summit of White Rock Mtn. is 570 ft.

The White Rock Trail takes the right fork and continues north, descending to a wet area (0.9 mi.). The trail then climbs around numerous boulders at or near the ridge to its terminus at the Waterbury Trail (1.5 mi.). To the right it is a steep 0.2-mi. ascent to the south summit of Mt. Hunger. From the Middlesex Trail to the summit of Mt. Hunger is 915 ft.; the White Rocks Trail ascends 915 ft.

SKYLINE TRAIL

Distance: 9.2 mi. (14.8 km)
Elevation Change: 2,058 ft. ascent
Hiking Time: 5½ hr. (reverse 6 hr.)

Constructed by the Vermont Youth Conservation Corps in the late 1980s, the Skyline Trail traverses the spine of the

Worcester Range to connect Mt. Hunger in the south with Worcester Mtn. in the north. The trail is marked with blue blazes or rock cairns in open areas, but can occasionally be obscure in the absence of a well-worn treadway. The Hogback Trail, which connects the Skyline Trail with Stowe Pinnacle, provides a shorter hiking route and access from the west side of the ridge. The trail here is described northbound from the south summit of Mt. Hunger.

DESCRIPTION: From the south summit of Mt. Hunger (0.0 mi., USGS Stowe) at the junction of the Waterbury and Middlesex Trails, the Skyline Trail leaves north at a sign and follows the exposed rock ridge. After making a brief descent east, the trail climbs to regain the ridge (0.1 mi.), soon reaching an unmarked junction where a spur trail south leads to views of Mt. Hunger as well as Camel's Hump and Mt. Abraham to the south and southwest. The trail skirts the base of a series of ledges and gradually ascends to the north summit of Mt. Hunger (0.6 mi.). Here, as well as at other points along the ridge, gaps in the canopy of balsam fir can be attributed to the cyclical succession of this species. Known as fir waves, older trees exposed to the wind are blown over, opening up space and light for saplings to take root. These gaps also provide natural vistas both east and west, the inspiration for the name of the trail.

Continuing north, the trail descends steadily into a saddle and eventually reaches an unmarked junction (1.1 mi.) where the closed Worcester Trail (not to be confused with the Worcester Mountain Trail, page 242) once ascended Mt. Hunger from the east. Bearing left, the Skyline Trail continues along moderate grades atop the ridge, winding over puncheon through wet and marshy terrain. The trail then begins an ascent, occasionally scrambling over exposed rocks, to reach a spur trail leading east to an impressive vista and an informal trail register (2.4 mi.).

From this point the trail quickly climbs through a horseshoe-shaped rock formation and continues along the

5

ridge to the highest point in the Worcester Range on the wooded summit of an unnamed mountain (3,642 ft.) (2.8 mi.). After a short descent, the trail reaches a junction (3.0 mi.) where the Hogback Trail departs left and descends about 1.0 mi. to the Stowe Pinnacle Trail. Bearing right at the junction and dropping steeply, the Skyline Trail zigzags through interesting rock formations, eventually reaching an outcropping with excellent views north (3.7 mi.).

The trail continues atop the ridge, with modest changes in elevation, before finally starting a steady climb, leading first to a false summit (3,278 ft.) (5.4 mi.), then the true summit (3,477 ft.) (6.0 mi.) of a nameless peak (USGS Mt. Worcester). The trail descends into a saddle (7.7 mi.) and, after another level section, begins a final ascent up the southwest ridge of Mt. Worcester. Gradual climbing soon gives way to a more laborious approach over boulders and rock outcroppings along the west side of the ridge before the trail reaches the exposed rock summit (9.2 mi.). Mt. Worcester is the northern terminus of the Skyline Trail; to the east, the blue-blazed Worcester Mountain Trail descends 2.5 mi. to a public road in the town of Worcester.

WORCESTER MOUNTAIN

Distance: 2.5 mi. (4.0 km)
Elevation Change: 1,970 ft. ascent
Hiking Time: 2¼ hr. (reverse 1¼ hr.)

Located in the northwest corner of the town of Worcester, the summit (3,293 ft., USGS Mount Worcester) offers good views of the Green Mountains, the Lamoille Valley, and the northern White Mountains.

To the Trail: From the town hall in Worcester (0.0 mi.), continue north on Vt. 12 a very short distance and take the first left on Minister Brook Road. Follow this road west to Hampshire Hill Road (1.5 mi.).

Turn right on Hampshire Hill Road and ascend steadily.

After passing Hancock Brook Road, which doubles back to the right (3.8 mi.), veer left into a narrow lane immediately after crossing Hancock Brook (3.9 mi.) and just before a small, red remodeled schoolhouse. Continue up the lane and bear right by a mobile home on the left (4.0 mi.), bypassing a private drive straight ahead. Continue past an overgrown road on the right to a clearing with ample parking (4.1 mi.).

DESCRIPTION: From the clearing (0.0 mi.), the blue-blazed Worcester Mountain Trail begins near the Putnam State Forest sign and follows the course of an old road northwest into the woods. Soon crossing a stream, the trail bears right at a woods road junction as indicated by a small sign, bypassing a more distinct woods road leaving left. The trail crosses two small streams, eventually assuming a course parallel to Hancock Brook for some distance. Passing a small unmarked spur to the right and bearing left (0.6 mi.), it reaches a level, grassy area. The trail crosses another stream (0.8 mi.) before beginning a moderate ascent, then makes another stream crossing (1.1 mi.) and passes between two large boulders (1.3 mi.). It makes three more stream crossings before beginning a steeper ascent toward the ridge crest.

The trail eases its ascent at a shallow sag (2.2 mi.) where it turns sharply back to the left, although a partially obstructed dead-end path continues straight ahead. Now following blue blazes mostly on the rocks, the trail begins a rough, steep ascent, at times following a beautiful quartz vein in the rocks, through thick scrub to the small open summit of Mt. Worcester (2.5 mi.). The view here includes the main range of the Green Mountains to the west with the Stowe Valley in the foreground, the southern Worcester Range, and the White Mountains in the distance to the east. From the summit, the blue-blazed Skyline Trail begins a long traverse of the high ridge of the Worcester Range, eventually ending some 9.0 mi. to the south atop Mt. Hunger.

5

MOSS GLEN FALLS

Distance: 0.4 mi. (0.6 km)
Elevation Change: 150 ft. ascent
Hiking Time: 20 min. (reverse ¼ hr.)

This attractive falls, owned by the state of Vermont, is in the northeast corner of the town of Stowe. It should not be confused with the spectacular falls of the same name in Granville Gulf in Granville, Vermont.

TO THE TRAIL: From Vt. 100, 3.1 mi. north of the intersection of Vt. 100 and Vt. 108 in Stowe village, turn right onto Randolph Road (0.0 mi.). At the next fork, turn right again (0.4 mi.) on the gravel Moss Glen Falls Road and continue to a parking lot on the left (0.9 mi.) at a bend in the road before crossing Moss Glen Brook.

DESCRIPTION: From the parking lot, the trail proceeds generally southeast through forest dominated by hemlock trees, then turns to follow the stream. The trail makes a short steep ascent to the first of several viewpoints into the bowl of the falls before continuing its climb and reaching a terminus on an old woods road (0.4 mi.). Note: Extreme caution should be exercised when viewing the falls from the adjacent ledges.

• • • • • • • • • • • • • • • •

STERLING FALLS GORGE

Distance: 3.1 mi. (5.0 km)
Elevation Change: 700 ft. ascent
Hiking Time: 2 hr. either direction

Sterling Falls Gorge (USGS Sterling Mtn.) is in the northeast corner of the town of Stowe at the former site of the High Bridge Mill (1860–1920). The gorge lies within the 1,600-acre Watson Forest purchased by the town of Stowe in 1996. Sterling Brook bisects the property, entering it at roughly 3,600 ft. in elevation, then falling nearly 2,000 ft. The elevation and geology create a bowl that is cool in summer and holds snow well into spring. In addition to the loop described here, there is an interpretive trail with a small historical display.

TO THE TRAIL: From the intersection of Vt. 100 and Vt. 108 in the village of Stowe (0.0 mi.), follow Vt. 100 north to West Hill Road (1.0 mi.). Turn left on West Hill Road and continue past Mayo Farm Road (1.5 mi.) to the junction with the Moran Loop and Sterling Valley Road (4.0 mi.). Turn left to follow the Sterling Valley Road uphill to the parking lot at the end (6.0 mi.).

DESCRIPTION: There are two trailheads at the entrance to the gorge parking lot. The nearest one is marked with blue Catamount Trail diamonds and yellow Stowe Trails and Greenways triangles. To complete the loop, follow the yellow triangles. The trail follows the brook west (0.0 mi.), climbing steadily through a beech-birch forest. With the gorge on the left, the trail bears left and right several times before reaching the top of the gorge where it turns sharply left at a series of Catamount Trail signs (2.3 mi.). Crossing the brook on steppingstones, it turns left again to begin the gradual descent back to the parking area. The trail passes through a swampy area (2.7 mi.), crosses the stream, then a VAST trail (3.0 mi.), before reaching a junction with the Catamount Trail. The loop trail continues 150 yds. to a left turn and the parking lot.

•••••••••••••••

LITTLE RIVER AREA

The Little River area of the Mount Mansfield State Forest includes more than 10,000 acres of mountainous terrain, bounded on the east by Waterbury Reservoir and on the west by Woodward and Ricker Mtns. (USGS Bolton Mtn., Waterbury). Little River State Park lies within the state forest and straddles Stevenson Brook on the west shore of the reservoir. Established in 1962, the park offers camping facilities but is not open for day-use beyond the hiking trails described here. In season, a fee is charged for day-use of the hiking trails. The park makes a good base camp for hiking in the greater Waterbury-Stowe area. During the summer months, a swim in the reservoir is just the right thing to cool off after a hike. A state-run beach and picnic area is available for day-use off Vt. 100 in Waterbury Center.

The Little River trails generally follow former town roads, some of which are now used for logging roads and snowmobile trails as well as for hiking. The trails are good for walking, cross-country skiing, and snowshoeing. Mountain biking is allowed on some trails. The trails are marked with blue paint blazes. The trail system in the Little River area is accessible from the vicinity of Waterbury Dam on the south side and from Moscow (a settlement on the south side of Stowe) on the north side.

In November 1927, Vermont was inundated by torrential rains, which caused widespread flooding and destruction in almost every major watershed in the state. Waterbury Dam was constructed as a flood control project on the Little River by the Civilian Conservation Corps (CCC) between 1934 and 1938. Below the dam, on the west side of the access road, only a few stone chimneys remain to identify the location of eighty buildings in the camp, which served as the living facilities for the 2,000 men who worked on the dam construction.

Lying west of the reservoir, the Little River area encompasses the drainage basins of Stevenson Brook and Cotton Brook. In the late 1700s, settlers began clearing the area for farms, and it was well populated in the nineteenth century. The inhabitants eked out a meager living from subsistence farming and logging, but depletion of the thin soil, the harsh environment, and better economic

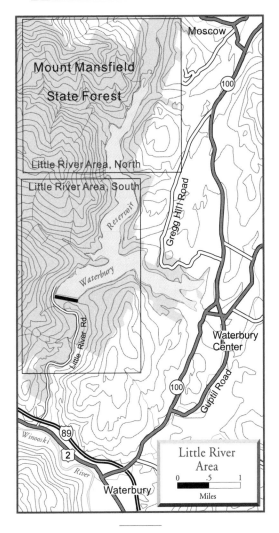

opportunities elsewhere led to gradual depopulation of the area. The settlement was almost totally abandoned when the land was acquired for the construction of Waterbury Dam. Stonewalls, cellar holes, cemeteries, clearings, apple trees, and lilac bushes remain as reminders of the past.

In 2000, the state of Vermont drew down the Waterbury Reservoir to make critical repairs to the dam. A visit to the reservoir is well worth the trip to view the landscape as it was before the dam was built. The reservoir will be refilled.

SOUTHERN ACCESS

TO THE TRAIL: From exit 10 on I-89 near Waterbury (0.0 mi.), travel south on Vt. 100 a short distance to the junction with U.S. 2 (0.1 mi.). Turn right on U.S. 2 and proceed west. Turn right onto Little River Road (1.5 mi.), then pass under I-89. Continue past the unsigned Woodward Hill Trail on the left (3.0 mi.). Pass a large state parking lot on the left (3.3 mi.) and continue to a parking area near the top of the western dam abutment (4.2 mi.). A formidable gate blocks the access road when the state park is closed (from mid-October to mid-May). The park contact station lies a short distance further along the access road (4.8 mi.).

Parking is available at two lots within the park. From the contact station, bear left, then turn right at an intersection (5.0 mi.) to cross Stevenson Brook on a highway bridge. The Nature Trail parking lot is on the right (5.3 mi.), shortly before another parking lot on the right signed for history hike parking (5.5 mi.).

WOODWARD HILL TRAIL

Distance: 3.7 mi. (6.0 km)
Elevation Change: 1,270 ft. ascent
Hiking Time: 2½ hrs (reverse 2½ hr.)

The trail follows a series of gravel roads making it appropriate for early season walks when other trails may be wet

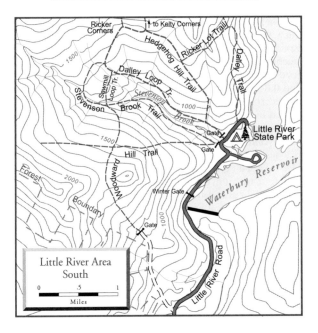

Little River Area
South

0   .5   1

Miles

and subject to erosion. A loop hike is possible by walking 1.8 mi. along the Little River Road. One end of the trail is accessible from outside the park gate, while the other end is near the park contact station. The trail is described from Little River Road to the contact station.

To the Trail: There are two access points for this trail. One is via a class 4 town road that departs Little River Road 1.2 mi. below the state gate at Waterbury Dam (follow the directions on page 248 to the southern access of the Little River area). Parking is available either at a nearby lot on the access road or near the gate itself; both areas are accessible when the park is closed. The other access is in the park near the contact station.

5

DESCRIPTION: The trail starts at a road junction, by following a woods road, which diverges westerly from Little River Road just beyond the last house. The trail ascends fairly steeply from an initial elevation of 500 ft. It passes a woods road branching left (0.6 mi.) and two deer camps (0.7 mi. and 0.8 mi.), which are on private holdings on the left side of the road. A state gate is reached (1.0 mi.), which is locked in the summer. (Cars may be driven to this gate in summer and parked in a log-loading area on the left.)

Beyond the gate, the trail continues to ascend and reaches a saddle on the east shoulder of Woodward Mtn. (1.8 mi.) at an elevation of 1,770 ft. The trail then descends to a four-way junction (2.4 mi.) where a snowmobile trail goes straight ahead and an improved logging road goes left and right. The trail bears right at the intersection, coinciding with the logging road and descends to reach another gate (3.5 mi.). Continuing straight ahead, the trail follows the road to the park contact station (3.7 mi.), from which point it is an additional 1.8 mi. down the Little River access road to reach the junction at the start of the trail.

STEVENSON BROOK TRAIL

Distance: 2.4 mi. (3.9 km)
Elevation Change: 750 ft. ascent
Hiking Time: 1½ hr. (reverse 1¼ hr.)

TO THE TRAIL: The blue-blazed Stevenson Brook Trail starts at a gate at a road junction located 0.2 mi. beyond the contact station where there is a trail sign. (This trail begins at the same place as the northern end of the Woodward Hill Trail.) Day-users may inquire at the contact station about parking somewhere between the station and the road junction/trailhead beyond it; otherwise, parking is available at the Nature Trail parking lot across Stevenson Brook.
DESCRIPTION: The Stevenson Brook Trail follows a long-abandoned road upstream, first paralleling the paved park

road through a hemlock grove. Stevenson Brook soon comes into sight. Continuing on easy grades for a short distance, the trail follows along the western side of Stevenson Brook. It crosses the brook (1.0 mi.), then crosses it again (1.2 mi.) over two footbridges. The trail then crosses a small tributary of Stevenson Brook (1.5 mi.), also over a bridge.

The trail comes to an intersection with the Sawmill Loop Trail, which leads 0.3 mi. north to the Dalley Loop Trail. Immediately after the junction, the Stevenson Brook Trail reaches the site of the former sawmill of the Waterbury Last Block Company (1.6 mi.), which features the remains of a locomotive-sized boiler as well as parts of old band saws and a truck chassis. The sawmill was constructed in 1916 and operated until 1922. From the sawmill site, the trail continues northwesterly along the west side of Stevenson Brook and widens into a woods road. It crosses Stevenson Brook (2.0 mi.) on a substantial snowmobile bridge. Proceeding easterly over a rise, the trail passes the farm site (on the north side of the trail) of the first settler to this area, George Kenyon, who arrived in 1790. The trail then reaches its end at the Dalley Loop Trail (2.4 mi.).

STEVENSON BROOK NATURE TRAIL

Distance: 0.75 mi. (1.2 km) loop
Elevation Change: minor
Hiking Time: ¾ hr.

This short trail was developed by the Department of Forests, Parks and Recreation to showcase the cultural and natural history of Little River State Park. *Stevenson Brook Nature Trail*, a trail guide describing the botanical, geological, and cultural features of the circuit, is available from the park office. Numbered posts along the trail correspond with the guide; the trail is marked with blue markers.

To the Trail: To reach the nature trail parking, follow the directions to the Little River State Park contact station (page 248). From the office, take the park road toward Camping Area B. After crossing Stevenson Brook on a bridge, park in the parking lot on the right.

Description: Follow the signs and numbered posts. The trail is an out and back with a short loop at its far end.

History Hike Loop via
Hedgehog Hill Trail and Dalley Loop Trail

Distance: 3.8 mi. (6.1 km) loop
Elevation Change: 650 ft. ascent
Hiking Time: 2½ hr. either direction

The historic sites along this loop are numbered and described in "History Hike," a pamphlet available at the Little River State Park contact station or from the Barre district office of the Department of Forests, Parks and Recreation. The hike makes a loop following two trails, the Hedgehog Hill Trail and the Dalley Loop Trail.

To the Trail: The trail starts opposite the History Hike parking lot, which accommodates a half-dozen cars. Follow directions to the southern access on page 248.

Description: Passing through a gate, the trail shortly reaches a signed junction where it follows the Hedgehog Hill Trail to the right to traverse the loop in a counterclockwise direction. The trail ascends steadily with a generally moderate grade to reach a parallel detour (0.3 mi.) on the left.

> **Junction:** The parallel detour (from 0.3 mi. to 0.6 mi.) begins with a very steep grade and avoids an eroded portion of the original road. The detour rejoins the Hedgehog Hill Trail at an unmarked intersection with a road departing right.

> **Junction:** This road leads to the Ezra Fuller farm site. While unblazed and unmaintained, the road follows the

northerly side of a stonewall to a junction with the presently maintained north side of the Ricker Lot Trail. This trail loops back to the park access road near Camping Area B, campsite number 59.

Continuing northwesterly, the Hedgehog Hill Trail soon reaches the Ricker Family Cemetery (0.7 mi.) on the left. (For an instance of nineteenth-century longevity, note Phoebe Ricker's tombstone.) The trail then comes to an intersection (0.8 mi.) where a trail to the Ricker sugarhouse site branches right at a sign for the Ezra Fuller Farm and eventually connects with the Ricker Lot Trail.

Continuing to ascend on a northerly and northwesterly course, the Hedgehog Hill Trail ascends to a height of land (1.1 mi.) at an elevation of 1,500 ft., then takes a short detour right necessitated by beaver activity and reaches an intersection (1.5 mi.) where a right turn leads to Kelty Corners and Moscow. A schoolhouse was once located at this intersection.

Junction: To the right, the Little River Trail ascends to cross over the ridge between the Stevenson Brook and Cotton Brook drainage basins (0.3 mi.), passes an obscure intersection on the left with the Patterson Trail (0.5 mi.), and reaches Kelty Corners (0.6 mi.).

Junction: The Patterson Trail starts opposite two signs pointing in opposite directions to Ricker Corners and Kelty Corners. It goes westerly along the northerly flank of the ridge, then turns left, passing over the ridge and descending to the Patterson farm site. It then follows a discernable road to Ricker Corners where there is a sign for the Patterson Trail to Kelty Corners. The trail is about 1.0 mi. long.

From the schoolhouse intersection, the Hedgehog Hill Trail continues straight ahead, descending gradually to Ricker Corners (1.8 mi.) where the so-called upper cemetery is located on the westerly side of the intersection.

Here, the trail turns left onto Dalley Loop Trail, descending southwesterly to a corner (2.2 mi.) and the intersection with the western end of the Stevenson Brook Trail at a sign for the Sawmill Trail. Turning left, the Dalley Loop Trail goes southeasterly, shortly passing another intersection (2.3 mi.) for the Sawmill Loop Trail and another sign for the Sawmill Trail.

Junction: The Sawmill Loop Trail makes a fairly direct descent to Stevenson Brook opposite the site of the sawmill of Waterbury Last Block Company. Since there is no bridge across Stevenson Brook, use of the trail is not recommended. The trail is about 0.5 mi. long.

The Dalley Loop Trail continues southeasterly, passing the Bert Goodell farmhouse, the only original building still standing in the Little River Area, and returns to the History Hike parking lot (3.8 mi.).

NORTHERN ACCESS

TO THE TRAIL: From exit 10 on I-89 near Waterbury, travel north on Vt. 100. Pass the Cold Hollow Cider Mill (3.3 mi.) in Waterbury Center and the Green Mountain Club headquarters (4.4 mi.) to the Moscow Road on the left (7.3 mi.). Bear left on Moscow Road, which crosses Little River, and continue through the namesake village. Continue past Barrows Road and Trapp Hill Road on the right to a bridge across Miller Brook (9.4 mi.) and an immediate left fork. Bear left on the gravel Cotton Brook Road where ample parking is available on both sides of the road at a large state lot (9.6 mi.) found immediately after the fork. In the summer it is feasible to drive another 0.5 mi. to two small parking lots on the left shortly before a state gate. This area also provides canoe access to Waterbury Reservoir.

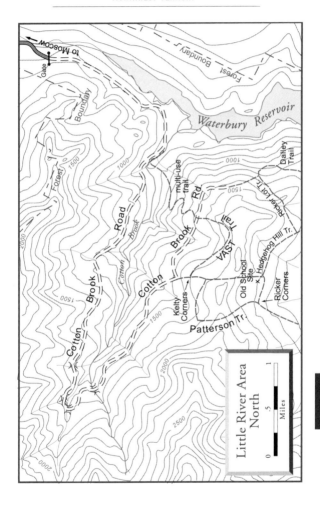

Little River Area
North

0 .5 1
Miles

5

COTTON BROOK LOOP VIA KELTY CORNERS

Distance: 11.0 mi. (17.7 km)
Elevation Change: 1,470 ft. ascent
Hiking Time: 6 hrs. either direction

None of this route is blazed, and there are very few signs; however, it does follow a series of old gravel roads and snow-mobile trails. In season, this loop is also open to bicycles. Skiers enjoy this trail in winter, but must share it with snow-mobiles. Along the route are sites of the old Little River set-tlement, including former homes, sawmills and a school.

DESCRIPTION: From the large state parking lot, the trail co-incides with a wide gravel road and follows the westerly shore of Little River and Waterbury Reservoir to the state gate (0.5 mi.). At the gate, a multiuse trail diverges left and runs parallel to Cotton Brook Road for a distance before rejoining the road (1.4 mi.). Beyond the gate, the trail co-incides with a continuation of Cotton Brook Road, which is an improved gravel logging road passable for bicycles as well as hikers. The trail proceeds along the easterly side of Cotton Brook. At an unmarked junction (1.7 mi.) just be-yond a utility shed, the return end of the loop enters left.

Continuing right, the trail ascends gradually, passing several sites of historic interest. Three streams are crossed, two on concrete bridges (4.1 and 4.5 mi.), and a third on a plank-surfaced bridge, before the trail swings south at the crossing of the main branch of Cotton Brook (5.0 mi.) on a large steel culvert. The trail crosses the larger left fork of Cotton Brook (5.4 mi.) on a concrete bridge. On a fairly level course, it comes to an intersection (6.7 mi.) with an uphill spur right where a trail sign points up the spur. The spur is an unmaintained segment of the original road and ascends to Kelty Corners (7.0 mi.).

From the intersection with the spur, the trail gradually descends in a southeasterly direction, offering a 0.8-mi. shortcut to bypass Kelty Corners. Kelty Corners is on the east side of the ridge separating the Cotton Brook and

Stevenson Brook drainage basins. From Kelty Corners, the trail currently takes a sharp left turn to follow a VAST snowmobile trail, which has an uneven surface and is muddy in places. It proceeds southeasterly, descending and ascending gradually to a left turn (7.3 mi.), from which it descends northeasterly on a moderately steep grade to a four-way intersection (7.8 mi.). At this intersection, the shortcut via the road comes in on the left. To the right, the road continues 0.4 mi. to a log-loading area beyond which is the closed and unmaintained trail connecting to the Ricker Lot Trail.

Straight ahead, the trail follows a smooth logging road/snowmobile trail, which zigzags downward to a substantial bridge (8.8 mi.) across Cotton Brook. The trail then follows the easterly side of the brook downstream until it swings away from the brook (9.1 mi.) and makes a very steep ascent to rejoin the easterly side of the loop (9.3 mi.), just beyond the utility shed. The outbound leg is then retraced to the large state parking lot (11.0 mi.).

• • • • • • • • • • • • • • • •

Mount Norris

Distance: 1.8 mi. (2.9 km)
Elevation Change: 1,320 ft. ascent
Hiking Time: 1½ hr. (reverse 1 hr.)

Located in the town of Eden, the summit (2,580 ft.) and several lower vantage points on this distinctively shaped peak (USGS Albany) offer good local views south and more distant views of the Worcester Range and the Green Mountains. The trail is maintained by the campers and staff of the nearby Mount Norris Scout Reservation. (The Larry Dean Trail, named for a dedicated Green Mountain Club member and a veteran Boy Scout, used to leave from the same trailhead and create a loop hike, but it has not been maintained and is impassable.)

5

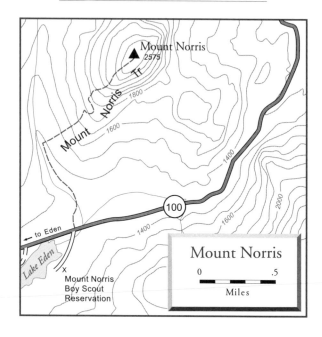

To the Trail: The trail begins on the west side of Vt. 100, just north of the entrance to the scout reservation, 2.0 mi. north of Eden Mills and 6.1 mi. south of Vt. 58 in Lowell village. The unmarked trailhead is at a gravel pit road, which heads west through an old field. Ample parking is available beside the highway or a short distance south at the boat access.

Description: This steep and direct route to the summit is blazed with an eclectic mix of faded red and blue paint, green arrows on rocks, and red, blue, or pink flagging. From Vt. 100 (0.0 mi.), the trail follows the gravel pit road west a short distance, then angles right onto an overgrown old road before reaching a line of trees (0.2 mi.) and a brook. An arrow nailed to a tree points left, and the first blue blazes appear. The trail follows the washed-out road upstream at an easy grade, following orange and blue tree markings for some distance before coming into the lower end of a large clearing (0.7 mi.). Crossing to the upper edge of the clearing, the road divides and the Mount Norris Trail enters the woods to the right at a trail register. It ascends steadily for some distance on an old woods road following blue and orange markings. It then turns right at a big rock. Continuing upward, the trail swings right of a huge rock at the base of a rock ledge (1.1 mi.) to begin a steep and winding climb around the ledge.

Resuming a northerly direction, the trail continues a steep, difficult upward climb through rocks to a partially open rock area where there are good views south and east (1.3 mi.). Pink ribbons tied on tree branches are used along with the blue and orange flagging to mark the trail from here to the summit.

The trail, now narrow and mostly overgrown, passes several more limited views before ascending to what appears to be a wooded summit. Now only a short distance from the real summit, the trail reaches a 6-ft. drop-off and another short descent before it begins its final ascent to a large rock hogback and the open summit (1.8 mi.).

• • • • • • • • • • • • • • • •

BURNT MOUNTAIN

5

Distance: 2.0 mi. (3.2 km)
Elevation Change: 1,500 ft. ascent
Hiking Time: 2 hr. (reverse 1¼ hr.)

Burnt Mtn. (2,626 ft., USGS Hazen's Notch) is the highest point on a spur ridge that trends northwesterly from Haystack Mtn. about 2.0 mi. south of Hazen's Notch. The trail was established by the Hazen's Notch Association and is part of a 30-mi. trail system maintained in association with the Hazen's Notch Cross-Country Ski Area. Most of these trails are for winter use by skiers and snowshoers, but a few trails are open without charge to hikers in the summer season. An area map is available from the association and several stores in the Jay-Montgomery area.

TO THE TRAIL: From Vt. 118 in Montgomery Center, turn east on Vt. 58 (0.0 mi.), continue past the Hazen's Notch Cross-Country Ski Area and turn right onto Rossier Road (2.0 mi.). This road is about 9.0 mi. west of Vt. 100 in Lowell. Continue uphill, past a fork to the left, until the road ends at the High Ponds Recreation Area parking lot, near an abandoned farmhouse in a small field (2.5 mi.). Since all trails maintained by the Hazen's Notch Association are on private property, care should be taken to observe the rules posted nearby.

DESCRIPTION: The Burnt Mountain Trail departs left from the Twin Ponds Trail, 0.1 mi. south of the parking lot and a short distance past the two namesake bodies of water. From this signed junction (0.0 mi.), the trail, well-blazed with blue plastic diamonds, soon crosses a small brook and trends southeasterly on an old woods road. Turning sharply right off this road (0.2 mi.) the trail ascends southerly along an old skid road with rough and wet footing and arrives at a junction with the Catamount Trail (0.6 mi.). Turning left, the trail follows the Catamount Trail a short distance, then bears right on a less distinct woods road (0.7 mi.) and climbs more steeply. It ascends to Window Rock (1.1 mi.) where there are fine views east of Hazen's Notch, Sugarloaf Mtn., and Buchanan Mtn.

At Window Rock, the trail swings right to begin a steep and winding climb, eventually reaching and crossing the east side of the ridge (1.5 mi.). The trail continues on easy grades through tall ferns and paper birches to pass near the minor north summit before descending into a sag. It then makes a final ascent through spruces to the top of a series of ledges, which it follows to its terminus on the south summit (2.0 mi.).

From various points along the small, open summit ridge, there are impressive views north to three of the Jay Peaks and east to Hazen's Notch itself. Although the high ridge of the main range of the Green Mountains to the east and the Cold Hollow Mountains to the west preclude views in those directions, there is a good view northwest of the Champlain Valley extending into Quebec. The view northeast includes the Lake Memphremagog area of the Northeast Kingdom, parts of northern New Hampshire, and several Quebec summits.

●●●●●●●●●●●●●●●●●

EAGLE MOUNTAIN

Distance: 2–3 mi. (3.2–4.8 km)
Elevation Change: 560 ft. ascent
Hiking Time: 1 hr. (reverse ½ hr.)

Eagle Mtn. in Milton sits on the shore of Lake Champlain, overlooking the Champlain Islands. It is relatively unknown and is a quick getaway in populous Chittenden County. The property was conserved by the Lake Champlain Land Trust in 1995 and is managed by the Milton Conservation Commission. Only pedestrian recreation is allowed. The trails are well marked and obvious, and the terrain is suitable for beginners and children, as well as dogs.

TO THE TRAIL: From the U.S. 7 bridge over the Lamoille River at the Arrowhead Lake Dam in the village of Milton (0.0 mi.), travel north on U.S. 7 for 0.6 mi. and turn left on Lake Road. Follow Lake Road 2.9 mi. to a farm and turn left on Everest Road (3.5 mi.). Continue 0.5 mi. to a stop sign and turn right (4.0 mi.). After 1.4 mi. (there is a red barn on the left), turn right on Beebe Hill Road (5.4 mi.) and follow it 0.6 mi. to Cold Spring Road (6.0 mi.). Turn left and continue a short distance to where the road curves left; the Eagle Mtn. trailhead is marked by a white

5

bulletin board. There is parking for two to three cars. Please do not block this private road.

DESCRIPTION: The trails on the Eagle Mtn. property are marked with green diamonds, numbered to correspond to the trail map on the trailhead bulletin board. The network of trails forms several loops, and the numbering can be confusing. There are two main trails, one leading to the summit and the other to a beautiful lookout over the lake. The side trails are short enough that the best option is to just wander about. A thorough exploration of the area involves a walk of no more than 2.0 or 3.0 mi.

•••••••••••••••••

WINOOSKI VALLEY PARK DISTRICT

The Winooski Valley Park District was formed to preserve or acquire natural areas of regional significance and special interest. The park district includes the municipalities of Burlington, Colchester, Essex, Jericho, South Burlington, Williston, and Winooski. The district maintains more than seventeen properties totaling 1,736 acres for passive recreation and environmental protection. Several small, but interesting, locations in Chittenden County providing boat access, picnic areas, or wildlife sanctuaries are described in the district's "Six Easy Walks," a flyer available from the district. Two of the larger district parks that may be of interest to the day hiker are described below. For more information, contact the Winooski Valley Park District, Ethan Allen Homestead, Burlington, Vermont 05401; (802) 863-5744; wvpd@together.net.

ETHAN ALLEN HOMESTEAD

The Ethan Allen Homestead was once the home of Ethan and Fanny Allen. The property offers walking trails, guided tours of the restored farmstead, a multimedia show, and museum exhibits as well as picnicking. The trails are open year-round from dawn to dusk. The homestead is open Monday through Saturday, 10:00 A.M. to 5:00 P.M., and Sunday from 1:00 P.M. to 5:00 P.M. during spring, summer, and fall. During winter, the hours are 12:00 P.M. to 4:00 P.M. on weekends or by appointment Monday through Friday.

TO THE TRAIL: To reach the homestead, take the North Avenue Beaches exit off Vt. 127 (Beltline/Northern Connector) in North Burlington and follow the small green highway signs. The driveway to the homestead begins off this exit ramp. Proceed to the education center where trail maps are available from the nearby information stand or from the office. Ample parking is available.

DESCRIPTION: There are five trails on the property. Two are short wetland trails named Wetlands Walk South and Wetlands Walk North. The three others, each less than a mile long and within easy walking distance of the education center, are the Peninsula Loop, Homestead Loop, and River Loop. Natural features of the Intervale, such as the mature floodplain forests, may be seen from all these trails.

COLCHESTER POND NATURAL AREA

Distance: 2.9 mi. (4.7 km)
Elevation Change: minor
Hiking Time: 1½ hr. (reverse 1½ hr.)

This 694-acre park, opened by the Winooski Valley Park District in 1997, encircles the mile-long Colchester Pond. This natural area is contiguous with the Indian Brook Reservoir Park (page 265) to the east owned by the town of Essex. No vehicles, motorized boats, or electric motors are permitted in the natural area, which is open dawn to dusk. The one hiking trail in the park circumnavigates Colchester Pond and is marked with yellow blazes and wooden directional signs.

To the Trail: From the junction of U.S. 2 and U.S. 7 with Vt. 2A in Colchester (0.0 mi.), proceed east on Vt. 2A to the center of Colchester village and turn north (left) on East Road (1.0 mi.). Turn right at the next intersection (1.2 mi.) on Depot Road and proceed past the railroad tracks (1.9 mi.) to a fork (2.3 mi.). Bear left on Colchester Pond Road and proceed past Curve Hill Road on the right to the parking area on the right (2.6 mi.). The gravel lot contains parking for twenty cars and provides access to both the pond and the hiking trail.

Description: From the parking lot (0.0 mi.), the trail descends along a tree line to the western shore of the pond, which it then follows northerly for some distance through three meadows before ascending the shoulder of a small hill. The trail meets an unmarked junction (0.8 mi.) where it bears right, then meets another unmarked junction where a spur trail right leads to the shore. Continuing left through mature pines, the trail follows the north end of the pond until it intersects the Peninsula Trail (1.2 mi.), which leads 0.1 mi. to the pond's edge.

Continuing straight, the trail crosses a stream on a wooden bridge (1.3 mi.) before meeting and following a logging road (1.6 mi.) along the east side of the pond. The trail follows this road through three hay fields, bisecting each on an indistinct path. Near an electrical transmission line at a gate and fence, the trail turns right to follow the southern shore of the pond back to the dammed outlet and bridge. The parking lot is a short walk to the right on the road. This last stretch along the southern edge of the pond is often muddy. Special care should be taken to respect the private property of the residents

• • • • • • • • • • • • • • • • •

INDIAN BROOK RESERVOIR PARK

This 575-acre preserve was formerly used as a municipal water supply and is now managed by the Essex Town Parks and Recreation Department. The 66-acre reservoir was created by damming Indian Brook and is attractive for small muscle-powered watercraft. The principal hiking trail in the park circumnavigates the reservoir but is only intermittently signed or blazed. A second trail ascends a ridge east of the reservoir where there is a view west.

CIRCUMFERENTIAL TRAIL

Distance: 1.8 mi. (2.9 km)
Elevation Change: none
Hiking Time: 55 min. either direction

To the Trail: From the junction of Vt. 289 and Vt. 15 in the town of Essex (0.0 mi.), travel east on Vt. 15 and turn left on Old Stage Road (0.2 mi.). Passing Lost Nation Road on the left, take the next left (0.6 mi.) onto Indian Brook Road and continue into the park at a boundary sign (1.8 mi.). Bear right past two parking lots to reach a third lot located near the boat launch.

Description: From the north end of this parking lot (0.0 mi.), the Circumferential Trail begins its loop around the reservoir by paralleling the east shore. Bearing right at an intersection (0.4 mi.) where a spur leads left to the shore, the trail follows an old road northward to a corner where a blue arrow on a tree points left. Bearing left, the trail swings south to an unmarked intersection (0.8 mi.) where it turns right and crosses Indian Brook on a plank bridge. Bypassing an unmarked trail to the right (1.0 mi.), the trail reaches another intersection (1.2 mi.) marked by a second blue arrow. Bearing left as the arrow indicates, the trail flanks the western edge of the pond, bypassing a spur on the right (1.6 mi.) before reaching a signpost (1.8 mi.) marking the western end of the trail. A short gravel path

5

from this spot leads below the reservoir's dam back to the access road and lower parking lots.

OVERLOOK TRAIL

Distance: 1.0 mi. (1.6 km)
Elevation Change: 300 ft. ascent
Hiking Time: 40 min. (reverse 30 min.)

TO THE TRAIL: The trail leaves the east side of the parking lot for the Circumferential Trail, described previously.

DESCRIPTION: The Overlook Trail leaves the parking lot on its east side (0.0 mi.) and proceeds southeast as a mowed path before swinging north after being joined by another path from the right. Marked by blue blazes, the trail soon empties into an old road and crosses a stone fence (0.3 mi.). Here, the trail makes a sharp left turn (unmarked) off the road and follows a narrow path past a sharp right turn (0.4 mi.) to two lookouts (0.7 mi.). From the second of these lookouts the trail makes a sharp turn right and continues its northward ascent of the ridge. The end of the trail is reached at a ledge from which there is a distant view of Lake Champlain (1.0 mi.).

•••••••••••••••••

RAMBLES

SHELBURNE FARMS

Shelburne Farms was established in 1886 as the model agricultural estate of William Seward and Lila Vanderbilt Webb. Today, it is open to the public as a nonprofit environmental education center and 1,400-acre working farm. The many historic farm buildings, footpaths and unobstructed views of Lake Champlain make this an interesting destination any time of year. The grounds and welcome center are open year-round. From mid-May to mid-October, a fee is charged for admission to the grounds and buildings. There is no fee from mid-October to mid-May, and the trails are open from 10:00 A.M. to 5:00 P.M. Tickets, information, and a map of the grounds are available at the welcome center. For more information, contact Shelburne Farms at (802) 985-8686 or shelburnefarms.org

TO THE TRAIL: From the intersection of Shelburne Road (U.S. 7) and Bay Road north of Shelburne village, turn west on Bay Road and follow it 1.8 mi. to a four-way intersection. The visitors center and parking lot are across the intersection on the right.

CENTENNIAL WOODS NATURAL AREA

Centennial Woods is a designated natural area of the University of Vermont (UVM). It encompasses 70 acres of mature conifer and mixed hardwood forests, streams, and wetlands used as an ecology laboratory for students. Centennial Woods is notable for its relatively pristine state despite its location along the eastern edge of Burlington, Vermont's largest city. The area is open to the public for foot travel, and UVM's Environmental Program maintains a trail loop. Just over 1.0 mi. in length, the trail is blazed sparingly with white paint and some arrows at important turns. For more information, contact University of Vermont Environmental Program, 153 South Prospect Street, Burlington, Vermont 05405; (802) 656-4055.

TO THE TRAIL: From the jug-handle intersection of Williston Road (U.S. 2), Spear Street, and East Avenue, turn north on East Avenue and proceed a short distance to the first traffic light. Turn right and continue to the second driveway in front of the Instrumentation & Model Facility at 280 East Avenue where there are four metered spaces reserved for natural area visitor parking. The trailhead is across the road near a wooden sign.

DESCRIPTION: At the entrance to the trail there is a ledger box, which may contain copies of a UVM field guide with descriptions corresponding to numbered stations along the trail. The trail heads northeast to cross a wet area on puncheon before reaching a bridge crossing a stream at the bottom of a ravine. It then ascends a short distance to a junction, marking the beginning of the trail loop. Following an arrow to the right to make a counterclockwise circuit, the trail ascends steeply to a plateau, then meanders along a ridge covered with towering white pine trees, many of which are more than 100 years old. The trail passes municipal boundary markers, crossing into South Burlington, then back into Burlington, before descending steeply into a ravine and its northernmost point at an electric transmission line. The trail climbs over a small shoulder to follow a southerly course along the east side of a stream back to the junction with the access trail.

EAST WOODS INTERPRETIVE TRAIL

Owned by the University of Vermont, East Woods is a 40-acre woodland in South Burlington, exemplary of a mature northern forest. UVM students use the area as an ecology laboratory; it is open to the public for foot travel. An interpretive loop trail, under 1.0 mi. in length, winds through the site's towering pines, hemlocks and oaks and is sparsely marked with wooden rectangles inscribed with arrows.

TO THE TRAIL: From the jug-handle intersection of Williston Road (U.S. 2), Spear Street, and East Avenue (0.0 mi.), turn south onto Spear Street and continue to a traffic light (2.1 mi.). Turn right onto Swift Street and proceed west a short distance to the entrance to East Woods Natural Area, which is on the right and marked by a large wooden sign (2.5 mi.).

Alternatively, from the intersection of Shelburne Road and Swift Street (0.0 mi.), just south of the I-189 interchange, turn left on Swift Street to the entrance, which appears shortly on the left (0.6mi.). Ample parking is available along the side of the street at the entrance.

DESCRIPTION: From the entrance, the trail leads a few hundred feet to an informative bulletin board and ledger box, which is usually empty. The trail continues westerly and passes a junction on the left (0.1 mi.) with the return trail. Bearing right at this junction to make a counterclockwise circuit, the trail descends steeply to approach Potash Brook, which meanders through the woods on its way to Lake Champlain. It crosses a slight depression (0.2 mi.), a remnant of the railbed of the Burlington and Hinesburg Railroad, which was graded in 1898 but abandoned before any track was laid.

Adjacent to this railbed, the trail crosses the more conspicuous and parallel railbed of the Burlington and Lamoille Railroad, which was completed in 1877. The tracks here were used for only a few years before being removed. Directly across the B&L railbed, the trail descends to an elbow of Potash Brook, then swings back to recross the two railbeds (0.4 mi.). (Turning left on the B&L railbed is a shortcut.) After ascending a small shoulder, the trail descends to follow the south shore of Potash Brook downstream to the west. It then arcs 180 degrees, rising easterly on undulating terrain to reach the return end of the loop (0.9 mi.). From here, the trail may be retraced back to the entrance (1.0 mi.).

RED ROCKS PARK

Located in South Burlington, Red Rocks Park occupies the former site of a private estate, with interconnected carriage paths that lead through pleasant pine woods to vantage points on the shore of Lake Champlain. The park is maintained by the South Burlington Recreation Department.

TO THE TRAIL: From U.S. 7 (Shelburne Road), immediately south of the I-189 interchange, turn west on Queen City Park Road. After crossing a one-lane bridge, turn left on Central Avenue and continue a short distance to the park entrance on the right. A parking fee is charged from late June to Labor Day, but pedestrians may enter the park without charge at any time.

DESCRIPTION: From the parking lot designated Parking 1 (0.0 mi.), a trail leads west along the top of a bluff on the north shore of Shelburne Bay, eventually reaching an overlook with a fine view south (0.4 mi.). The trail continues to a turnaround loop at the west end of Red Rocks Point, about 50 ft. beyond a right turn where another trail descends to a loop on the east shore of the lake (0.6 mi.). From this latter lookout, there is a magnificent vista across the broad lake to the Adirondacks.

North of this main trail are three loops, each 0.6 mi. long, which may be used to return to the park's entrance. The westernmost loop departs the main path before the turnarounds on Red Rocks Point and circles a 240-ft. knob before returning to the main trail. At this junction, the middle loop leaves north to cross the park's 280-ft. wooded summit, passing red rock ledges. This path continues east, ending at a junction. To the right, a short path returns to the main trail; while to the left, the easternmost loop heads north to the park boundary before bearing east and ending at the park entrance.

BURLINGTON RECREATION PATH

This 7.6-mi. multipurpose path has many access points along Burlington's scenic waterfront and provides links to other recreation trails in the area. Generally following the former Rutland Railway rail bed, there are striking views across Lake Champlain toward the Adirondack High Peaks.

Local Motion, a nonprofit organization promoting walking and cycling, is working to extend this trail northward from Burlington to Canada on the historic Rutland Railroad Island Line and existing roads. The Island Flyer train ran on these tracks through the Lake Champlain islands from 1901 to 1961.

The Burlington Recreation Path connects to the South Burlington Recreation Path to the south and recreation paths in Colchester to the north. The South Burlington path is more a spider web of trails than a path. From Oakledge Park, it is roughly 0.5 mi. on Austin Drive to link up with the network.

In 1999, a group of trail advocates established a bike ferry across the Winooski River (the northern terminus of the Burlington Recreation Path) to connect the Burlington Recreation Path with the recreation path in Colchester. That ferry has now been replaced by a pedestrian/ bike bridge. On the Colchester side, the recreation path continues 1.0 mi. before connecting with the Mallets Bay Causeway, described on page 272.

To learn more about Local Motion's work to unite existing trails into a regional Island Line Trail, contact Local Motion, 1 Steele Street, Suite 103, Burlington, Vermont 05401; (802) 652-BIKE; info@localmotionvt.org; or localmotionvt.org.

TO THE TRAIL: To reach the path's southern terminus, from the rotary on U.S. 7 at the head of Shelburne Road, proceed south about 0.7 mi. Turn west on Flynn Avenue and continue about 0.5 mi. to Oakledge Park where ample parking is available (a fee may be charged). Parking is also available at the Burlington Boat House.

DESCRIPTION: The southern terminus of the paved recreation path is at Austin Drive (0.0 mi.) 0.3 mi. south of Oakledge Park. The trail continues north, reaching the waterfront at Roundhouse Point and Perkins Pier (2.2 mi.) where there is a ferry dock and parking, and continuing north past the foot of College Street, the Lake Champlain Science Center, and Burlington Boat House. The path ascends a tiny hill (3.6 mi.) before reaching North

5

Beach (4.1 mi., parking) and continuing through a wooded area to Leddy Park (5.2 mi., parking). After crossing Starr Farm Road (6.2 mi.), the path crosses another side road (7.3 mi.) before crossing the Winooski River (7.6 mi.) on the pedestrian/bike bridge.

MALLETS BAY CAUSEWAY

At the turn of the twentieth century, the Rutland Railroad constructed a causeway between Mills Point in Colchester and Allen Point in South Hero, commencing rail service through the Champlain Islands in January 1901. Although rail service was discontinued in 1961 and the tracks were removed in 1964, the massive marble blocks of the causeway remain intact, stretching more than 3.0 mi. into the broad lake

TO THE TRAIL: There are two ways to access the causeway, by the Burlington Recreation Path or by car. After crossing the Winooski River on the pedestrian/bike bridge, travel 0.5 mi. on boardwalks and a dirt path through Delta Park (a beautiful lakeshore natural area). Continue 0.5 mi. on bike lanes through a quiet, residential neighborhood. The bike lanes connect into Airport Park where the causeway path picks up.

Or, to reach the causeway by car (or bike): from Vt. 127, about 1.2 mi. north of the Heineberg Bridge over the Winooski River, follow Porter's Point Road (0.0 mi.) northwest to a four-way intersection (1.9 mi.). Turn left on Airport Road and proceed to Airport Park on the right (2.4 mi.) where ample parking is available.

DESCRIPTION: From the park (0.0 mi.), follow a path leading west, which parallels Airport Road at the edge of Colchester Bog. The path joins the old railroad bed, which turns northwesterly to cross the bog, shortly reaching Mills Point Road (1.1 mi.). The trail continues to the edge of the lake (1.5 mi.) before continuing out onto the marble-block causeway. Beyond the first bridge (2.7 mi.), the causeway narrows a bit as the thin ribbon continues out into the lake, eventually reaching its end at a gap where the railroad's drawbridge once stood (3.0 mi.). From this point, there are fine views in all directions from this unique, low-level perspective. The shore of South Hero lies 0.5 mi. north, and to the east the main range of the Green Mountains is clearly visible over the scattered foothills of the Champlain Valley.

Local Motion (see page 271), a nonprofit organization promoting walking and cycling, is developing a bike ferry, replacing the missing turnstile bridge, to link the Colchester side of the causeway with the South Hero side. Once linked, it will be possible to walk, run, or cycle through the lake between Vermont's mainland and islands.

GRAND ISLE STATE PARK

Grand Isle State Park takes its name from, and is located on, the east shore of Lake Champlain's largest island. A short trail opposite the park entrance leads to an observation deck and is the only park facility open for day use.

TO THE TRAIL: From the intersection of Vt. 314 and U.S. 2 in South Hero (0.0 mi.) near Keeler Bay, proceed north on U.S. 2 to an intersection on the right with State Park Road (1.8 mi.) where there is a large sign for Grand Isle State Park. Turn east on State Park Road and proceed straight through an intersection with East Shore Road (2.7 mi.) before reaching the contact station (2.8 mi.) where parking is available. A day-use fee is charged in season.

DESCRIPTION: Opposite the park entrance, on the southwest corner of the State Park Road and East Shore Road intersection, is a nature trail sign marking the trailhead of the counterclockwise loop. The trail immediately reaches a junction where a spur left leads directly to the observation deck. Continuing straight ahead, the trail crosses several

5

marshy areas on puncheon, then two watercourses. It passes from cedar woods into a young hardwood forest as it crosses an open rock knob and the corner of an agricultural field. After ascending a flight of wooden steps, the trail reaches an unmarked four-way intersection. About 70 ft. to the right is a well-constructed, 10-ft.-tall wooden observation deck with good views over the lake to the east. Straight ahead, the trail emerges from the woods to its terminus, 60 ft. south of the trailhead.

ALBURGH RECREATION TRAIL

This nearly 4.0-mi. multiuse trail follows the abandoned East Alburgh to Alburgh branch of the former Central Vermont Railway. Owned by the state of Vermont and maintained by the Department of Forests, Parks and Recreation in cooperation with a local snowmobile club, the trail is obvious but unsigned and unblazed.

TO THE TRAIL: The western terminus of the trail is at the easterly end of the Alburgh Industrial Park and is reached by the paved Industrial Park Road that leaves U.S. 2 opposite the Alburgh Volunteer Fire Department. Ample parking is available at this trailhead.

DESCRIPTION: The trail departs the parking lot (0.0 mi.) easterly along the flat roadbed before entering the Mud Creek Waterfowl Area (0.8 mi.). Managed by the Department of Fish and Wildlife, the waterfowl area attracts a variety of wildlife, especially in late summer and early fall. The trail continues through areas of marsh and open water before crossing a bridge over Mud Creek (1.6 mi.) and reaching the eastern boundary of the waterfowl area at Vt. 78 (1.7 mi.), about 1.0 mi. east of its junction with U.S. 2. Parking areas are located a short distance east and west.

Continuing across Vt. 78, the trail, now less used, passes intermittently through areas of open farmland before crossing a farm road (2.3 mi.). It continues through a narrow band of trees to cross the paved Blue Rock Road (2.6 mi.), then the private gravel McGregor Point Road, both within sight of Vt. 78. The trail passes behind a series of private residences and through a wet area to reach an uncertain end in East Alburgh, terminating at an active railroad spur track a short distance west of the posted East Alburgh trestle (3.6 mi.). Here, a road leads a short distance to Vt. 78 at the west end of the Missisquoi Bay Bridge.

BURTON ISLAND STATE PARK

Burton Island is one of three island state parks in the northern part of Lake Champlain and accessible by boat or ferry from St. Alban's Kill Kare State Park. At 253 acres, it is the largest of the three state-owned islands. Both Woods Island State Park and Knight Island State Park are nearby.

Burton Island has 3.0 miles of shoreline, hiking trails, a nature center and museum, a park store and food service, rowboat and canoe rentals, and places to swim and picnic. It is popular for family recreation with seventeen tent sites, twenty-six lean-to sites, fifteen boat moorings, and a 100-slip marina with dockside electricity, fuel service, and a marine holding-tank pump-out facility. For more information, call (802) 524-6353 in season, (802) 241-3655 in the winter months, or log on to vtstateparks.com/htm/burton.cfm.

TO THE TRAIL: At the T intersection of Vt. 36 (Lake Street) and Lake Shore Road in St. Albans Bay (0.0 mi.), travel north on Lake Shore Road and bear left on Hathaway Point Road (0.8 mi.). Continue to Kill Kare State Park at the end of the road where parking is available (3.7 mi.). The ferry runs 9:00 A.M. to 6:00 P.M. and is $4.00 one-way per person. The state park day-use fee is $2.50 per adult, $2.00 for children four to thirteen years. For a current ferry schedule, log on to vtstateparks.com/htm/documents/ferry.pdf.

DESCRIPTION: Three different named trails connect and circle approximately 2.5 miles of the island. The North Shore

5

Trail starts at the westerly end of the campground and connects with the West Shore Trail at the northern shore. This trail leads to a clearing where it connects to the Southern Trip Trail, which circles back to the southerly side of the park facility. A descriptive brochure of the trails is available at the island's Nature Center, and an interactive map of the North Shore Trail can be found online at vtstateparks.com/htm/hike/trailhed/htm.

MISSISQUOI VALLEY RAIL TRAIL

Following 26 mi. of the former Central Vermont Railway-Richford Subdivision, this smooth gravel trail generally follows Vt. 105 and the Missisquoi River northeast from the town of St. Albans through Swanton, Fairfield, Sheldon, Enosburg, and Berkshire before ending in Richford. This multipurpose trail, the longest continuous rail trail in Vermont, is owned by the Vermont Transportation Agency and maintained by the Department of Forests, Parks and Recreation with volunteer assistance. A flyer describing the access, history, and permitted uses is available from the Northwest Vermont Rail Trail Council and sometimes from register boxes located at major road accesses. The trail is described eastbound from St. Albans.

TO THE TRAIL: Although access to the trail is possible at a number of road crossings, parking is not always available. There is ample parking at a designated lot at the junction of U.S. 7 and Vt. 105 in St. Albans.

DESCRIPTION: From this point (0.0 mi.), the trail bears northeasterly, passing under I-89 and traversing a series of farm fields before crossing Vt. 105 near an old cemetery at the hamlet of Greens Corners (3.0 mi.). It soon crosses an interesting marshy area before passing high above the forest floor on the built-up roadbed and eventually crossing Vt. 105 again near Sheldon Springs. After passing through the village, the trail reaches Vt. 105 a third time (8.6 mi.).

It crosses a restored railroad bridge over the Mississquoi River, then departs the river to the left into the midst of an active grain mill (9.0 mi.). The trail follows the Misisquoi River upstream, eventually making a road crossing in North Sheldon (11.4 mi.) before recrossing Vt. 105 (14.4 mi.) a short distance south of a parking area near a bend in the river.

The trail continues through a series of pastures, crossing Vt. 236 in South Franklin (13.5 mi.) and Vt. 105 twice more (13.9 mi., 15.8 mi.) before crossing a wooden railroad trestle (16.2 mi.) near Enosburg Falls. After passing through the center of town (16.6 mi.), the trail again departs through farm fields and follows the river before making the first of six crossings of Vt. 105 (18.9 mi.). At the last of these crossings, beyond East Berkshire, the trail reaches the east side of Vt. 105 (22.0 mi.) and passes a view up the Trout River to Hazen's Notch and Sugarloaf Mtn. A short distance beyond, the trail crosses the Missisquoi River on a large single-span truss trestle (23.2 mi.), then continues through rural landscape to reach its terminus on the Troy Road/Vt. 105 (26.1 mi.) in the village of Richford.

MISSISQUOI NATIONAL WILDLIFE REFUGE

This 6,345-acre area, managed by the U.S. Fish and Wildlife Service, was established in 1943 to provide feeding and resting habitat for migratory waterfowl. Lying in the Atlantic Flyway, the refuge occupies much of the Missisquoi River delta on the eastern shore of Lake Champlain (USGS East Alburgh) and consists of marsh, open water, and wooded swamp. Most of the refuge is inaccessible to foot travel.

TO THE TRAIL: The refuge headquarters building is on the south side of Vt. 78, 2.4 mi. west of its junction with U.S. 7 in Swanton village. Parking is available behind the building.

5

About 1.5 mi. of foot trails on a small tongue of land extending southwest between Maquam Creek and Black Creek are open during daylight hours throughout the year. **DESCRIPTION:** The trailhead is at an informational kiosk at the rear of the parking lot. An unblazed but obvious access trail follows a refuge road across the field behind the headquarters building, over the active New England Central Railroad tracks and past a woodcock management area.

At a signed junction, the Maquam Creek Trail departs right and closely follows the shore of the meandering waterway. The trail soon arrives at a signed junction where the Black Creek Trail leaves left. Straight ahead, the Maquam Creek Trail continues about 0.5 mi to reach its end at Lookout Point, deep in the heart of the swamp.

Bearing left at the junction, the Black Creek Trail crosses an impressive series of bridges before wandering along the south shore of the peninsula. The trail leaves the water's edge to reach its end on the refuge road at the start of the Maquam Creek Trail, a short distance from the headquarters.

MONTPELIER AREA

Long home to beloved Hubbard Park, the city of Montpelier and nearby East Montpelier now have an extensive trail network. Walkers and cross-country skiers can enjoy trails connecting Hubbard Park, the North Branch River Park, and East Montpelier.

HUBBARD PARK

In 1899, John E. Hubbard donated 125 acres to the city of Montpelier. Today the park contains 185 acres and nearly 7.0 mi. of hiking and skiing trails, as well as picnic areas, a soccer and softball field, a sledding hill, and a 54-ft. observation tower with spectacular views of the Montpelier area and the surrounding mountain ranges. A map of the Hubbard Park Trails is published by the Montpelier Parks Commission and is available at the city clerk's office in City Hall or at montpelier-vt.org-parks-index.cfm. A self-guiding Nature Trail booklet is sometimes available at the beginning of the trail. Bikes are not permitted on the trail system, but are allowed on park roads. For more information, contact Montpelier Parks Department (802) 223-7335.

A range of habitats is found in the park, including meadows, softwood and hardwood stands, swamps, and thickets. Hubbard Park has several impressive stands of white pine, red pine, and hemlock. The center area is a designated natural area. Near the tower are majestic red oaks, which are at the northern end of their range.

TO THE TRAIL: There are several entrances to Hubbard Park, and it is easily reached by foot from town or by vehicle from access roads with parking. A road also passes through the park leading to many trails as well as a short hike to the tower. The new Statehouse Trail begins on Court Street, 70 yds. east of the statehouse, and leads 3,000 ft. to the tower.

Other entrances to the park are at the end of Winter Street and at the end of Hubbard Park Drive. To reach the Winter Street access, from the intersection of Main and State Streets in downtown Montpelier, proceed north on Main Street for three blocks. At the roundabout, turn left onto Spring Street. At the stop sign, turn right, onto Vt. 12 (Elm Street). Turn left on Winter Street and proceed uphill a short distance to the park entrance and parking.

NORTH BRANCH RIVER PARK

5

With lands protected by the Montpelier Conservation Commission, the North Branch River Park added 179 acres to Montpelier's parks. Approximately 4.0 mi. of trails are available for walking and skiing. A trail and new bridge connect Hubbard Park trails with the Vermont Institute of Natural Science's North Branch Nature Center. The nature center has additional trails including a self-guided nature trail. A trail also leads from the nature center to conserved lands at Sparrow Farm; this trail is open to snowmobiling. A mountain bike trail will be added through North Branch River Park to connect the Elm Street trailhead to the East Montpelier trail systems above Sparrow Farm.

TO THE TRAIL: To access the North Branch trails, park at the city pool parking lot on Elm Street and cross the bridge near the tennis courts or park at the end of Cummings Street or at the nature center.

EAST MONTPELIER TRAILS

A nice addition to the Montpelier areas trails, this 8.0-mi. trail network passes through farm fields and forests. The trails give a glimpse into the working landscape of Vermont as they pass through sugar stands, cornfields, and logged areas. They allow walking, skiing, snowshoeing, and access to and from hunting areas. Biking, horseback riding, and snowmobile use are also permitted on some sections. The trail system is gradually expanding and includes a link with the North Branch River Park in Montpelier and the VINS nature center. For access points or a map, contact the East Montpelier town clerk's office.

SHORT TRAIL

Rich with information on Vermont's natural history, the half-mile loop on the GMC's campus in Waterbury Center is the ideal destination for families with young children.

TO THE TRAIL: Take exit 10 off of I-89 (Waterbury/Stowe exit). Proceed north on Vt. 100 for approximately 5.0 miles (you will pass Ben & Jerry's and the Cold Hollow Cider Mill). GMC is on the left (west) side of Vt. 100.

DESCRIPTION: On the Short Trail, you can see evidence of the glaciers that lingered in Vermont within the last 10.000 years, the stone fences from the early 1800s "sheep fever," and signs of a beaver population on the move. Educational signage is posted along the way, and for those who would like more information in interpreting the landscape, a new guide, *The Short Trail: A Footpath Through History*, is available for $1.50 at the GMC's Hiker Center.

STOWE RECREATION PATH

An internationally recognized 5.5-mi. greenway, this scenic, paved, nonmotorized recreation path follows the West Branch of the Littler River from the village of Stowe to the field at Topnotch Resort and Spa. Along the way, there are gorgeous views of Mt. Mansfield, Vermont's highest peak. With seven access points and four designated parking lots, the path is easily accessible for walking, cycling, inline skating, and cross-country skiing. Bikes, skates, and skis may be rented at nearby stores. For more information, contact 800-24STOWE or locally (802) 253-7321.

WEISSNER WOODS

This 80-acre parcel of woodland was donated to the Stowe Land Trust in 1993 in memory of Fritz Weissner by his family. The trust has established walking trails designed to minimize impact to the site. A map and guide is available from the Stowe Land Trust describing the site and guidelines for its use; visitors should take care to abide by these rules. For more information, contact Stowe Land Trust, P.O. Box 284, Stowe, Vermont 05672; (802) 253-7221.

TO THE TRAIL: From Vt. 100 in Stowe village (0.0 mi.), follow Vt. 108 north and turn right onto Edson Hill Road (3.5 mi.). Continue past the entrance to the Stowhof Inn and take the next drive on the right (3.9 mi.). Parking is available off this private road in a lot on the left.

DESCRIPTION: Two trail loops emanate from a four-corners found about 0.2 mi. from the parking area. To the left, the Meadow Trail, 1.1 mi. long, offers views of Mt. Mansfield and points south along the main range of the Green Mountains. To the right, the Hardwood Ridge Trail and Sugar House Loop make a 1.6-mi. loop.

LAMOILLE COUNTY NATURE CENTER

Located in Morristown, this 40-acre nature center is owned by the nonprofit Lamoille County Natural Resources Conservation District. A self-guiding nature trail examines the characteristics of the northern spruce-fir forest and related management practices and land stewardship principles. For more information, call (802) 888-9218.

TO THE TRAIL: From Vt. 100 about 1 mi. south of Vt. 15A in Morrisville, turn west on the Morristown Corners Road (0.0 mi.). Staying on Morristown Corners Road, bear left at the first intersection (0.1 mi.) and continue straight through the village of Morristown at a four corners (0.7 mi.). Bear left at the next intersection (1.0 mi.) on Walton Road and left again on Cole Hill Road (1.3 mi.). Continue past the Mud City Loop Road to the nature center parking area on the right (about 3.7 mi.).

DESCRIPTION: The main nature loop starts to the left of the signposts and proceeds about 100 yds. to the first station on the trail where pamphlets are available. A short trail to the right of the signposts leads to a wildflower garden, which attracts many types of butterflies in season. The area is open from dawn to dusk.

Northeast
Vermont

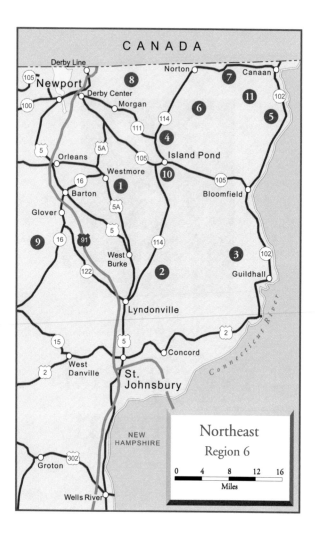

CANADA

Derby Line
Newport
Derby Center
Morgan
Norton
Canaan
Orleans
Westmore
Island Pond
Barton
Bloomfield
Glover
West
Burke
Guildhall
Lyndonville
Concord
West
Danville
St.
Johnsbury
NEW
HAMPSHIRE
Groton
Wells River
Connecticut River

Northeast
Region 6

0   4   8   12   16
Miles

Northeast Vermont

K nown as the Northeast Kingdom, this region is a rugged, heavily forested, and sparsely populated land. Much of the region's interior is accessible only by woods roads, and many people still make their living from traditional use of the land. Geologically, this area has more in common with neighboring New Hampshire than most of the Green Mountain state.

Unlike the major north–south mountain ranges that dominate much of Vermont, this region consists of more than 125 randomly scattered mountains and high hills, many of them nameless. Geologists refer to it as the Northeast Highlands. Heavy glacial tilling formed several large lakes and ponds, among them Maidstone and Averill Lakes. Lake Memphremagog and Lake Willoughby are the best known. The classic profile of the Lake Willoughby gateway is the most notable example of the role played by glaciation in creating this landscape. In many areas, poor drainage has created extensive swamp and muskeg, making foot travel and route finding difficult.

While these mountains once supported an extensive series of fire towers, used from before the advent of aviation until the 1970s to protect the area's vast timberland, only four of these historic towers are still standing on the mountains located east of I-91. On Monadnock Mtn. (Lemington), Bald Mtn. (Westmore), and Burke Mtn., the towers are well maintained and open to the public. On many other summits, including Gore Mtn. and Stone Mtn., the towers have been removed. The only other fire tower to be found in this area is privately owned and closed to public access. Please respect the owner's wishes by not visiting this site.

LAKE WILLOUGHBY AREA

Long acclaimed as one of the most scenic areas in Vermont, Lake Willoughby (USGS Sutton, Island Pond, Westmore) has become the center of an extensive trail system. Although the peaks are relatively low, their dramatic cliffs, the deep waters of the lake, and the scenic views make this an exceptional hiking destination.

Mt. Hor and Mt. Pisgah drop dramatically into Lake Willoughby with some viewpoints looking straight off the mountain to the ice cold waters over 1,000 ft. below. The two mountains form the Lake Willoughby gateway, visible from many mountaintops in northern Vermont and New Hampshire.

Trail maintenance in this area is shared by the Westmore Association, the Department of Forests, Parks and Recreation (FPR), the Northeast Kingdom Conservation Service Corps, and the Northeast Kingdom Section of the Green Mountain Club. Many of the trails are on land that is privately owned. Please respect the generosity of these landowners by not camping or building fires on their property.

The trails are divided into those west of and those east of Lake Willoughby. The *Willoughby State Forest Guide*, available from FPR, contains useful information on the

6

western portion of the region. See page 329 for contact information.

WHEELER MOUNTAIN TRAIL

Distance: 1.3 mi. (2.1 km)
Elevation Change: 690 ft. ascent
Hiking Time: 1 hr. (reverse ½ hr.)

Despite its relatively low elevation, Wheeler Mtn. (2,371 ft., USGS Sutton) offers some of the finest and most varied views in the Lake Willoughby area. Located on private property, this white-blazed trail to the summit and Eagle Cliff is maintained by the Westmore Association. An alternate red-blazed route is steeper and creates a loop.

TO THE TRAIL: The trail begins on the Wheeler Mountain Road (Sutton Town Road 15), which leaves the north side of U.S. 5, 8.3 mi. north of Vt. 5A in the village of West Burke and 5.0 mi. south of Vt. 16 in Barton. From the highway, this unpaved road climbs steadily past Wheeler Pond (1.0 mi.) and the beginning of the Wheeler Pond Trail (1.3 mi.) before arriving at a small parking area on the left (2.0 mi.), beyond the second house on the right. (Please do not park in front of this last house.) Additional roadside parking can be found farther up the road. The Wheeler Mountain Road becomes very rough and potentially impassable approximately 1.0 mi. beyond this point, limiting access from the north.

DESCRIPTION: From the parking area, the hike begins down the road a few feet at the trailhead on the right (0.0 mi.). Passing through a tree line, the trail quickly reaches an overgrown field and a junction where an alternate route begins (0.1 mi.).

> **Junction:** To the right, a shorter and more difficult red-blazed route quickly enters the woods, begins a steep and winding climb over the rocks (where there are views of Mt. Norris and Wheeler Pond), and rejoins the main

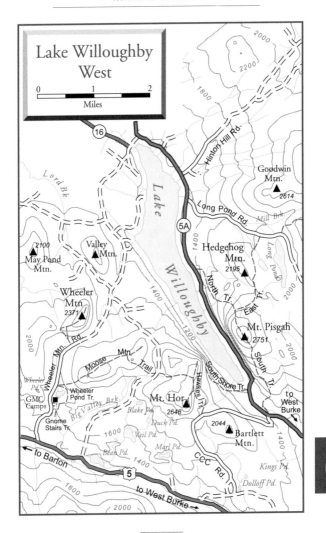

Lake Willoughby
West

0   1   2
Miles

16

Hinton Hill Rd.

Goodwin
Mtn.
▲ 2614

Lord Bk

Lake

Long Pond Rd.

Mill Brk

5A

1400

Long Pond

Valley
▲ Mtn.

2100
▲
May Pond
Mtn.

Hedgehog
Mtn.
▲ 2195

North
Tr.

East Tr.

Wheeler
Mtn
2371 ▲

1400

1200

Willoughby

Mt. Pisgah
▲ 2751

2000

South
Tr.

2000

Wheeler Mtn. Rd.

Moose   Mtn.   Trail

Hawkes Tr.

South Shore Tr.

to
West
Burke

Wheeler
Pd.

GMC
Camps

Wheeler
Pond Tr.

Big Valley Brk.

Blake Pd.

Mt. Hor
▲ 2648

Gnome
Stairs Tr.

Duck Pd.

2044
▲ Bartlett
Mtn.

to Barton

1600

Vail Pd.

Marl Pd.

CCC   Rd.

1400

Bean Pd.   1400

5

1600

to West Burke

2000

Kings Pd.

Dolloff Pd.

6

trail in 0.3 mi. The main trail takes the left fork and follows a less demanding route.

From the junction, the main trail soon enters the woods and ascends easily for some distance before beginning a short but stiff climb (0.4 mi.). After turning sharply right, the trail continues on easier grades past a view of Wheeler Pond (0.5 mi.) to an open rock area where the red-blazed alternate route rejoins the main trail (0.7 mi.). A short distance beyond, an unsigned and unblazed spur on the left ascends 125 ft. to a view, which includes Jay Peak to the northwest.

From the spur junction, the trail winds through spruce and birches for some distance then returns to open rock (0.9 mi.). Remaining well away from the cliffs comprising the southeast face of the mountain, the trail climbs steadily in the open, past ever-widening views of Lake Willoughby, Mt. Pisgah, Burke Mtn., and Bald Mtn. to an impressive vantage (1.1 mi.) where the panorama also includes Jay Peak, Mt. Mansfield, and many other peaks in the Green Mountain Range.

Beyond the lookout, the trail climbs gradually in the open for some distance, then enters the woods near the summit (1.2 mi.) and descends through spruce and balsams to the end of the trail at Eagle Cliff (1.3 mi.). Here, there is an especially grand view of Lake Willoughby, with the open fields in the foreground providing a contrast to the sheer cliffs of Mt. Pisgah and the numerous mountains in the background.

WHEELER POND TRAIL

Distance: 0.5 mi. (0.8 km)
Elevation Change: 80 ft. ascent
Hiking Time: 20 min. either direction

TO THE TRAIL: This trail begins on the Wheeler Mountain Road (follow directions to the Wheeler Mountain Trail,

page 288) at a small parking area 1.3 mi. north of U.S. 5.
DESCRIPTION: From the parking lot (0.0 mi.), the trail, marked with blue blazes, immediately crosses a footbridge over Wheeler Brook to a junction with the Moose Mountain Trail. The Wheeler Pond Trail bears right at the junction and continues through the woods, offering occasional glimpses of Wheeler Pond. The trail meets and joins a woods road (0.3 mi.) that parallels the south shore of the pond; it then arrives at a clearing with a limited view of the pond and an old beaver den (0.4 mi.).

Following the road, the trail turns left and begins a gentle climb before departing the woods road right and continuing along the south branch of Wheeler Brook. After crossing the brook, the Wheeler Pond Trail ends at the start of the Gnome Stairs Trail (0.5 mi.). Straight ahead are the Wheeler Pond Camps owned and operated by the GMC (see page 328). The Wheeler Mountain Road lies 0.1 mi. past these camps, and the parking area is an additional 0.4 mi. north on the road.

GNOME STAIRS TRAIL

Distance: 0.3 mi. (0.5 km)
Elevation Change: 120 ft. descent
Hiking Time: 15 min. (reverse 20 min.)

The Gnome Stairs Trail leads from the Wheeler Pond Trail a short distance to a series of small cascades.
TO THE TRAIL: Follow the Wheeler Pond Trail to Gnome Stairs Trail (0.5 mi.).
DESCRIPTION: The blue-blazed Gnome Stairs Trail leaves the Wheeler Pond Trail near the GMC camps on Wheeler Pond (see Wheeler Pond Trail, page 290), then follows Wheeler Brook in a southerly direction away from the pond. The trail gently descends and meanders along both sides of the brook before reaching its scenic destination (0.3 mi.). The unique series of small steplike waterfalls found here gives the trail its name.

6

MOOSE MOUNTAIN TRAIL

Distance: 3.6 mi. (5.8 km)
Elevation Change: 1,500 ft. ascent
Hiking Time: 2½ hr. (reverse 1¾ hr.)

The blue-blazed trail provides a route between Wheeler Mountain Road and the east branch of the Hawkes Trail on Mt. Hor. At its eastern terminus, it is identified as the Wheeler Pond Trail.

TO THE TRAIL: The trail begins on the Wheeler Mountain Road at a small parking area, 1.3 mi. north of U.S. 5. This also provides access to the Wheeler Pond Trail.

DESCRIPTION: From the parking lot (0.0 mi.), the trail immediately crosses a footbridge over Wheeler Brook to a junction where the Wheeler Pond Trail departs right. Bearing left, the Moose Mountain Trail climbs moderately through a hardwood forest to a second junction (0.5 mi.). From this point, a short spur trail departs right to an outlook with views from southeast to west, including Wheeler Pond.

Bearing left at the junction, the trail climbs more steeply over a series of switchbacks and up a boulder-strewn slope to the west summit. Here, the trail descends briefly, passes by a vernal pool, then follows a broad ridge east as it makes a gradual ascent to the wooded main summit (1.2 mi.). From here the trail begins an easy descent along the scenic ridge to another junction (2.1 mi.).

Junction: From this point, the Lake Willoughby Vista Trail proceeds straight ahead, and in 0.3 mi. reaches a short spur path on the right, which leads to the first of two lookouts. The second lookout, with views of Bald Mtn. and Lake Willoughby, is 250 ft. beyond this spur in an area of deep crevasses. Hikers with small children or dogs should use caution

At the junction, the Moose Mountain Trail bears right and descends, steeply at first, to a forest road in a broad clearing (2.5 mi.). On the south side of the road, the trail enters the woods and soon crosses a small stream. Ascending at an easy grade and staying east of a larger stream, the trail reaches another woods road in a muddy area (3.0 mi.). Turning right onto this road, the trail crosses a small brook on flat stones (3.1 mi.) and narrows into a footpath. Then, ascending more steeply, the Moose Mountain Trail reaches its terminus at the east branch of the Hawkes Trail (3.6 mi.).

MOUNT HOR

HAWKES TRAIL

Distance: 1.4 mi. (2.3 km)
Elevation Change: 700 ft. ascent
Hiking Time: 1 hr. (reverse ¾ hr.)

Forming the west side of the Lake Willoughby gateway, Mt. Hor (2,648 ft., USGS Sutton) is notable for the sheer cliffs that rise more than 1,000 ft. above the lake. The blue-blazed Hawkes Trail, named in honor of trail-builder Herbert Hawkes, provides access to three lookouts on the mountain; two are on the longer east branch of this trail, while the third is just beyond the wooded summit to the west. The total round-trip distance to all three lookouts is 3.4 mi.

TO THE TRAIL: To reach the trailhead from Vt. 5A, follow the CCC Road (0.0 mi.) west from the Mt. Pisgah South Trail parking lot. Bear right at a fork and continue to the trailhead 1.8 mi. from Vt. 5A. There is a small parking area on the right.

DESCRIPTION: From the CCC Road (0.0 mi.), the Hawkes Trail ascends steadily, for the most part on an old woods road. Turning sharply left where the road peters out (0.4 mi.), the trail climbs moderately at first, then quite steeply past a piped spring (0.6 mi.) to a junction (0.7 mi.) with

6

the East Branch and West Branch, just below the summit ridge. These two trails each lead to a viewpoint.

Junction: From the junction, the West Branch turns left. After climbing steadily for most of its ascent, the trail continues on easy grades to a point just below the summit, then quickly descends to the Summit Lookout (1.0 mi.). In the foreground are ten small ponds, among them Bean, Wheeler, Blake, Duck, Vail, and Marl. Burke Mtn. is visible on the left, while Hazen's Notch and several of the northern Green Mountain peaks lie to the northwest.

From the junction (0.7 mi.), the East Branch turns right and continues just below ridgeline to a junction with the Moose Mountain Trail (also known as the Wheeler Pond Trail) on the left (1.0 mi.). The East Branch continues straight through this junction, with little change in elevation, to a final junction. From here, the right spur descends 170 ft. to the East Lookout (1.3 mi.), some 1,200 ft. above Lake Willoughby and directly opposite the cliffs of Mt. Pisgah. Back at the junction, the left spur makes a noticeably longer descent before it ends at the North Lookout (1.4 mi.). Here, there is a sweeping view of the north end of Lake Willoughby, beyond which can be seen the lower end of Lake Memphremagog and several peaks along the Vermont-Quebec border. Bald Mtn. is left of Mt. Pisgah.

SOUTH SHORE TRAIL

Distance: 1.3 mi. (2.1 km)
Elevation Change: 150 ft. ascent
Hiking Time: 40 min. either direction

This short but rough trail slabs the east side of Mt. Hor, 150 ft. above Lake Willoughby, reaching a terminus under the Mt. Hor cliffs.

TO THE TRAIL: The trailhead is at a gated parking area on Vt. 5A, 5.2 mi. south of its junction with Vt. 16 at the north end of Lake Willoughby and 6.2 mi. north of U.S. 5 in the village of West Burke. This lot is 0.5 mi. north of the Mt. Pisgah South Trail parking lot on Vt. 5A.

DESCRIPTION: From the parking area (0.0 mi.), the blue-blazed trail leads 150 yds. to a clearing where it bears left onto a woods road for 50 yds. before leaving the road on the right at a small sign. The trail climbs at a moderate pitch in a westerly direction before turning north and becoming rougher. It then ascends to its terminus in a large gully under the open cliff face of Mt. Hor (1.3 mi.). From this point, there are limited views through the trees toward the lake.

MOUNT PISGAH

Forming the east side of the classic Lake Willoughby profile, Mt. Pisgah (2,751 ft., USGS Sutton, Westmore) has long been popular with hikers. From the sheer cliffs, which rise more than 1,000 ft. above the lake, there are numerous vantage points with fine local and distant views. Two blue-blazed trails from Vt. 5A form a continuous route over the mountain. Completion of the loop, however, requires a scenic 3.0-mi. walk along narrow Vt. 5A. A third trail, maintained by the Westmore Association, provides indirect routing to the summit from Long Pond Rd.

The spur paths near the cliffs may be closed between March 15 and August 1 if peregrine falcons are nesting in the area. (See page 11 for more information.)

SOUTH TRAIL

Distance: 1.7 mi. (2.7 km)
Elevation Change: 1,450 ft. ascent
Hiking Time: 1¾ (reverse 1 hr.)

6

TO THE TRAIL: This trail begins on the east side of Vt. 5A, opposite a state parking area and the beginning of the CCC Road, 5.8 mi. south of the junction of Vt. 16 at the

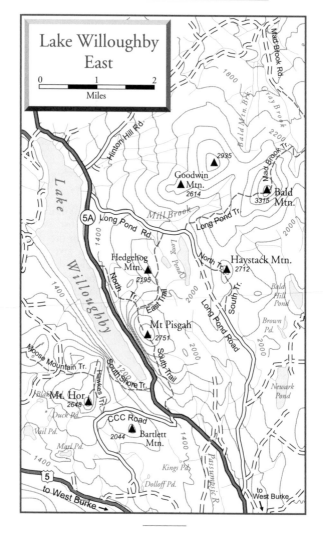

Lake Willoughby East

0   1   2

Miles

north end of Lake Willoughby and 5.8 mi. north of U.S. 5 in the village of West Burke.

DESCRIPTION: From the road (0.0 mi.), the trail descends an embankment and quickly crosses a swampy area on two boardwalks. Turning left, the trail follows a hogback to a woods road junction (0.2 mi.). Here, it turns right and ascends for some distance through rocky terrain before again turning sharply left (0.4 mi.) and beginning a steep climb. Soon after negotiating a switchback (0.5 mi.), the trail continues on much easier grades before reaching Pulpit Rock (0.9 mi.), where there is a dramatic view of Lake Willoughby and Mt. Hor.

From Pulpit Rock, the trail bears right to begin a steady climb, eventually reaching the South Lookout where there are views of the White Mountains, Victory Basin, Newark Pond, Burke Mtn., and some of the Green Mountains. From here, the trail continues a short distance to the summit and the upper end of the North Trail (1.7 mi.).

Continuing over the summit via the North Trail, it is an additional 0.3 mi. to the last of three lookout spurs providing outstanding views of Lake Willoughby, Lake Memphremagog, and the Green Mountains, and 2.2 mi. to Vt. 5A. Continuing on the North Trail requires a car spot or a 3.0 mi. road walk.

NORTH TRAIL

Distance: 2.2 mi. (3.5 km)
Elevation Change: 1,530 ft. ascent
Hiking Time: 2 hr. (reverse 1¼ hr.)

TO THE TRAIL: The trail begins on the east side of Vt. 5A, 3.0 mi. south of its junction with Vt. 16 near the north end of Lake Willoughby and 3.0 mi. north of the beginning of the South Trail. Limited parking is available near the trailhead.

DESCRIPTION: From the highway (0.0 mi.), the trail ascends a steep bank and soon enters the woods, following old woods roads on easy grades. After crossing two brooks

6

(0.6 mi. and 0.8 mi.), the trail follows steeper grades to a third brook crossing, the last certain water on the trail (1.0 mi.). Beyond the third crossing, the trail turns sharply left to climb fairly steeply on an old road. Soon turning right off the road (1.2 mi.), the trail climbs steeply on rough footing to a junction with the East Trail (1.5 mi.), which climbs Mt. Pisgah from Long Pond Road.

Passing this junction, the trail continues its steep climb over rough ground to the first of three spur trails on the right (1.9 mi.). The lower spur leads 350 ft. northwest to the North Lookouts; the nearby middle spur leads west 90 ft. to the West Lookout. Although the views are about the same from each vantage point, the differences in elevation and angle of view provide different perspectives. From the West Lookout, some 1,400 ft. directly above the lake and the road, the views include Mt. Hor, Wheeler Mtn., and other local peaks to the west; Lake Memphremagog, Owl's Head, Bear Mtn., and other Quebec summits to the north; many of the Green Mountain peaks from Jay Peak south to Camel's Hump; and Burke Mtn. and a number of New Hampshire peaks to the south, including Mt. Moosilauke.

Farther on, the trail passes a third lookout spur as it approaches the summit of Mt. Pisgah and the north end of the South Trail (2.2 mi.).

From the summit, the South Trail quickly passes the South Lookout as it leads 1.7 mi. down to Vt. 5A. Taking this route requires a car spot or a 3.0 mi. road walk.

East Trail

Distance: 1.9 mi. (3.0 km)
Elevation Change: 350 ft. ascent
Hiking Time: 1¼ hr. (reverse 1 hr.)

This trail, also known as the Long Pond–Mt. Pisgah Trail, provides an indirect link between the other trails on Mt. Pisgah and the trails on Bald Mtn. and Haystack Mtn. to the east. Maintained by the Westmore Association, most of the route is on a signed but unblazed truck road, while the upper portion is marked with white blazes. The trail joins the North Trail 0.7 mi. below the summit.

To the Trail: Trailhead parking is on Long Pond Road at a truck road junction 1.8 mi. east of the Willoughby Lake Store on Vt. 5A in Westmore and 0.3 mi. west of the Long Pond Fishing Access.

Description: From Long Pond Road (0.0 mi.), the trail descends southerly on the truck road to a brook crossing (0.3 mi.), then ascends to a small clearing on the left (1.0 mi.), which offers a view of Bald Mtn. and Haystack Mtn. The trail then continues to a junction in a large clearing (1.4 mi.). Here, it turns sharply right to cross a tiny stream and a waterbar and enters an older grassy woods road. Continuing with minor elevation changes, the trail bears left at a fork (1.5 mi.) and follows the road for some distance before turning sharply left off the road into the woods (1.6 mi.). White blazing begins at this point. The trail climbs easily for some distance before ascending more steeply to a junction (1.9 mi.) with the North Trail to Mt. Pisgah. From this point, it is 0.7 mi. south to the summit of Mt. Pisgah or 1.5 mi. north (downhill) to Vt. 5A.

Bald Mountain, Westmore

Sometimes referred to as Westmore Mtn., Bald Mtn. (3,315 ft., USGS Island Pond) has a recently restored fire tower on its heavily wooded summit. The tower provides extensive views that include Lake Willoughby, various local peaks, and much of the Green Mountain Range to the west; Lake Seymour, Lake Memphremagog, and several Quebec mountains to the north and northwest; Island Pond, Percy Peaks, the Columbia Range, and northern White Mountain peaks to the east; and Burke Mtn., Umpire Mtn., and the Presidential Range to the south.

6

Currently, two maintained trails lead to the summit: the Long Pond Trail from the southwest and the Mad Brook Trail from the northeast. A third trail, the long-abandoned Lookout's Trail (also known as Telegraph Trail), which ascends from the north, is nearly impossible to follow through a logged section.

LONG POND TRAIL

Distance: 2.1 mi. (3.4 km)
Elevation Change: 1,450 ft. ascent
Hiking Time: 1¾ hr. (reverse 1 hr.)

TO THE TRAIL: Located mainly on private property, this trail begins on a truck road that leaves the Long Pond Road, 2.1 mi. east from the Willoughby Lake Store on Vt. 5A in Westmore and 0.1 mi. east of the Long Pond fishing access area. Ample parking is available at the trailhead. Except for the unblazed truck road portion where signs mark critical turns, the trail is marked with blue blazes.

DESCRIPTION: From the gate at the trailhead (0.0 mi.), the trail ascends northerly on the truck road, bears right at a fork (0.2 mi.), and climbs steadily northeast until it enters a large clearing (0.5 mi.). The trail turns sharply right at the top of the clearing and follows an old woods road for a short distance before turning sharply left at a trail sign (0.6 mi.) where the blazing begins.

Ascending very gradually easterly through pleasant open woods, the trail eventually reaches an old woods road junction (1.0 mi.). Here, it turns sharply left, descends gradually to cross a brook (1.1 mi.), then resumes its ascent, crossing three smaller streams and a larger brook (1.3 mi.)

Beyond the brook crossing, the trail ascends steadily for some distance, then continues on easier grades to an old woods road junction (1.5 mi.). Here, the trail turns sharply right and begins an increasingly steep climb easterly. After swinging around a large rock outcrop (1.8 mi.), the trail continues a steady winding ascent for some distance before bearing left (2.0 mi.) and climbing on easy grades to the summit and the fire tower (2.1 mi.).

MAD BROOK TRAIL

Distance: 2.9 mi. (4.6 km)
Elevation Change: 1,415 ft. ascent
Hiking Time: 2¾ hr. (reverse 1½ hr.)

Caution: This trail may not be suitable for everyone. The presence of a deceptively aggressive dog at a house near the parking area could make this trail a poor choice for hikers with children or dogs. The noticeably shorter Long Pond Trail can be reached from this direction by taking Westmore Road to Hinton Hill Road, which in turn leads to Vt. 5A at the first junction north of Long Pond Road.

TO THE TRAIL: This trail begins at the gated terminus of Mad Brook Road in East Charleston. From the junction of Vt. 105 and Vt. 114 outside Island Pond, follow Vt. 105 west 3.1 mi. to Hudson Road on the left. Leaving Vt. 105 (0.0 mi.) follow Hudson Road briefly before turning left onto Westmore Road (0.3 mi.). Stay on Westmore Road to Mad Brook Road (1.5 mi.). Turning left, follow Mad Brook Road to a small parking lot on the right (2.8 mi.). Please do not block the nearby gate or driveway when parking.

DESCRIPTION: From the parking area (0.0 mi.), the trail follows this road beyond the gate for over a half mile before passing a second house on the right and entering an open meadow. The trail continues straight through the meadow where it meets a woods road marked by a trail sign high on a tree. Climbing on easy grades as it follows the grassy road for a significant distance, the trail swings west where it descends briefly to a brook crossing (1.7 mi.) at the base of the mountain. From here, the trail climbs gradually via a large switchback, then more steeply toward the summit (2.9 mi.).

6

HAYSTACK MOUNTAIN

Just below the heavily wooded summit of this aptly named mountain (2,712 ft., USGS Sutton, Westmore) are three lookouts providing excellent views to the west, south, and east. Two trails, located on private property, lead to the summit. The North Trail is the steeper of the two routes. Both trails, with a 1.2 mi. road walk, make a nice loop hike.

NORTH TRAIL

Distance: 1.0 mi. (1.6 km)
Elevation Change: 875 ft. ascent
Hiking Time: 1 hr. (reverse ½ hr.)

TO THE TRAIL: This yellow-blazed trail begins at the entrance to a small clearing on Long Pond Road, 2.6 mi. southeast of Vt. 5A at the Willoughby Lake Store in Westmore and 0.6 mi. beyond the Long Pond fishing access area. Parking space is very limited and care should be taken not to obstruct the narrow public road.

DESCRIPTION: From the road (0.0 mi.), the trail quickly passes through an overgrown clearing and climbs steadily in an easterly direction on an old woods road. Eventually assuming a southerly direction (0.4 mi.), the trail continues for some distance on easier grades before beginning a moderately steep climb (0.7 mi.) past views of Bald Mtn. and Long Pond (0.8 mi.) to a junction (1.0 mi.).

> **Junction:** To the left, it is 75 ft. to the summit, which is marked by a large cairn. To the right, a spur descends easily 150 ft. to West Lookout where there are views of Long Pond, Lake Willoughby, Wheeler Mtn., and Jay Peak. From the summit, the South Trail descends 0.1 mi. to the East Lookout and 0.2 mi. to the South Lookout.

SOUTH TRAIL

Distance: 1.1 mi. (1.8 km)
Elevation Change: 525 ft. ascent
Hiking Time: ¾ hr. (reverse ½ hr.)

TO THE TRAIL: This yellow-blazed trail begins on Long Pond Road, 3.8 mi. southeast of Vt. 5A at the Willoughby Lake Store in Westmore, 1.2 mi. south of the North Trail trailhead. Although ample parking is available at the trailhead, the 1.2 mi. section of the minimally maintained Long Pond Road between the North Trail parking area and the beginning of the South Trail may not be passable for vehicles with low clearance.

DESCRIPTION: From Long Pond Road (0.0 mi.), the trail ascends gradually in a northeasterly direction on an old road to a junction in a large overgrown clearing (0.6 mi.). Here, the trail turns left, passes the ruins of an old camp and continues on easy grades through a series of small, overgrown clearings before entering the woods. Soon turning sharply left (0.8 mi.), the trail begins a steep and winding ascent around rocks and ledges to a junction on the east side of the ridge (0.9 mi.). To the left, a spur leads 125 ft. to South Lookout where there are views of Burke Mtn. and Newark Pond

From the junction, the trail ascends to the East Lookout (1.0 mi.) where there are views of Bald Mtn., Bald Hill Pond, East Haven Mtn., and various White Mountain peaks. From the East Lookout, the trail continues to a large cairn marking the summit of Haystack Mtn. (1.1 mi.). A short distance beyond, the trail reaches a junction with the North Trail (page 302) on the right. Continuing straight through this junction, a spur path leads 150 ft. to the West Lookout

6

•••••••••••••••••

BURKE MOUNTAIN

Located in East Burke, Burke Mtn. (3,267 ft., USGS Burke Mountain) is home to a ski area, private campground, toll road, and communications facilities on its west slopes and summit. The mountain's hiking trails offer good views of the surrounding area. The Burke Cross-Country Ski Center offers excellent groomed ski trails. In recent years, business owners and local residents founded the Kingdom Trails Association, which publishes a map that includes hiking trails on Burke Mtn. and a network of mountain bike trails.

The summit of Burke Mtn. was one of the earliest fire tower sites in Vermont. The station was established in 1912 when Elmer A. Darling built a camp and tower on the mountaintop. The original tower collapsed in 1932 due to a buildup of ice and snow. A new wooden tower was constructed, but lasted only six years when it fell victim to the 1938 hurricane, which also destroyed the original fire tower atop nearby Bald Mtn. The steel tower with an enclosed cab, currently occupying the summit, was used as a fire lookout until 1984.

TOLL ROAD

Built by the Civilian Conservation Corps, the 2.5-mi. Toll Road leads to a parking area just below the summit. A fee is charged for vehicles, but hikers may walk the road for free. From the parking area near the summit, the Summit Trail and the Profile Trail lead to scattered lookouts around the main summit and the West Peak. Descriptions for these trails follow.

TO THE TRAILS: From downtown East Burke, follow Vt. 114 north a short distance to the turn for Mountain Road (the access road to Burke Mountain Ski Area) on the right (0.0 mi.). Follow Mountain Road to where the Toll Road branches left (2.0 mi.). From here the Toll Road leads 2.5

mi. to the summit parking lot. Mountain Road ends at the Mid-Burke Lodge parking area (2.5 mi.). Please park here if you plan to walk the Toll Road.

SUMMIT TRAIL

From the south end of the parking area at the top of the Toll Road (0.0 mi.), the Summit Trail trends easterly to a junction with the Profile Trail (0.2 mi.). Here, the Summit Trail turns left and ascends northerly in the woods to the base of the summit fire tower (0.3 mi.).

PROFILE TRAIL

The Profile Trail (also known as the Under Profile Trail) coincides with the Summit Trail between the parking area and the junction (0.2 mi.), at which point the Profile Trail turns right to follow a separate routing. After a brief gradual descent, the trail swings left into a ravine and ascends along the base of the ledges before climbing to a junction with a short lookout spur. Continuing, it rejoins the Summit Trail, which it follows for a very short distance to the fire tower (0.5 mi.).

CCC ROAD

Distance: 3.2 mi. (5.1 km)
Elevation Change: 450 ft. ascent
Hiking Time: 1¾ hr. (reverse 2 hr.)

This is a moderate, multiuse trail built by the Civilian Conservation Corps.

TO THE TRAIL: Blazed with blue diamonds, this multiuse trail leaves the Toll Road at a signed junction, 0.6 mi. above the ski area access road. Limited parking is available at a small lot 300 ft. below the junction or along the Toll Road a short distance uphill from the junction.

6

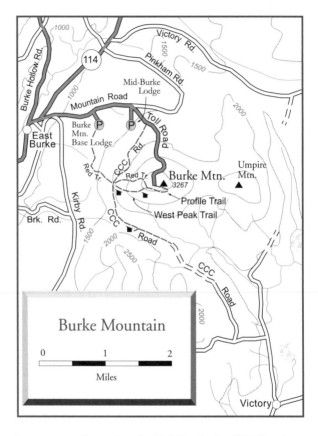

Burke Mountain

0   1   2

Miles

DESCRIPTION: Departing the Toll Road, the CCC Road ascends south on easy grades, crossing several ski trails that offer good views west. Continuing in the woods, the road reaches its highest point at an intersection with the Red Trail (1.3 mi.). (The Red Trail and the nearby West Peak Trail both lead to the summit area from here.) From the height of land, the CCC Road descends easily southeast into the shallow notch between Burke Mtn. and Kirby Mtn. to the south. Soon after passing a lean-to on the right (2.1 mi.), the trail reaches a junction with a privately maintained snowmobile trail (blazed with orange diamonds), which leaves right (2.2 mi.) and heads westerly for about 1.25 mi. to the public East Burke Road between North Kirby and East Burke. Beyond the junction, the CCC Road descends on easy grades past the state forest boundary to a woods road junction (3.2 mi.).

Junction: Straight ahead from the junction, an old road descends on easy grades for about 1.25 mi. to the beginning of a public road which leads south for about 3.5 mi. to the Victory-Granby Road, about 1.0 mi. south of the Mitchell's Landing parking area.

WEST PEAK TRAIL

Distance: 1.1 mi. (1.8 km)
Elevation Change: 960 ft. ascent
Hiking Time: 1¼ hr. (reverse ¾ hr.)

The West Peak Trail (sometimes referred to as the Blue Trail because of its blazing) climbs the west side of Burke Mtn. while connecting with the Red Trail near the CCC Road for a possible loop hike.

TO THE TRAIL: This trail leaves the Red Trail just above an intersection with the CCC Road (page 305) at its highest point, 1.3 mi. south of the Toll Road.

DESCRIPTION: From the CCC Road junction, the Red Trail climbs 200 ft. to the site of a log lean-to and a junction with the lower end of the West Peak Trail (0.0 mi.). Departing right, the West Peak Trail begins a sustained climb through secluded forest to another lean-to at the wooded summit (3,150 ft.) of the West Peak (0.8 mi.).

Quickly reaching a good view to the south, the trail circles around the south and east slope to the upper terminus of the Red Trail (0.9 mi.), which departs left. The West

6

Peak Trail then gradually descends to a ski trail (1.0 mi.), which it follows uphill to the south end of the Toll Road parking area (1.1 mi.).

The West Peak Trail ends at this point, but the blue-blazed Summit and Profile Trails (page 305), which can be combined into an interesting loop, provide routing to the summit fire tower.

RED TRAIL

Distance: 2.5 mi. (4.0 km)
Elevation Change: 1,600 ft. ascent
Hiking Time: 2 hr. (reverse 1¼ hr.)

Blazed with red paint, this trail provides an alternate route to the summit area of Burke Mtn. for those who want to avoid the Toll Road and the ski slopes.

TO THE TRAIL: From downtown East Burke, follow Vt. 114 north a short distance, then turn right onto Mountain Road (0.0 mi.). Follow Mountain Road to the Base Lodge Road on the right (1.1 mi.). Take this road to the lower parking lot of the Burke Mountain Ski Area. The trailhead kiosk is located at the far south end of this parking lot (1.3 mi.).

DESCRIPTION: From the kiosk (0.0 mi.), the route follows the gated woods road south as it climbs on easy grades. The Red Trail leaves this road at a signed junction on the left (0.6 mi.). Heading southeast, the footpath travels through an area that is usually very wet. The trail soon begins a sustained climb on drier terrain, staying away from any signs of the ski resort. This trail continues its climb through a mature forest until it reaches an intersection with the CCC Road (1.7 mi.).

After crossing the CCC Road, the Red Trail climbs 200 ft. to a junction with the lower end of the West Peak Trail at the site of a log lean-to. Turning left at this junction, the Red Trail passes between the lean-to and a rock outcrop as it begins a side hill traverse. The trail eventually swings around to the north slope of the West Peak where it approaches, but generally remains hidden from the nearby ski trails. It ends at a junction with the West Peak Trail (2.5 mi.), 0.1 mi. east of West Peak and 0.2 mi. below the parking area at the top of the Toll Road.

• • • • • • • • • • • • • • • • •

MAIDSTONE STATE FOREST

Distance: 1.8 mi. (2.9 km)
Elevation Change: 270 ft. ascent
Hiking Time: 1 hr. (reverse: 55 min.)

Lying deep within the Northeast Kingdom, Maidstone Lake was created during the last glacial age, when tremendous forces carved out a deep basin in a preexisting valley. When the glaciers retreated some 12,000 years ago, a clear, cold lake was formed, typical of many in the region.

The Department of Forests, Parks and Recreation operates two facilities along the east side of the 796-acre lake. Maidstone State Park offers day-use activities (including a beach), while Maidstone State Forest contains a variety of camping facilities. Three short trails, totaling less than 2.0 mi., encircle the camping areas in the state forest. A brochure describing the area is available and a fee is charged in season.

TO THE TRAIL: From Bloomfield, follow Vt. 102 south for about 5.0 mi., then turn west onto the gravel Maidstone Lake Road at a Maidstone State Park sign (0.0 mi.). Continue through the state park (5.8 mi.) before reaching the state forest contact station (6.9 mi.), where you can inquire about day-use parking, then follow the access road to the Camper's Beach (7.2 mi.).

DESCRIPTION: The trailhead (0.0 mi.) is at the south end of the Camper's Beach. From this point, the Shore Trail

6

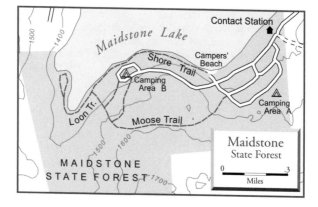

follows the lake's undeveloped south side along flat grades to reach its terminus at a junction (0.6 mi.) with the Loon Trail. From the junction, a spur of the Loon Trail continues straight ahead, passes very close to a beaver lodge (0.7 mi.) and ends in a small loop at the southwest corner of the lake (0.9 mi.).

At the junction, the Loon Trail ascends left gently to reach the south side of Camping Area B where two spur trails leave left and enter the campground. The Moose Trail then continues to climb very moderately to three large boulders at the top of a wooded slope, before descending to Camping Area A near the parking lot and trailhead (1.8 mi.).

●●●●●●●●●●●●●●●●●

BLUFF MOUNTAIN

Located in Brighton (USGS Island Pond), Bluff Mtn. rises steeply from the village of Island Pond and extends northeasterly forming the northwestern boundary of the Nulhegan River Basin and overlooking the eastern headwaters of the Clyde River.

BLUFF MOUNTAIN COMMUNITY TRAIL

Distance: 1.7 mi. (2.7 km)
Elevation Change: 1,080 ft. ascent
Hiking Time: 1¼ hr. (reverse ¾ hr.)

The Bluff Mountain Community Trail climbs to the lower summit and lookout on Bluff Mtn. Although it has existed for many years, portions of the trail have been relocated and stabilized because of recent logging and damage from the 1998 ice storm.

TO THE TRAIL: The blue-blazed trail, restored and maintained by the Northeast Kingdom Conservation Service Corps, begins on the north side of Mountain Street in Island Pond. From the junction of Vt. 105 and Vt. 114 in downtown Island Pond, follow Vt. 105 past the historic railroad station going east. Turn left onto South Street immediately after crossing the bridge over the railroad tracks. The turn for Mountain Street is on the right, directly opposite the upper entrance to Island Pond's impressive downtown footbridge. Continue on Mountain Street for about 0.6 mi. to a small parking area on the left. The total distance from downtown is less than one mile.

DESCRIPTION: From the parking area, the trail climbs moderately north through a red pine plantation before bearing west, over two small stream crossings (0.2 mi.), into a mixed forest. From here, the trail begins to climb steadily northwest through open mixed hardwoods, crosses an old woods logging road (0.4 mi.), and follows a small ridge until it crosses a game trail and turns sharply left (0.6 mi.). The trail soon turns right and, climbing more steeply, follows another small ridge before turning left again. Now turning westward, the trail descends slightly, crosses a small ravine, and follows a wooded sidehill where limited views of Island Pond and the Nulhegan Basin are seen to

6

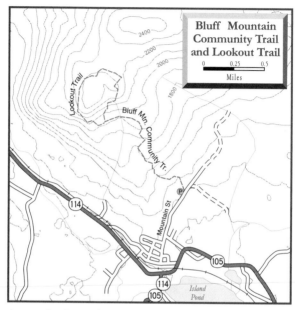

the south. Soon the trail turns sharply left to descend a short steep grade before bearing right where it continues to follow a sidehill and again descends to the junction with the now-abandoned old trail (0.9 mi.).

From here, the trail turns northward again and, within a few yards, passes a stream crossing and the lower junction of the historic Lookout Trail (1.0 mi.). Continuing north, the main trail passes through a heavily cut area before climbing more steadily north and east through an improved section of stone steps and a series of switchbacks. After cresting a small knoll (1.3 mi.), the trail makes a short descent before turning steeply left, up a second series of steps and switchbacks, to the summit ridge where there are views of the Nulhegan Basin and the surrounding hills to the south and east.

From the top of the steep section (1.5 mi.), the trail continues through a high-elevation gully, winds northward, and drops into a small moose hollow (1.6 mi.) where it crosses a wet area and again climbs up onto the summit ridge. After a few hundred yards, the trail reaches the short summit spur trail on the right and the historic Lookout Trail directly ahead (1.7 mi.). From the summit, Bald Mtn. is evident to the southeast.

LOOKOUT TRAIL

Distance: 0.5 mi. (0.8 km)
Elevation Change: 760 ft. ascent
Hiking Time: 40 min. (reverse 25 min.)

The yellow-blazed Lookout Trail is the last remaining portion of the original Bluff Mountain Trail. From the cliff lookouts near the summit, extensive views of Island Pond, East Mtn., Burke Mtn., and a number of other small peaks are visible to the south and west. Caution: The Lookout Trail is steep and rocky in places and may not be suitable for some hikers.

DESCRIPTION: From the lower junction of the Bluff Mountain Trail, the Lookout Trail crosses a small stream and climbs gently through a large clearcut. At the far edge (0.2 mi.), the trail enters a gradually more mature hardwood forest and bears right. Here, it climbs steeply at times to the base of the lookout. The trail continues up, with several small switchbacks, over open rock faces to a lower lookout (0.3 mi.) with views of the Nulhegan Basin to the south.

From the lower lookout, the trail continues to climb steeply to the main lookout (0.4 mi.) with more extensive views of the surrounding area. From the lookout, the trail continues moderately to the summit spur and upper junction of the Bluff Mountain Trail (0.5 mi.).

6

• • • • • • • • • • • • • • •

MOUNT MONADNOCK

Distance: 2.5 mi. (4.0 km)
Elevation Change: 2,108 ft. ascent
Hiking Time: 2½ hr. (reverse 2 hr.)

Only slightly lower than the more famous Mt. Monadnock of southern New Hampshire and far less frequently visited, this mountain rises abruptly from the banks of the Connecticut River in the town of Lemington. The mountain is especially impressive when seen from the Mohawk Valley between Colebrook and Dixville Notch, New Hampshire. The fire tower at the summit (3,148 ft., USGS Monadnock Mtn.) was restored in 2005 after many years of neglect. Significant improvements to the trail are also in progress.

To the Trail: The trail begins on the west side of Vt. 102 at a gravel pit, 0.1 mi. north of the Lemington-Colebrook Bridge where there is ample parking in the designated area on the far left side of the pit.

Description: From the parking area (0.0 mi.), the trail leaves the rear of the gravel pit and climbs the bank to a sign (0.1 mi.). Bearing left, it crosses an open field, then turns sharply right where it passes over some long berms and a snowmobile trail before entering the woods. Now blazed with yellow parallelogram-shaped markers, the trail soon passes through an overgrown field with limited views north along the Connecticut River Valley and east toward Dixville Notch in New Hampshire.

Returning to a mature mixed forest, the trail passes near and under several rock outcroppings. Farther on, it makes a sharp left turn before beginning a short, steep climb to the first of two brook crossings (0.7 mi.). After crossing the brook on steppingstones, the trail quickly joins the old road that originally provided access to the fire tower at the summit. It follows this road uphill, with a scenic gorge on the right, until it reaches a footbridge at the second brook crossing near a fine waterfall (1.1 mi.). While the mileage given

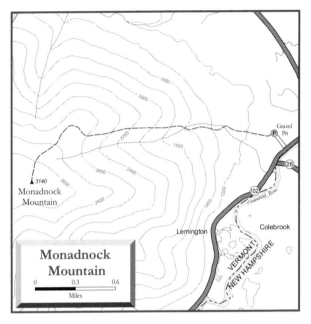

Monadnock
Mountain

0   0.3   0.6
Miles

here might suggest the halfway point of the hike, in reality it will take nearly twice as long to finish the remaining climb as it took to reach this point.

As it gradually diverges from the brook, the trail begins a rough and rocky ascent along a shoulder of the mountain. It continues this relentless climb through a section of forest, badly damaged during the ice storm of 1998. Passing through some wet areas, the grade eases somewhat before reaching the summit and fire tower (2.5 mi.) in a dense growth of fir. The foundation of the fire lookout's cabin is nearby. This summit area provides habitat for the rare spruce grouse, commonly known as the fool bird.

●●●●●●●●●●●●●●●●

GORE MOUNTAIN

Distance: 3.8 mi. (6.1 km)
Elevation Change: 1,972 ft. ascent
Hiking Time: 3½ hr. (reverse 2 hr.)

Located in Avery's Gore (USGS Norton Pond), Gore Mtn. (3,332 ft.) forms the northern boundary of the Nulhegan River Basin. The wooded summit has a remote feeling and offers limited views. The recently restored Gore Mountain Trail follows much of the historic fire warden's trail used to access the summit cabin and lookout tower. While the cabin is still standing, the tower has been removed.

To the Trail: The trailhead is in Norton off Vt. 114 across from a pull-off between Lake Station Road and DeVost Road at the north end of Norton Pond. The white-blazed trail, built and maintained by the Northeast Kingdom Conservation Service Corps, enters the woods through a small opening on the east side of the road.

Description: From the trailhead, the trail makes a short climb, follows an unnamed brook for a short way, then climbs gradually for the first mile along the old woods road, originally used to access the summit. After the initial ascent from Norton Pond, the trail levels and crosses several boggy areas using bog bridges and steppingstones. A short spur trail leads left to a beaver meadow (0.6 mi.) where the wooded summit of Gore appears eastward in the distance.

From here, the trail climbs gradually, following a series of beaver meadows, and crosses two more small brooks before reaching the most recently abandoned beaver pond (0.9 mi.). The trail skirts the northern edge of the opening and turns eastward, continuing straight for some time through more boggy areas and a logged forest. After passing some abandoned machinery on the right, the trail soon bears left at a signed junction (1.2 mi.) and crests a small knoll (1.3 mi.). From the height of land, the trail descends gradually, winding until it reaches the edge of a wet area and, immediately thereafter, a tributary of Station Brook

(1.5 mi.). It follows the southern bank of the brook a short distance and, after crossing it, emerges on the edge of an expansive logged area (1.6 mi.). The trail passes through and skirts the logged area, winding through small hardwood stands before turning northeastward and climbing more steeply to the crest of a second knoll. Here, the trail continues for a short distance through a young forest to the edge of a large timber company road (2.0 mi.). The marked trail continues on the opposite side of the clearing.

After crossing the logging road, the trail climbs a short, steep grade and bends right where it soon reaches the junction with the Lookout Trail (2.1 mi.).

Junction: The Lookout Trail leads 300 ft. westward down a gradual grade to the edge of an old sandpit and

6

the timber company road. From here, local views of Middle Mtn. and the Hurricane area are visible to the west.

From the lookout junction, the trail turns left and continues, at a moderate grade, to a second road crossing (2.4 mi.) where it continues opposite the road and, after a short distance, climbs steeply through moderately open hardwoods along the northwest ridge of the mountain. There are occasional views along the way. To the north are Brousseau and Round Mtns.; Coaticook and the Eastern Townships of Quebec are to the northwest; and to the west are the Bill Sladyk (Hurricane) Wildlife Management Area lands in Norton and Holland.

After passing an old skid road (3.0 mi.), the trail turns left to begin a more persistent climb into the higher elevation spruce-fir forests of the summit. The trail bears south and continues steeply over granite bedrock to the shoulder of the mountain. Continuing, it enters the summit forest and turns eastward (3.5 mi.), winding its way until emerging at the edge of the summit clearing (3.8 mi.). Here, the abandoned fire warden's cabin still stands, and an outhouse is located north of the clearing down a short spur trail. From the summit, there are limited views of the Nulhegan Basin to the south.

●●●●●●●●●●●●●●●●

BROUSSEAU MOUNTAIN TRAIL

Distance: 0.8 mi. (1.3 km)
Elevation Change: 614 ft. ascent
Hiking Time: 1.0 hr. (reverse ¾ hr.)

Located in the town of Norton, Brousseau Mtn. (2,714 ft., USGS Averill) offers a spectacular view of Little Averill Lake and the former Champion Lands. A short trail, maintained by the Northeast Kingdom Conservation Service Corps, gives access to the top of the mountain's extensive south-facing cliffs.

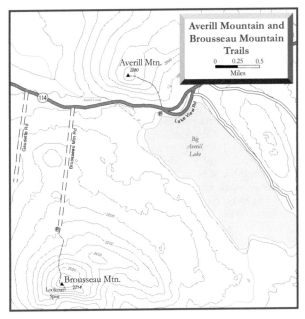

Averill Mountain and
Brousseau Mountain
Trails

0   0.25   0.5
Miles

Averill Mtn.
2280

114

Averill Creek

Lake View Rd

Big
Averill
Lake

Gaudette Rd

Brousseau Mtn Rd

2000

2200

2400

2600

Brousseau Mtn.
2714

Lookout
Spur

Note: Brousseau Mtn. provides one of the few poten-
tial nesting sites in northern Vermont for the peregrine falcon. While this bird is no longer listed as endangered, it
remains a protected species. Please plan to hike here after
August 1, if possible, to avoid the spring to summer incu-
bation and nesting period when these birds and their
young are most easily disturbed. (See page 11 for more
information.)

To the Trail: Limited parking is available at the gated terminus of Brousseau Mountain Road, which leaves Vt. 114
at an unmarked junction located 2.9 mi. east of the border
crossing in Norton and 1.5 mi. west of the Lake View
Store in Averill. The unpaved and unsigned Brousseau
Mountain Road (not maintained in winter) follows a

6

nearly straight course south from Vt. 114. Climbing uphill at first, this road soon descends to a flat stretch before it reaches the gate at 1.2 mi. Please do not block the gate or camp access when parking.

DESCRIPTION: From the gate, continue straight on the road for almost 350 ft. to the start of the trail at a sign on the left. As it begins a mostly gradual climb, the trail passes through an overgrown field before entering a recently cut mixed forest. After the trail crosses a logging road, it enters a mature softwood forest. The footway now travels over granite bedrock (which is often wet and slippery) until it reaches the wooded summit (0.8 mi.).

Beyond the summit, the trail descends for nearly 350 ft. to the dramatic cliff-top lookout. This last section of the trail might be closed between March 15 and August 1 if nesting falcons are present.

• • • • • • • • • • • • • • • • •

AVERILL MOUNTAIN TRAIL

Distance: 0.7 mi. (1.1 km)
Elevation Change: 540 ft. ascent
Hiking Time: ¾ hr. (reverse ½ hr.)

Located just south of the Canadian Border in the town of Norton, Averill Mtn. (2,240 ft., USGS Averill) offers an excellent view of Big Averill Lake and the mountains of northern Vermont.

TO THE TRAIL: This trail leaves the north side of Vt. 114 at an inconspicuous trailhead located 3.9 mi. east of the border crossing in Norton and 0.5 mi. west of the Lake View Store in Averill. Roadside parking can be found nearby at the west junction of Lake View Road and Vt. 114. (The east junction is directly across from the store.) There is room to park on the south shoulder of the highway leading into Lake View Road.

DESCRIPTION: The trail begins across Vt. 114, a short distance west and is marked by two small signs near the roadside. Heading north, the trail crosses a wet area on planks as it enters the woods. This well-worn footpath is marked with blue and orange flagging. Climbing on easy to moderate grades as it swings gradually west, the trail stays well away from the steep terrain of the mountain's south slope. After passing near the top (0.6 mi.), the trail drops steeply into a small saddle and an unmarked junction. The two pathways leading from here form a very short loop before reaching the lookout. The more direct route continues straight through the junction and climbs steeply out of the saddle to the second junction. Turning left, the lookout is at the end of a short spur path. The other side of this summit loop provides an easier (but slightly longer) approach between these two junctions.

• • • • • • • • • • • • • • • •

BILL SLADYK WILDLIFE MANAGEMENT AREA

Administered by the Department of Fish and Wildlife, the Bill Sladyk Wildlife Management Area (WMA) comprises about 10,000 acres in the towns of Holland, Norton, Warren's Gore, and Warner's Grant. There are no officially marked or maintained hiking trails; most of the area is restricted to travel by foot or snowmobile.

In addition to the many miles of old woods roads, there are several miles of wildlife habitat management access roads and numerous privately maintained snowmobile trails, some of which have signs and orange diamond markers at junction points. The map on page 323 shows only a couple trails to small ponds in the area.

Because this is a large area with few conspicuous landmarks, hikers should be especially observant and familiar with the use of map and compass. Using a USGS map is highly recommended.

6

ROUND POND, BEAVER POND, AND LINE POND

Distance: 2.0 mi. (3.2 km)
Elevation Change: 200 ft. ascent
Hiking Time: 1 hr. (reverse 1 hr.)

Located in the northwest corner of the wildlife management area, these primitive natural ponds are reached from the west side of Holland Pond (USGS Morgan Center).

TO THE TRAIL: From Vt. 111, a short distance west of Morgan Center and just beyond the Seymour Lake fishing access, turn north onto the paved and signed Valley Road (0.0 mi.). After reaching the village of Holland and passing the town garage and a white church, continue straight ahead onto the unsigned and gravel Selby Road (also known as Holland Pond Road) at a point where the paved road swings sharply left (4.8 mi.). After passing straight through a crossroad (6.1 mi.), turn right onto the unsigned and unpaved Holland Pond Road at the next intersection (7.8 mi.). Ignoring a road to the left (8.3 mi.), bear left at the next fork (9.9 mi.) and continue to the end of the road at the Holland Pond fishing access area where ample parking is available. From here, the access road leading to the WMA is rough. Vehicles with low clearance should park at the fishing access. Note: Hikers parking here at the Holland Pond fishing access should add 0.6 mi. to all mileages.

From the fishing access (0.0 mi.), follow a narrow private camp road north across Holland Brook. Ignore two forks to the right and continue straight ahead onto a woods road (0.1 mi.) to reach a small clearing, a sign for the WMA and a gate (0.6 mi.). Vehicles other than snowmobiles are not permitted beyond this point.

DESCRIPTION: From the WMA gate (0.0 mi.), the trail follows the old woods road easterly on high ground above the north shore of Holland Pond to an unmarked trail junction on the left (0.3 mi.).

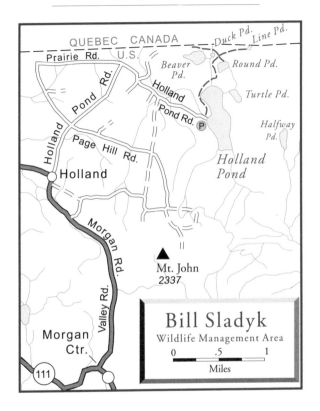

Junction: From the junction (0.0 mi.), the trail to the left ascends northerly on an old woods road, which is badly washed out in places. After crossing the height of land (0.4 mi.), the trail descends steadily to a small clearing on the southeast shore of Beaver Pond (0.6 mi.). The ridge opposite the pond is in Canada. From the WMA gate to the southeast shore of Beaver Pond it is 0.9 mi.

6

Continuing straight ahead from the Beaver Pond trail junction, the main trail crosses a small brook on the rocks just below a beaver swamp. A short distance beyond, the trail turns sharply left at a junction on the right with an old woods road (0.6 mi.). After briefly separating and rejoining the road (1.0 mi.), the trail continues to an unmarked spur on the left (1.1 mi.), which descends 100 ft. to the south shore of Duck Pond. The main trail then trends easterly to another unmarked trail junction on the left (1.3 mi.).

Junction: From this junction (0.0 mi.), the trail to the left trends northerly then westerly on high ground above the north side of Duck Pond. After crossing a small inlet brook (0.3 mi.), the spur trail continues to its terminus at a small open area on the north shore of Beaver Pond opposite a tiny island (0.8 mi.). It is 2.1 mi. from the WMA gate to the north shore of Beaver Pond.

Continuing straight ahead from the second Beaver Pond trail junction, the main trail soon reaches another unmarked junction on a patch of exposed bedrock (1.4 mi.). Here, a spur trail continues straight ahead for 225 ft. to a log lean-to at the upper end of a large clearing just above the north shore of Round Pond.

The main trail turns left at the junction with the Round Pond spur trail and ascends northeasterly in the woods to its final junction, marked by a small birch blowdown and pieces of flagging (1.5 mi.). Hikers should be sure to take the left fork, as the right fork soon swings to the south and continues to the Hurricane Brook area.

Following an old woods road, which is wet in places, the trail reaches its highest point (1.8 mi.), then gradually descends to its terminus on the west shore of Line Pond, which straddles the U.S.-Canada boundary (2.0 mi.). The boundary, unmarked at this point, is the centerline of the cleared swath around both sides of the pond.

• • • • • • • • • • • • • • • •

RAMBLES

BARR HILL NATURE PRESERVE

Located in the Town of Greensboro (USGS Caspian Lake), this 256-acre natural area was donated to The Nature Conservancy in 1972 by the Philip Gray family. In 1983, students and staff of Sterling College built a nature trail on the site. An excellent guide is available at the trailhead.

While the summit of Barr Hill is wooded, several vantage points on two short loop trails offer excellent views of four mountain ranges: the main range of the Green Mountains lies to the west, with the Worcester Range slightly south, while southeast is the Presidential Range of the White Mountains and, to the north, Mt. Tremblant in the Canadian Laurentians. One loop is 0.3 mi. long, and the other is 0.7 mi

TO THE TRAIL: Located on both the south shore of Island Pond and the west shore of Spectacle Pond, Brighton State Park is reached by following Vt. 105 east from the village of Island Pond for about 2.0 mi., then following the paved Lakeshore Drive/Pleasant Street south for about 0.75 mi. The park entrance and contact station are on the east side of the road.

BRIGHTON STATE PARK

ABOUT THE TRAIL: The park has a variety of campsites, as well as developed day-use facilities. An entrance fee is charged in season. A nature trail guide and map of the park's trail system are available at the contact station.

TO THE TRAIL: Located on both the south shore of Island Pond and the west shore of Spectacle Pond, Brighton

6

State Park is reached by following Vt. 105 east from the village of Island Pond for about 2.0 mi., then following the paved Lakeshore Drive/Pleasant Street south for about 0.75 mi. The park entrance and contact station are on the east side of the road.

DESCRIPTION: The park contains four relatively flat interconnecting trails totaling about 2.0 mi. The Shore Trail leads to three scenic vistas of Spectacle Pond and, with the Red Pine Trail, leads to a fine natural stand of mature red pines with an understory of boreal plant species. This plant community, uncommon in Vermont and especially in this region, has been designated a state natural area. Portions of three trails are combined into a 0.5-mi. nature trail that focuses on the forests of the Northeast Kingdom.

CHAMPION LANDS

In 1998, roughly 132,000 acres in Essex County that formerly belonged to Champion International were protected for public access through a complex land deal involving the state of Vermont and other parties. About 84,000 acres of the parcel are owned by the Essex Timber Co. and are subject to a public access easement; 22,000 acres are owned by the state of Vermont as the West Mountain Wildlife Management Area; and 26,000 acres have been added to the federal Sylvio O. Conte Wildlife Refuge.

The Champion Lands offer recreational opportunities for hikers, cross-country skiers, nature enthusiasts, hunters, fishermen, and snowmobile riders. Although only a limited number of hiking trails cross the property, there are many places to explore in this remote corner of the state. Planning for the use of the Champion Lands is underway. The Green Mountain Club, through its Northeast Kingdom Section, will play an active role as the designated corridor manager for hiking trails. The GMC anticipates providing information about selected hikes in the next edition of the *Day Hiker's Guide to Vermont.*

Useful Addresses

Appalachian Trail Conference, 799 Washington St., P.O. Box 807, Harpers Ferry, WV 25425; (304) 535-6331; general@atconf.org; appalachiantrail.org. *Coordinates the work of the organizations and individuals who maintain the Appalachian Trail from Maine to Georgia. Publishes guidebooks to the Appalachian Trail.*

Ascutney Trails Association, P.O. Box 147, Windsor, VT 05089. *Maintains trails and shelters on Mt. Ascutney. Publishes* Mount Ascutney Guide.

Catamount Trail Association, 1 Main St., Suite 308A, Burlington, VT 05401; (802) 864-5794; ctamail@aol.com; catamounttrail.org. *Maintains 280-mile Catamount Trail. Publishes* Catamount Trail Guide.

Cross Vermont Trail Association, c/o Cross Vermont Trail Coordinator, 81 East Hill Rd., Plainfield, VT 05667; georges@together.net. *The CVT will be Vermont's first east-west, long-distance, multiuse trail extending 75 miles from the Connecticut River to Lake Champlain.*

Equinox Preservation Trust, P.O. Box 46, Manchester Village, VT 05254; (802) 362-4700; ept@sover.net. *Maintains and protects trails on Mt. Equinox and near Equinox Pond.*

Friends of West River Trail, P.O. Box 25, Jamaica, VT 05343. *Maintains West River Trail.*

Green Mountain Club, 4711 Waterbury-Stowe Rd., Waterbury Center, VT 05677; (802) 244-7037, (fax) (802) 244-5867; gmc@greenmountainclub.org; greenmountainclub.org. *Maintains, manages, and protects 445-mile Long Trail System. Publishes* Long Trail Guide *and quarterly newsletter, the* Long Trail News.

Green Mountain National Forest, Forest Supervisor's Office, Rte. 7, 231 North Main St., Rutland, VT 05701; (802) 747-6700; fs.fed.us/r9/gmf/. *Maintains foot trails and multiuse trails as well as camping and other recreation areas. Forest map, day hiking guides, and other publications available. District ranger offices in Manchester, Middlebury, and Rochester.*

Hazen's Notch Association, P.O. Box 478, Montgomery Center, VT 05471; (802) 326-4799; info@hazensnotch.org; hazensnotch.org. *Promotes land conservation, environmental education, outdoor recreation, scientific research, and stewardship of natural resources.*

Kingdom Trails Association, P.O. Box 204, East Burke, VT 05832; info@kingdomtrails.org; kingdomtrails.org. *Protects, develops, and promotes recreational trail network in Northeast Kingdom.*

Merck Forest and Farmland Trust, Route 315, P.O. Box 86, Rupert, VT 05768; (802) 394-7836; merck@vermontel.net; merckforest.com. *More than 2,800 acres devoted to education, conservation, and recreation. Publishes free trail map of 26-mile trail system.*

The Nature Conservancy, 27 State St., Montpelier, VT 05602; (802) 229-4425; kward@tnc.org; nature.org/states/ vermont. *Preserves plants, animals, and natural communities.*

New England Trail Conference, c/o Forrest House, 33 Knollwood Dr., East Longmeadow, MA 01028; wapack

.org/netrails/index.htm. *Clearinghouse for organizations and public agencies that maintain and manage trails in New England.*

Putney Mountain Association, P.O. Box 953, Putney, VT 05346; (802) 387-6635. *Protects and maintains trails on Putney Mountain ridge.*

Rivendell Trails Association, P.O. Box 202, Fairlee, VT 05045.

Sterling Falls Gorge Natural Area, 91 Sterling Gorge Rd., Stowe, VT 05672; gander07@realtor.com.

Stowe Land Trust, P.O. Box 284, Stowe, VT 05672; (802) 253-7221; stowelandtrust@pshift.com; stowelandtrust.org. *Conserves land in the Stowe area, especially Lamoille Country and the Worcester Range.*

Taconic Hiking Club, c/o Katharine Wolfe, 45 Kakely St., Albany, NY 12208. *Maintains Taconic Crest Trail. Publishes Taconic Crest Trail Guide.*

Vermont Department of Fish and Wildlife, 10 South Building, 103 South Main St., Waterbury, VT 05671-0501; (802) 241-3700; information@fwd.anr.state.vt.us; anr.state.vt.us/fw/fwhome/. *Manages state's fisheries and wildlife resources.*

Vermont Department of Forests, Parks and Recreation, 103 South Main St., 10 South, Waterbury, VT 05671-0601; (802) 241-3655; parks@state.vt.us; vt-stateparks.com. *Maintains hiking and multiuse trails, campgrounds, picnic areas and other recreational facilities in state parks and forests. Publishes maps, brochures. Free trail maps available at many parks or from agency regional offices in Barre, Essex Junction, Rutland, St. Johnsbury, and Springfield.*

Vermont Department of Travel and Tourism, 6 Baldwin St., Drawer 33, Montpelier, VT 05633; 1-800-VERMONT; (802) 828-3237; 1-800-vermont.com.

Vermont Institute of Natural Science, Montpelier, North Branch Nature Center, 713 Elm St., Rte. 12, Montpelier, VT 05602; (802) 229-6206.

Vermont State Police Headquarters, Waterbury State Complex, 103 South Main St., Waterbury, VT 05676; (802) 244-8727; dps.state.vt.us. *In case of emergency, call 911.*

Westmore Association, c/o Paul Moffat, RD 2, Orleans, VT 05860. *Maintains trails in the Lake Willoughby area. Publishes free map and guide of area trails.*

Williams Outing Club, Williams College, Williamstown, MA 01267. *Maintains trails in southwest Vermont and northwest Massachusetts.*

Windmill Hill–Pinnacle Association, 218 Barnes Road, Putney, VT 05346-9007. *Manages trails and protects portions of the Windmill Mountain ridgeline in Westminster.*

Winooski Valley Park District, Ethan Allen Homestead, Burlington, VT 05401; (802) 863-5744; wvpd@together.net. *Protects land and funds recreation and education programs along the lower Winooski River.*

GMC Publications

Books

Long Trail Guide (25th edition, 2003). Describes the Long Trail System and the Appalachian Trail in Vermont. Comprehensive guide with sixteen topographical maps, trail summaries, trailhead directions, suggested hikes, and winter hiking suggestions.

The Long Trail End-to-Ender's Guide. This supplement to the *Long Trail Guide* provides up-to-date information on trail conditions, overnight accommodations, equipment sales and repairs, trail towns, mail drops, and transportation.

360 Degrees: A Guide to Vermont's Fire and Observation Towers. Gives driving directions and trail descriptions to Vermont's twelve remaining fire towers and five observation towers that are open to the public.

Snowshoeing in Vermont: A Guide to the Best Winter Hikes. A compilation of the favorite winter hikes of GMC trip leaders. Includes maps, trail descriptions and winter hiking tips.

A Trip Leader's Handbook: Advice for Successful GMC Outings. A handy reference for GMC sections, school groups, outing clubs, and camps. This booklet covers everything a trip leader needs to know to plan and run a successful outdoor trip. Topics include clothing and equipment, emergencies, trail etiquette, and leadership.

Brochures and Newsletters

Long Trail News. GMC's quarterly membership newsletter provides trail and shelter updates, hiking, statewide trail information, club history, and a club activities calendar.

"The Long Trail: A Footpath in the Wilderness." Information about the Long Trail System. Free with self-addressed stamped envelope.

"The Tundra Walk: An Interpretive Guide to the Mount Mansfield Alpine Region." A brochure with illustrations that describes a one-half-mile section of the Long Trail on the ridge of Mount Mansfield.

Additional Reading

Shop online at greenmountainclub.org.

Natural History and Field Guides

The Nature of Vermont: Introduction and Guide to a New England Environment, Charles W. Johnson, University Press of New England, 1998.

Newcomb's Wildflower Guide, Lawrence Newcomb, Little, Brown & Co., 1989.

The Peterson Field Guides Series, Houghton Mifflin Co. and The Stokes Nature Guides, Little Brown & Co.

Reading the Mountains of Home, John Elder, Harvard University Press, 1998.

Tracking and the Art of Seeing: How to Read Animal Tracks and Sign, Paul Rezendes, Harper Resource Books, 1999.

Hiking How-to Books

Mountaineering First Aid: A Guide to Accident Response and First Aid Care, Jan D. Carline et al., Mountaineers Books, 1996.

Ethics and History of Outdoor Recreation

Backwoods Ethics: Environmental Issues for Hikers and Campers, Laura and Guy Waterman, Countryman Press, 1993.

Forest and Crag: A History of Hiking, Trail Blazing, and Adventure in the Northeast Mountains, Laura and Guy Waterman, AMC Books, 1989.

Wilderness Ethics: Preserving the Spirit of Wildness, Laura and Guy Waterman, Countryman Press, 1993.

Green Mountain Trail Guides and Maps

Long Trail Map, Wilderness Maps.

Appalachian Trail Guide to New Hampshire–Vermont, Appalachian Trail Conference, 2001.

Best Hikes with Children: Vermont, New Hampshire, & Maine, Cynthia C. Lewis, Thomas J. Lewis, The Mountaineers, 2000.

Fifty Hikes in Vermont, Green Mountain Club, Backcountry Publications, Countryman Press, 1997.

Guide to the Taconic Crest Trail, Taconic Hiking Club, 1992.

Hiker's Guide to the Mountains of Vermont, Jared Gange, Huntington Graphics, 2001.

Mt. Ascutney Guide, Ascutney Trails Association, 1992.

Index

GMC Membership

Become a member — help protect and maintain trails and support outdoor education throughout Vermont. We have two types of membership — section and at-large. See page 20 for information about dues and more details.

GMC Sections

Enjoy year-round outings — hiking, biking, cross-country skiing, canoeing, potlucks, and more. Help maintain trails and shelters. Meet people who enjoy outdoor activities in one of these sections:

- Bennington, Vermont
- Brattleboro, Vermont
- Bread Loaf (Middlebury), Vermont
- Burlington, Vermont
- Killington (Rutland), Vermont
- Laraway, Northwestern Vermont
- Manchester, Vermont
- Montpelier, Vermont
- Northeast Kingdom, Vermont
- Northern Frontier (Montgomery), Vermont
- Ottauquechee (Woodstock), Vermont
- Sterling (Stowe-Morrisville), Vermont
- Connecticut
- Worcester, Massachusetts (eastern Massachusetts)

At-large Membership

The club also offers an at-large membership for those who wish to support the GMC but are not interested in affiliating with a section.

Green Mountain Club

*Providing and Protecting
Vermont's Hiking Trails
Since 1910*

Your membership or
gift supports hiking in
Vermont and the protec-
tion of the Green Mountains.
Thank you for considering a
contribution to the GMC at
4711 Waterbury-Stowe Road,
Waterbury Center, Vermont 05677;
(802) 244-7037;
www.greenmountainclub.org.

TRAIL
NOTES

TRAIL NOTES

Date: ....

Trail (*Described on page #_____*):

....

....

Mileage: ....

Time: ....

Hiking Party: ....

....

....

Weather: ....

....

....

Comments: ....

....

....

....

....

....

....

TRAIL NOTES

Date: ....

Trail (*Described on page #_____*):

....

....

Mileage: ....

Time: ....

Hiking Party: ....

....

....

Weather: ....

....

....

Comments: ....

....

....

....

....

....

....

PLEASE CONTACT GMC (GMC@GREENMOUNTAINCLUB.ORG) TO REPORT
ERRORS, CHANGES, OR PROBLEMS ENCOUNTERED. THANK YOU!

TRAIL NOTES

Date: ....

Trail (*Described on page #_____*):

....

....

Mileage: ....

Time: ....

Hiking Party: ....

....

....

Weather: ....

....

....

Comments: ....

....

....

....

....

....

....

TRAIL NOTES

Date: ....

Trail (*Described on page #_____*):

....

....

Mileage: ....

Time: ....

Hiking Party: ....

....

....

Weather: ....

....

....

Comments: ....

....

....

....

....

....

....

TRAIL NOTES

Date: ....

Trail (*Described on page #_____*):

....

....

Mileage: ....

Time: ....

Hiking Party: ....

....

....

Weather: ....

....

....

Comments: ....

....

....

....

....

....

....

Date: ....

Trail (*Described on page #_____*):

....

....

Mileage: ....

Time: ....

Hiking Party: ....

....

....

Weather: ....

....

....

Comments: ....

....

....

....

....

....

....

PLEASE CONTACT GMC (GMC@GREENMOUNTAINCLUB.ORG) TO REPORT
ERRORS, CHANGES, OR PROBLEMS ENCOUNTERED. THANK YOU!

TRAIL NOTES

Date: ....

Trail (*Described on page #_____*):

....

....

Mileage: ....

Time: ....

Hiking Party: ....

....

....

Weather: ....

....

....

Comments: ....

....

....

....

....

....

....

TRAIL NOTES

Date: ....

Trail (*Described on page #_____*):

....

....

Mileage: ....

Time: ....

Hiking Party: ....

....

....

Weather: ....

....

....

Comments: ....

....

....

....

....

....

....

TRAIL NOTES

Date: ....

Trail (*Described on page #_____*):

....

....

Mileage: ....

Time: ....

Hiking Party: ....

....

....

Weather: ....

....

....

Comments: ....

....

....

....

....

....

....

PLEASE CONTACT GMC (GMC@GREENMOUNTAINCLUB.ORG) TO REPORT
ERRORS, CHANGES, OR PROBLEMS ENCOUNTERED. THANK YOU!

TRAIL NOTES

Date: ....

Trail (*Described on page #_____*):

....

....

Mileage: ....

Time: ....

Hiking Party: ....

....

....

Weather: ....

....

....

Comments: ....

....

....

....

....

....

....

TRAIL NOTES

Date: ....

Trail (*Described on page #_____*):

....

....

Mileage: ....

Time: ....

Hiking Party: ....

....

....

Weather: ....

....

....

Comments: ....

....

....

....

....

....

....

Date: ....

Trail (*Described on page #_____*):

....

....

Mileage: ....

Time: ....

Hiking Party: ....

....

....

Weather: ....

....

....

Comments: ....

....

....

....

....

....

....

TRAIL NOTES

TRAIL NOTES